MINJUNG
THEOLOGY

Heart's Fire

YANG SUNG-WU

Heart's fire—
forest fire in howling wind
flame and burn!
Flare up as sword from pursed lips
piercing painful flesh
tearing out every joint!
Heart's fire—
rather be an ocean,
long cold night on wooden floor,
an ocean of fire,
spewing flames of oil,
scattering soot, blackening empty sky.
Heart's fire—
stream of blood through valley snows
swell and flow!
Not just fists,
not just fists that strike me,
oh, fire in my heart,
burn, flaring, wailing!
I'd rather be an ocean baring teeth,
scattering soot, blackening empty sky,
I'd rather be an ocean of fire.

The woodcut on the cover is by Lee Chol-su and entitled "Fire of the Heart." This poem, by Yang Sung-wu, was written from a prison cell with a single window overlooking a forest and valley.

MINJUNG THEOLOGY

PEOPLE AS THE SUBJECTS OF HISTORY

Edited by
the Commission on Theological Concerns
of the Christian Conference of Asia
(CTC-CCA)

Zed Press
57 Caledonian Road
London N19DN

ORBIS BOOKS
Maryknoll, New York 10545

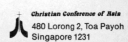
Christian Conference of Asia
480 Lorong 2, Toa Payoh
Singapore 1231

The Index was prepared by James Sullivan

Originally published by the Commission on Theological Concerns of the Christian Conference of Asia. Copyright © 1981 by Christian Conference of Asia, 480 Lorong 2, Toa Payoh, Singapore 1231.

This revised edition jointly published in 1983 by Orbis Books, Maryknoll, NY 10545; Zed Press, 57 Caledonian Road, London, N1 DN, U.K.; and the Christian Conference of Asia, 480 Lorong 2, Toa Payoh, Singapore 1231.

Library of Congress Cataloging in Publication Data

Main entry under title:

Minjung theology.

  Includes bibliographical references and index.
  1. Christianity—Korea—Addresses, essays, lectures.
2. Theology, Doctrinal—Korea—History—Addresses,
essays, lectures. I. Christian Conference of Asia.
Commission on Theological Concerns.
BR1325.M56 1983   230'.09519   83-7279
ISBN 0-88344-336-8 (pbk.)

British Library Cataloguing in Publication Data

Committee on Theological Concerns of the Christian Conference of Asia
  Minjung theology.
  1. Liberation theology—Korea (South)
  I. Title
  261.8 BT83.57

  ISBN 0-86232-190-5
  ISBN 0-86232-191-3 Pbk

CCA ISBN: 9971-948-05-2

Contents

Contributors   vii

Preface   *James H. Cone*   ix

Introduction   *D. Preman Niles*   1

Section One: Minjung and Theology in Korea

I. A Biographical Sketch of an Asian Theological Consultation   15
    Suh Kwang-sun David

II. Korean Theological Development in the 1970s   38
    Suh Kwang-sun David

Section Two: The Minjung Reality

III. A Theological Look at the Mask Dance in Korea   47
    Hyun Young-hak

IV. Towards a Theology of *Han*   55
    Suh Nam-dong

Section Three: The Minjung Roots of Korean Christianity

V. A Brief Sketch of Korean Christian History from the
Minjung Perspective   73
    Choo Chai-yong

VI. Korean Christianity as a Messianic Movement of the People   80
    Kim Yong-bock

Section Four: Minjung Perspectives in the Bible

VII. An Old Testament Understanding of Minjung   123
    Moon Hee-suk Cyris

VIII. Jesus and the Minjung in the Gospel of Mark   138
    Ahn Byung-mu

Section Five: Minjung Theology—Historical Vocation and Hope

IX. Historical References for a Theology of Minjung   155
        Suh Nam-dong

X. Messiah and Minjung: Discerning Messianic Politics over
     against Political Messianism   183
        Kim Yong-bock

Index   195

Contributors

Ahn Byung-mu, formerly Professor of New Testament, Hankuk Theological Seminary, Seoul, Korea. Director, Theological Institute, Seoul, Korea.

Choo Chai-yong, Professor of Church History, Hankuk Theological Seminary, Seoul, Korea.

Hyun Young-hak, formerly Professor of Christian Ethics, Ewha Women's University, Seoul, Korea.

Kim Yong-bock, Co-Director for Research, Christian Institute for the Study of Justice and Development, Seoul, Korea.

Moon Hee-suk Cyris, Professor of Old Testament, Presbyterian Theological Seminary, Seoul, Korea.

D. Preman Niles, Executive Secretary, Commission on Theological Concerns, Christian Conference of Asia, Singapore.

Suh Kwang-sun David, formerly Dean of Ewha Women's University, Seoul, Korea.

Suh Nam-dong, formerly Professor of Systematic Theology, Yonsei University, Seoul, Korea. Director, Institute for Mission-Education, Seoul, Korea.

Preface

JAMES H. CONE

"The history of Christianity has . . . been written by white, western, bourgeois hands,"[1] writes Gustavo Gutiérrez. This statement is an apt description
of the first 1900 years of the development of Christian theology. Whether
Protestant, Catholic, or Orthodox, Christian theology is a discipline that has
been primarily defined by the history and culture of Europe. European
theologians and their North American descendants identified the issues that
were regarded as appropriate for theology, and they also developed the cri-
teria by which others outside their historical and cultural context could participate in the theological enterprise. For any discourse to merit the name
"theology," liberal Protestants reacting to the impact of the Enlightenment
insisted that it had to be "rational," "scientific," and thus capable of "objective" verification. While Karl Barth and other twentieth-century neo-
orthodox oriented theologians softened the influence of the Enlightenment
upon Protestant theology, their impact was temporary, and they, like their
liberal brothers, also ignored human concerns outside of Europe. The political and social needs of oppressed classes and races were excluded from theological discourse. This is why one can still read accounts of modern and
contemporary European and North American white theology without en-
countering any references to African slavery and colonization. Why is it that
so-called Christian theologians can continue to write essays and books on the
God of the Exodus and of Jesus Christ and still fail to mention the oppressed
of the land in Asia, Africa, and Latin America? The answer to this question is
found in the history of Europe whose political, economic, and cultural dominance over the Third World continued unchecked for several centuries.

The recent emergence of Third World theologies has made it increasingly
more difficult for Europeans to exclude the issues of economic poverty and
political oppression from the subject matter of theology. As Europe's theological dominance is directly related to its political and economic power, the
rise of Third World liberation theologies is also similarly related to political
movements among oppressed peoples as they attempt to create an alternative
future for themselves. Theology emerges out of a particular social reality,

and it can never be understood independently of it. Theology is a "second step"[2]; it is human reflection arising out of the church's attempt to understand the meaning of God for a particular time and context.

As oppressed peoples began to liberate themselves from European colonization and cultural discrimination, it was only natural that they would also begin to develop theologies that would reflect their struggle to liberate themselves from political and economic oppression. Black theology in North America and South Africa emerged out of the political struggle of blacks on both continents to liberate themselves from white racism.[3] Feminist theology, primarily North American but also taking root in the Third World, represents a similar concern in women's attempt to overcome sexism.[4] Latin American liberation theology, strongly influenced by Marxist class analysis, was created out of the political struggle to close the gap between the rich and the poor on that continent.[5] African theology has focused on the terms "indigenization" and "Africanization" in order to indicate African people's search for a cultural identity in Christianity that is not defined by Europe but by their own pre-colonial heritage and also by their attempt to build new independent African nations.[6] A similar concern is found in Asian theology with its accent on "contextualization" and the biblical motif of creation.[7] The distinguishing characteristic of all theologies of the poor is their rejection of European theology and their affirmation of their own cultural history as a primary source for the doing of theology.

Minjung theology of South Korea is one of the most creative theologies emerging from the political struggles of Third World peoples. With roots stretching back to the late nineteenth and early twentieth centuries, it emerged as a fully developed theological voice in the 1970s. On the one hand, minjung theology is an example of what Korean Christians in particular and Asians generally are doing to liberate themselves from the stifling effects of European theology. But on the other hand, minjung theology is more than a rejection of European theology; it is an affirmation of Korean culture and history as the context in which Koreans must do theology. Korean theologians begin with the particularity of their own situation as defined by poor people's attempt to overcome their suffering. They make no universal claims, and thus do not attempt to speak for Christians everywhere. Minjung theology is *Korean* theology; it is a theology that is accountable to the liberating history and culture of poor people in Korea.

Since minjung theology is strongly influenced by the social biography of the minjung, it is perhaps appropriate for me to give a brief personal account of my encounter with the people who are creating this theology.[8] In May 1975, I was invited by the Korean Christian church in Japan to lead a series of seminars on the theme of "the Church struggling for the liberation of the people." I had never been to Japan or Korea, nor any other Asian land. Furthermore, my reading knowledge of Asian history generally and Korean history in particular were almost nil. The only preparation I had was the little reading I did immediately before my departure and a few conversations I had with people regarding the political and social situation of Koreans in Japan. I did not know what to expect, and I kept asking myself why Koreans wanted a *black* theologian, who knew so little about their social history, to lead their seminars. What did black theology have to say to Koreans in Japan or Asians anywhere?

The cultural shock that I experienced upon my arrival in Japan is very difficult to describe. Although I had been to Africa and Latin America, neither prepared me for Asia. For the first time I was in a completely different culture, unlike Africa which I could connect with my blackness and unlike Latin America which I could connect with my western identity. After only a short time on the continent of Asia, I realized that my theological perspective would be altered significantly. While I did not know what I would change or how I would change it (I needed more time to absorb and to reflect), yet I knew that the change would relate to christology and the need to enlarge my perspective beyond its narrow western orientation. In Asia Christianity is a minority religion, and western languages are not the primary means of communication. It is one thing to read about other religions in books and quite another to experience their powerful presence first-hand on the continent of Asia. What could I say to Koreans about the gospel when I knew neither their language nor much about their social situation in Japan? I felt that I had little to say to them, and they had much to say to me. However, Koreans insisted that I tell the black story of liberation in North America as defined by the black church tradition. They told me the Korean story of enslavement by the Japanese and their struggle to reclaim their humanity. We then compared our stories, identifying the similarities and the differences. Through the telling of our stories, we came to know and to love each other. It was an experience that I will never forget. I preached in Korean churches, ate in their homes; we laughed and told stories about our families, and I was transformed by the experience of being accepted by a people who knew so little about me and I about them. I began to realize much more clearly than before that God's liberating presence is found not only in the black liberation struggle but among *all* people who are fighting for freedom.

It was within the context of the Korean Christian community in Japan that I first heard about a new theology emerging from the history and culture of Korean people. The most surprising thing that happened during my visit was the Korean people's understanding and affirmation of my view of black theology. Before leaving home, I had been told by white Americans of the "conservative" nature of Korean Christianity and that my emphasis on liberation would be utterly rejected. Nothing could have been further from the truth. To be sure, I had to separate my view of liberation from the communists' use of the term in North Korea, but that only took a few minutes of talking about the black story of liberation as defined by our songs, prayers, and sermons. When I told them about our "blues," they told me about their "han." When I told Koreans that my nineteenth-century slave grandparents sang spiritual songs about the exodus of Hebrew slaves from Egypt, identifying themselves with the Hebrew slaves and white slaveholders with the Egyptians, Koreans smiled and then shared with me their "slave" songs about the exodus that they created during their servitude under the Japanese in the twentieth century. The similarities between Korean and black experiences of oppression and liberation astounded me. Later, when I preached at a Korean church on the theme "God the Liberator," I heard them singing a song in Korean whose melody sounded very familiar to me. When I asked my interpreter the name of the song, he said, "Were you there when they crucified my Lord?" "Do the people know that that is a black spiritual?!" I asked. He gave a negative answer. Here we were engaged in a profound cultural exchange and did not even know it. The Korean people's acceptance of the black experience created an openness in me to accept their history and culture.

The only rejection that I experienced in Japan came from white missionaries and affluent Japanese Christians. Both groups claimed that there was no such thing as black theology and Korean theology. Christian theology, they contended, refers to the writings of Barth, Brunner, and Bultmann. I always knew when I was speaking to a Japanese audience, even though I could detect no physical differences between them and Koreans. The difference had to do with their attitude toward me and Koreans which was always arrogant and condescending. My experience with whites in the United States prepared me well for the Japanese, and white missionaries in Japan helped to insure that I would not forget racism's true nature. The more white missionaries and Japanese Christians rejected black and Korean theologies, the more I and Koreans were determined to make theological sense out of our liberation struggles.

I was attracted to Korean theology because I liked Korean people. Like blacks, they had a history of suffering and had developed a culture that enabled them not to be determined by it. Like blacks, Koreans are a passionate people. They cry and laugh. They feel life at its depths and refuse to define reality in primarily rational terms.

I was also impressed by Korean lay people's ability to think theologically. Unlike some of their pastors who had been influenced too much by their study of and with Japanese and white theologians, Korean lay people use their common sense in their exegesis of the scripture. They read the Bible as a series of stories about what God has done to protect the little ones in extreme situations of oppression. They related the biblical stories to the Korean story of oppression under the Japanese and concluded that the God of Moses and of Jesus was present with them, sustaining them in their struggle to keep their identity.

Listening to Korean lay people tell their stories of struggle reminded me of how black theology was created. It did not start among professional black theologians who were teaching in seminaries and universities. Like whites, most professional black theologians rejected the very idea of a black theology until they realized that it would help secure their teaching posts in white seminaries and universities. Black theology began in the context of the civil rights and black power movements, largely defined by the ministries of Martin Luther King, Jr., and Malcolm X. It was during my participation in the black liberation struggle, in dialogue with laity and clergy, that the idea of a black theology became clear to me. I concluded that black theology had to be a theology of black people who were struggling to make sense of the gospel in their fight for freedom. Were not Koreans making the same point in their affirmation of the need for a unique Korean theology?

After nearly three weeks with Koreans in Japan, I took a flight to Seoul, Korea. In Seoul, I met many of the writers in this volume. Suh Kwang-sun David invited me to Korea, and Hyun Young-hak met me at the airport and served as my interpreter during my stay. Both introduced me to other Korean theologians and informed me of their struggle for democracy and human rights. The infamous "Presidential Emergency Measure No. 9" had just been issued (May 13, 1975), which allowed the police to arrest and imprison any person who criticized the Park regime. I met several persons who had been dismissed from their teaching posts in the universities,[9] many of whom were later imprisoned.

Since the universities had only been recently opened, my sponsors thought it wise not to hold my lecture in that context. I thought it best not to lecture at all because of the risks involved. Furthermore, what could I say to Koreans in a situation of political repression. I knew even less about Koreans in their own country than about Koreans in Japan. But despite the political risks and my lack of knowledge, everyone insisted that I speak. The lecture was held at the YMCA, and nearly half the audience were KCIA agents. Terribly anxious about the political dangers, especially for Koreans attending my lecture, I decided to lecture on the theme of "God the Liberator as Found in the Black Slave Songs in North America." Apparently the KCIA agents did not detect the double meanings in the spirituals and in my message, because no one was arrested. No questions were permitted following the lecture, and we closed with the singing of "We Shall Overcome."

I remained in South Korea for nearly a week, listening to many of the writers in this volume discuss Korean theology. Since I did not know much about Korean history and culture, I found it difficult to understand much of what they were advocating. The ethos of political repression was so dominant that they often found themselves speaking to each other in their own language, of which I understood nothing. They kept apologizing to me, but I tried to assure them that I was not troubled by not being able to understand. On one occasion given in my honor, one professor present had just received his "retirement" notice, and much of the time was spent "being with him," and other professors discussed when they too would receive their notice or be taken to prison.

It was in the context of Korean Christians' struggle for democracy and human rights that I first heard them speak about a new Korean theology. Although I had heard Koreans in Japan talk in a similar fashion, it was among Koreans in their own country where I saw an outline of it begin to be developed. They kept emphasizing the idea of "people as the subject of history," but *not* in a Marxist definition of the proletariat or of history. My western education had not prepared me for the creative insights of Korean theologians. But the black experience of oppression helped me to be open to new and unfamiliar voices. Korean theologians were patient with my slow understanding and assured me that I was making progress. My difficulty was with the language and the terms they used to express their theology. It was easy to associate the idea of the "people" with the "proletariat," but they assured me that what they meant by "people" could not be reduced to the Marxist idea of the working class. What they mean by people cannot be translated into English, they claimed. In Korean the word has a complex meaning that can only be understood in the context of Korean history and culture. I left South Korea with the determination to learn more about the history and culture that was giving birth to a new theology.

I knew that my search for a deeper understanding of Korean theology would involve acquiring some knowledge of Asia, especially in relation to the Christian presence on that continent. Through extensive reading and additional travels to Sri Lanka and India, meeting many lay people and clergy, I was introduced to the complexity of the Asian culture. My colleague Kosuke Koyama[10] and several Asian students at Union Theological Seminary instructed me in Asian theology. Particularly important has been Preman Niles of the Christian Conference of Asia, whom I met in connection with the Ecumenical Association of Third World Theologians (EATWOT).[11] We had many discussions about Asian and black theologies.

When I returned for the second time to South Korea in May 1979, I was ready to speak at a deeper level with Korean theologians. By this time, they were no longer just talking about the future development of a new Korean theology, but were actually creating it. They had given it the name "minjung theology." They were also making plans for the October 1979 theological consultation that produced this volume. I was invited to attend it, but the dates conflicted with another commitment. However, I will never forget the many hours we spent discussing minjung theology and its similarity with and difference from other Third World theologies.

The first thing that a non-Korean needs to understand about minjung theology is its uniqueness. It is a *Korean* theology defined by the culture and history of Korea. Although its identity is shaped by its commitment to the poor (as is true of other Third World liberation-oriented theologies), minjung theology is not identical with black, Latin, African, or even other Asian theologies. Rather it is a theology defined by the minjung reality. As Kim Yong-bock says, "The minjung reality is known only through its biography, its story, its hope and suffering."[12] It is the Korean story of suffering and hope that defines the essential nature of minjung theology. It cannot be explained rationally, as is true of European theology and some manifestations of liberation theology influenced by it. Again quoting Kim Yong-bock:

"Minjung" is not a concept or object which can be easily explained or defined. "Minjung" signifies a living reality which is dynamic. This living reality defines its own existence, and generates new acts and dramas in history; and it refuses in principle to be defined conceptually.[13]

If the reality of the minjung is dynamic, then a theology arising out of that experience must reflect a similar character. It cannot be explained in terms of concepts and ideas derived from another history and culture. To understand minjung theology, it is necessary to immerse oneself in the minjung story of suffering and hope. That is why the essays in this volume focus on the "underdogs" of Korean history. They tell the stories of the minjung, using their folklore and showing how they "kept the faith" in situations of extreme suffering. To know minjung theology is to know what it means to be a voiceless Korean in one's own land.

The second thing that a non-Korean needs to understand is that minjung theology is an *Asian* theology. This point is essential for non-Asians to understand. It is minjung theology's Asian identity that makes culture, including folklore, important in the structure and content of its discourse. Its strong affirmation of culture separates minjung theology from Latin American liberation theology with its almost exclusive attention to Marxist class analysis. The contrast between Latin American and minjung theologies is clearly indicated in Kim Yong-bock's distinction between the minjung and the proletariat.

This difference between the minjung and the proletariat entails different views of history. Minjung history has a strong transcendental or transcending dimension—a beyond history—which is often expressed in religious form. There is close relationship between religion and the minjung's perception of history. Even if minjung history does not involve religious elements in an explicit manner, its folklore or cultural elements play a transcending function similar to religion in the perception of history.[14]

Although Latin American theology has said much about the liberation of the poor, the form and content of their theology do not reflect much of the history and culture of the poor, especially among Indians and blacks on that continent. Latin American theologians are strongly influenced by Marxism, and thus they are suspicious that poor people's religion and culture is nothing but an opium.[15] This typically Marxist view of poor people's religion is utterly rejected by Korean theologians, and this rejection places them in solidarity with their Asian sisters and brothers and also in close company with African and black theologians in the United States. We have had many debates about the role of culture and class analyses in the Ecumenical Association of Third World Theologians, with many Latin Americans finding themselves alone defending the exclusive priority of class. We have learned much from each other, with most of us showing a greater appreciation of viewpoints different from our own.[16]

Korean theologians' rejection of European theology means that they recognize the role it has played in their political and economic oppression. Their affirmation of their own history and culture means that they believe in themselves. The poor can think! They can do theology. There is no need for them to depend upon their oppressors to tell them what the gospel is. How can the oppressors know what the gospel is when their lives contradict its essential meaning? When the poor begin to think, they become aware of an identity that transcends the world created and controlled by the oppressors. Hyun Young-hak calls this the "experience of critical transcendence."[17] On the basis of his modification of the meaning of the word "transcendence," by locating it in history, he can now say that:

> God is working and revealing his will in and through the minjung of Korea, especially the minjung's history and culture. God was not carried piggy-back to Korea by the first missionary. The minjung as the "cultural proletariat" has a messianic significance and role in Korea's history. Beginning to do theology in such a way is exciting, for you feel theology with your body and dance with it before you think it.[18]

The third thing that non-Koreans need to understand about minjung theology is its similarity with other Third World theologies. In its affirmation of culture, minjung theology not only expresses its solidarity with other Asian theologies but almost all theologies of the poor with the possible exception of Latin American liberation theology and a similar expression of it in the Philippines.[19] But as suggested earlier, some Latin Americans have begun to make significant modifications in their exclusive emphasis on class and have shown signs of a greater appreciation of the liberating function of culture.[20]

Like other Third World liberation-oriented theologies, minjung theology is a theology of the "underdog." Their focus on the "underdog" has led them to a re-reading of the scripture, and they speak of it in language similar to Latin American theologians. Suh Nam-dong expresses this point clearly:

> Theological activities do not end with the exposition of the biblical texts on salvation or liberation of [people] by God. In the Bible, the Exodus, the activities of the prophets, and the event of the Cross offer new insights, but these texts ought to be rediscovered and re-interpreted in the context of the human struggle for historical and political liberation today.[21]

All liberation theologians would agree with that statement. Although Latin Americans have done more exegetical work to demonstrate the biblical option for the poor than others,[22] the essays by Moon Hee-suk Cyris and Ahn Byung-mu in this volume show that Koreans are making an important contribution in biblical studies for the benefit of all students of the Bible.

There is no agreement among Korean theologians regarding the precise definition of the minjung. The term is dynamic. But most would agree that Han Wan-Sang's definition is useful. Hyun Young-hak interprets him as saying that "the minjung are those who are oppressed politically, exploited economically, alienated sociologically, and kept uneducated in cultural and intellectual matters."[23] With this definition of the minjung, a theology born of that reality must be inseparably connected with the "underdogs" of Korea. But minjung theology is more than a theological expression of the cultural history of the Korean poor. And it is this "more" that connects it with the universal church. Minjung is a theology of the cross and resurrection of Jesus. Therefore *all* people whose identity is defined by Jesus' cross in the struggle for freedom will be encouraged by reading this volume.

NOTES

1. "Two Theological Perspectives: Liberation Theology and Progressive Theology" in Sergio Torres and Virginia Fabella, eds., *The Emergent Gospel: Theology from the Underside of History* (Maryknoll, N.Y.: Orbis Books, 1978), p. 248.

2. The understanding of theology as a "second step" has been explicitly stated among Latin theologians, and it refers to its reflection upon praxis, the first step. According to Gustavo Gutiérrez, "Theology is reflection, a critical attitude. Theology *follows*; it is the second step. . . . The pastoral activity of the Church does not flow as a conclusion from theological premises. Theology does not produce pastoral activity; rather it reflects upon it" (cf. his *A Theology of Liberation*, trans. by Sister Caridad Inda and John Eagleson [Maryknoll, N.Y.: Orbis Books, 1973], p. 11). See also Virginia Fabella and Sergio Torres, eds., *The Irruption of the Third World: Challenge to Theology* (Maryknoll, N.Y.: Orbis Books, 1983), pp. 246–55; Marianne Katoppo, *Compassionate and Free* (Maryknoll, N.Y.: Orbis Books, 1980).

3. For an introduction to black theology in North America, see especially Gayraud S. Wilmore and James H. Cone, eds., *Black Theology: A Documentary History, 1966–1979* (Maryknoll, N.Y.: Orbis Books, 1979). On black theology in South Africa, see Basil Moore, ed., *The Challenge of Black Theology in South Africa* (Atlanta, Ga.: John Knox Press, 1974).

4. The best introduction to feminist theology in North America is Carol Christ and Judith Plaskow, eds., *Womanspirit Rising: A Feminist Reader in Religion* (New York: Harper, 1979). On Third World women's views, see especially Amba Oduyoye, "Reflections from a Third World Woman's Perspective: Women's Experience and Liberation Theologies" in Virginia Fabella and Sergio Torres, eds., *The Irruption of the Third World,* pp. 246–55.

5. An excellent introduction to Latin American liberation theology is José Míguez Bonino, *Doing Theology in a Revolutionary Situation* (Philadelphia: Fortress Press, 1975).

6. An important introduction to African theology is Henry Muzorewa, *African Theology: Its Origin and Development* (Maryknoll, N.Y.: Orbis Books, forthcoming); see also Kofi Appiah-Kubi and Sergio Torres, eds., *African Theology en Route* (Maryknoll, N.Y.: Orbis, 1979).

7. For an introduction to Asian theology, see Douglas J. Elwood, ed., *Asian Christian Theology: Emerging Themes* (Philadelphia: Westminster Press, 1980).

8. I have written about my experience in Japan and Korea in other places. See my "Introduction" to "Black Theology and Third World Theologies" in G. Wilmore and J. Cone, *Black Theology: A Documentary History*, pp. 455f.; and my "A Black American Perspective on the Asian Search for a Full Humanity" in Virginia Fabella, ed., *Asia's Struggle for Full Humanity* (Maryknoll, N.Y.: Orbis, 1980), pp. 177–190.

9. Several authors in this volume have lost their teaching posts.

10. See especially Koyama's *No Handle on the Cross* (Maryknoll, N.Y.: Orbis Books, 1977); *Waterbuffalo Theology* (Maryknoll, N.Y.: Orbis Books, 1974); *Three Mile an Hour God* (Maryknoll, N.Y.: Orbis Books, 1980).

11. EATWOT was organized in Tanzania (1976) and has held conferences in Ghana (1977), Sri Lanka (1979), Brazil (1980), India (1981) and Geneva (1983). It is an organization of African, Asian, Latin American, Caribbean, and North American black and Hispanic theologians. I first met Preman Niles at the Sri Lanka meeting.

12. See his essay "Messiah and Minjung: Discerning Messianic Politics Over Against Political Messianism" in this volume.

13. Ibid.

14. Ibid.

15. For this view, see especially José Miranda, *Being and the Messiah: The Message of St. John*, trans. by John Eagleson (Maryknoll, N.Y.: Orbis Books, 1977), pp. 39–42; see also José Míguez Bonino, "Popular Piety in Latin America" in *Cristianismo y Sociedad* (Buenos Aires), no. 47 (first issue, 1976), pp. 31–38, trans. James and Margret Goff. In this essay, Míguez Bonino writes: "From a theological as well as a political perspective the popular piety which used to exist and that still predominates in Latin America can only be considered a profoundly alienated and alienating piety, a manifestation of an enslaved consciousness and, at the same time, a ready instrument for the continuation and consolidation of oppression. The intent to transform the mobilizing power of that piety to the goals of transformation without altering the very content of the religious consciousness seems psychologically impossible and theologically unacceptable."

16. For my accounts of the tensions regarding class and culture between Latin Americans, on the one hand, and Asians, blacks, and Africans, on the other, see my " 'Asia's Struggle for a Full Humanity: Toward A Relevant Theology' (An Asian Theological Conference)" in G. Wilmore and J. Cone, eds., *Black Theology: A Documentary History*, pp. 593–601; "Introduction" to "Black Theology and Third World Theologies" in ibid., pp. 445–62; "Black Theology and Third World Theology" in Virginia Fabella and Sergio Torres, eds., *Irruption of the Third World*, pp. 235–45; "From Geneva to São Paulo: A Dialogue between Black Theology and Latin American Liberation Theology" in Sergio Torres and John Eagleson, eds., *The Challenge of Basic Christian Communities* (Maryknoll, N.Y.: Orbis Books, 1981), pp. 265–81.

One of the best accounts of this tension is found in the responses of the non-Latin Americans at the São Paulo, Brazil, Conference of EATWOT in *The Challenge of Basic Christian Communities,* pp. 235f. Note especially the responses of Preman Niles, Cornel West, and Tissa Balasuriya. For earlier accounts of this tension, see D. S. Amalorpavadass, "News and Comments: Ecumenical Dialogue of Third World Theologians" in *Indian Theological Studies,* vol. 14, no. 4, December 1977. Commenting on EATWOT's organizing meeting of Tanzania, he wrote: "The Latins were the whole time harping on socio-economic-political dimensions as the major or only reality, and applied rigorously the Marxian tool of analysis. All the other realities were so insignificant for them that they could be integrated into the economic-political domination or its consequences. This was questioned strongly by Asians and Africans though they agreed with the analysis and results of socio-economic-political reality." The most perceptive interpreter of the differences between Asian theology and Latin American theology is Aloysius Pieris of Sri Lanka. See especially his "Towards an Asian Theology of Liberation: Some Religio-Cultural Guidelines" in Virginia Fabella, ed., *Asia's Struggle for Full Humanity*, pp. 75–95; in this essay, Pieris says: "A liberation theopraxis in Asia which uses only the Marxist tools of *social* analysis will remain un-Asian and ineffective until it integrates the psychological tools of *introspection* which our sages have discovered" (p. 88). "The Place of Non-Christian Religions and Culture in the Evolution of Third World Theology" in Virginia Fabella and Sergio Torres, eds., in *Irruption of the Third World,* pp. 113–39; "The Asian Sense in Theology" in *Dialogue,* vol. VI, nos. 1 & 2, January–August 1979.

Other useful interpretations are J. C. Duraisingh and K. C. Abraham, "Reflections from an Asian Perspective" in V. Fabella and S. Torres, eds., *Irruption of the Third World*, pp. 209–16; Engelbert Mveng, "Third World Theology: What Theology? What Third World? Evaluation by an African Delegate" in ibid., pp. 217–21.

Regarding the significant movement of some Latin Americans toward an appreciation of religion and culture, see especially, Gustavo Gutiérrez, "Reflections from a Latin American Perspective: Finding Our Way to Talk about God" and Sergio Torres, "The Irruption of the Third World: A Challenge to Theology" in *Irruption of the Third World*, pp. 222–34 and 3–15 respectively. Reflecting upon EATWOT's five major conferences, from Tanzania (1976) to India (1981), Gutiérrez referred to the impact of Africans, Asians, and black and Hispanic North Americans upon his theology: "As a Latin American, I myself have been goaded by the life and death of my people. . . . I must confess that I had a tendency to shut myself up in those realities. But at these meetings I have come in contact with the forms of oppression experienced by other peoples and with their approaches to liberation and reflection on the faith. I have gained enormously from that contact. . . . When we began to talk explicitly about liberation theology (in 1968), we used three terms to talk about the poor and oppressed on our continent: class, race, and culture. This initial perception has acquired fresh urgency and content from our direct contact with other theologies and realities—that is, those of Africa, Asia, and the black and Hispanic minorities in the United States. Moreover, this contact has enabled us to better understand and appreciate certain features of our own people, which might otherwise have remained in the chiaroscuro of a theory with little or no relation to practice" (pp. 230–31).

17. See his "A Theological Look at the Mask Dance in Korea" in this volume.

18. Ibid.

19. There is a strong influence of Latin American liberation theology in the Philippines. This is partly due to the fact that Roman Catholic Christianity is the majority religion in that country. The tensions between Asians from the Philippines and persons from other parts of the continent emerged sharply at EATWOT's Sri Lanka Conference in January 1979. See especially Carlos H. Abesamis, "Faith and Life Reflections from the Grassroots in the Philippines" in Virginia Fabella, ed., *Asia's Struggle for Full Humanity*, p. 123-39.

20. In addition to the essays by Gutiérrez and Torres in Note 16, see especially Juan Carlos Scannone, "Theology, Popular Culture, and Discernment" in Rosino Gibellini, ed., *Frontiers of Theology in Latin America* (Maryknoll, N.Y.: Orbis Books, 1979).

21. See his "Towards a Theology of Han" in this volume.

22. See especially José Miranda, *Marx and the Bible*, trans. John Eagleson (Maryknoll, N.Y.: Orbis Books, 1974); *Being and the Messiah*, trans. John Eagleson (Orbis Books, 1977); Jon Sobrino, *Christology at the Crossroads*, trans. John Drury (Orbis Books, 1978); Leonardo Boff, *Jesus Christ Liberator*, trans. Patrick Hughes (Orbis Books, 1978); Elsa Tamez, *The Bible of the Oppressed* (Orbis Books, 1982); Severino Croatto, "Biblical Hermeneutics in the Theologies of Liberation," in Fabella and Torres, eds., *Irruption of the Third World,* pp. 140-68.

23. See Hyun, "Minjung the Suffering Servant and Hope," an unpublished lecture at James Memorial Chapel (April 13, 1982), Union Theological Seminary, N.Y. According to Hyun, Han Wan-song's definition appeared in his book, *Minjung and Society*. Han is a sociologist and formerly taught at Seoul National University.

MINJUNG
THEOLOGY

Introduction

D. PREMAN NILES

For quite some time now, Asian theologians have been debating the question of how one does theology in Asia. These have been, by and large, discussions *about* doing theology rather than the doing of theology itself.[1] Christopher Doraisingh, an Indian theologian, states the problem succinctly. "What theology is not in our context, we seem to know; but what it is, we still are not sure."

For the past few years, starting in 1978, the Commission on Theological Concerns (CTC) of the Christian Conference of Asia (CCA) has been wrestling with this problem; and the present volume, *Minjung Theology: People as Subjects of History*, is one of several breakthroughs in the task of doing theology in Asia.

In this introduction we will sketch the theological scene in Asia, answering as best as possible in a brief statement the problem posed by Christopher Doraisingh, so that Korean theology may be seen in the context of a wider theological ferment. We will limit ourselves to sketching the Asian theological scene, since in the first chapter of this volume, "A Biographical Sketch of an Asian Theological Consultation," David Suh introduces the Korean material in the context of a dialogue between Korean and other Asian theologians.

During the course of a debate on doing theology in Asia, Emerito Nacpil, a Filipino theologian, made an observation which both indicates the essential character of the context in which we do theology and the problem for theology itself. He said, "All the great religions in Asia have formed their own cultures. With the possible exception of the Philippines, Christianity has not." This situation poses a serious problem for doing theology in Asia, because we have to take these cultures into account, either negatively or positively, in trying to understand the presence and activity of Jesus Christ in Asia.

The problem of culture does not arise, or does not seem to be crucial, if one is concerned purely with the task of fishing out souls from a "non-Christian" world and fitting them out for heaven. In this case, it really does not matter whether the church is culturally and theologically Roman Catholic, Anglican, Methodist, Western, Eastern, or whatever. There may be some problems of adjustment for the new converts, but these are easily overcome as they have been in the course of Asian church history. In Asia, we call this phenomenon "Mission-compound Christianity."

However, if the task for theology is seen in more holistic terms as taking in the totality of individual and corporate life, one cannot ignore the whole complex of inter-relations, interactions, and mutual antagonisms between Christianity and other cultures which I have called elsewhere "the problem of the two stories."[2]

The usual approach to the second story (i.e., any Asian culture and spirituality) has been to deny its validity. It is deemed to be in the area of general revelation, i.e. it has its good points but is essentially worthless when one receives the gospel—the *full* story of Jesus Christ. It is therefore to be discarded when one becomes a Christian. This tendency is still evident, for example, in many of our theological schools where Western church history and Asian church history from a missionary perspective are taught, but seldom or never do we have courses on Asian history or culture. Even in the teaching of other religions one often begins to feel the implied prejudice that we are dealing with the less perfect in comparison to Christianity.

This stand was inadvertently strengthened by Kraemer at the Mission Conference in Tambaram, India (1938), when he raised the issue of syncretism which he called "the illegitimate mingling of different religious elements." Consequently, attempts to relate to Asian religions and cultures have often been stymied by the specter of syncretism. In actual fact, as M. M. Thomas points out,[3] Kraemer was not against the interaction of the two stories and indeed argued that it is imperative to "translate," "interpret," and "incarnate" Christianity against the background of other religions. He called this process "adaptation" and pointed to the fact that such adaptations or incarnations have taken place throughout church history. He went on to state, "Europeans can proffer no reasonable objection to adaptations in the sense of various characteristically Asiatic or African expressions, because their own national and regional Christianity, which they often cherish highly, are all adaptations."

Kraemer was a European Christian viewing other religions as alien stories in which the gospel had to be incarnated. Justice P. Chenchiah, a lay Indian Christian who disagreed with Kraemer, saw the gospel as the alien story which was breaking into the "Indian" story. It was his opinion that other faiths have a rightful place in the understanding of God's dealings with all humanity, so that other religious and historical traditions must be taken seriously as vehicles of divine revelation in Christian theological thinking.

In stating that other faiths also have a rightful place in understanding God's dealings with humanity, Chenchiah pointed out the inadequacy or narrowness of a theology that is based on salvation history as classically understood by the church. He himself spoke of a "Cosmic Christ" and emphasized the cosmic process of creation. Developing Chenchiah's insight, Paul Devanandan states, "God's act of redemption in Christ Jesus concerns the whole of his creation. Biblical faith repeatedly affirms that the work of Christ is of cosmic significance in that the redemption wrought in him has affected the entire creative process."[4]

This plea for widening the base for theological construction in Asia has led to three main distinguishable yet inter-related theological thrusts.

The Significance of Other Faiths for a Deeper Understanding of the Christian Faith

Even before Chenchiah, attempts were made to see the significance of other faiths in relation to Christianity. One of the earliest of these was that of J. N. Farquhar, who saw the best in other religions "reproduced in perfect form, completely fulfilled and completed in Jesus Christ." The title of his book, *The Crown of Hinduism*, is itself indicative of his approach that all religions find their fulfilment in Jesus Christ. Much later, Raymond Panikkar in his book entitled *The Unknown Christ of Hinduism* went much further in identifying Christic elements in one branch of Hindu faith. Panikkar's view is that Christianity is Hinduism which has died and risen again transformed. Panikkar for one makes a serious attempt to see how Hindu Scriptures can be related as an Old Testament to the New Testament.[5]

Without raising too sharply the issue of how other faiths may be seen in relation to Christianity or to Christ, attempts were made to use other faith categories to communicate the Christian faith. A good example of this is Robin Boyd's *Khristadvaita*, which uses Hindu religious concepts to communicate Christian doctrine.[6]

A similar attempt is made by Lynn de Silva, particularly in his article "Theological Construction in a Buddhist Context."[7] But he goes much further than Boyd in that he not only perceives conceptual similarities which make possible a communication of the Christian faith in Buddhist categories but also accepts and works on the possibility that Buddhism permits a deeper understanding of the Christian faith. A similar position is taken by Khin Maung Din in "Some Problems and Possibilities for Burmese Christian Theology Today."[8] Aloysius Pieris follows through with the same method and sees a greater complementariness between religions in his "Towards an Asian Theology of Liberation: Religio-cultural Guidelines."[9] Pieris breaks new ground in attempting to relate Marxian insights on liberation with religious experiences of liberation to forge a new theology for Asia. He declares that "theology in Asia is the Christian apocalypse of the non-Christian experiences of liberation." More recently Lakshman Wickremesinghe[10] has followed through the suggestions of his compatriot Pieris and argues that the only reasonable and viable option that the church in Asia can take is "indigenous Marxist socialism." To set out this ecclesiological stance he employs the story of Markandeya from the *Matsya Purana*, a Hindu sacred book. What is particularly challenging in this presentation is the methodological assumption that the experiences of an Asian church have already been symbolized in a Hindu myth so that it, rather than a biblical motif or symbol, would help to understand the church's predicament and the call to renewal.

An Option for Creation Rather than Salvation History (Redemption) as a Framework for Doing Theology in Asia

In his book, *Christian Mission in Reconstruction—An Asian Attempt*, Choan-seng Song rejects the ideology of Christendom as a theological undergirding for mission in Asia.[11] He points to two significant events which indicate that the Christendom era is clearly over.

> We have experienced two radical breaks in historical continuity: the breakdown of the effort on the part of the Western churches to incorporate the masses of humanity in Asia into "salvation history" as they saw it; and the resolute rejection of Christianity by China, which has become a communist state.[12]

Although the statement concerning China may now have to be tempered in the light of recent events in that country, the essential thesis of Song that Asian nations and peoples have chosen their own roads to "liberation" or "salvation" cannot be repudiated.

Having pointed to the break from Western mission history and a leap from Jerusalem to Asia, Song proposes the doctrine or framework of Creation for breaking out of a "Mission-compound Christianity" to a larger understanding of God's mission which recognizes the cultural and religious histories of other peoples.

While Song was essentially right in advocating the framework of Creation for theological construction in Asia, he was limited on two counts. *One*, he followed the German Old Testament theologian Gerhard Von Rad in treating Creation as ancillary to Redemption and as really no more than a backdrop to several "histories" or as a sum total of several redemption histories and not as a motif in its own right. *Two*, he tended to use the Christian or biblical experience or story as normative for viewing other histories. He regards other histories as exhibiting in a less concentrated way the salvation history intensely exhibited in the Bible.

Though agreeing with the basic position of Song, I took issue with him on both counts.[13] I argued that to take the biblical motif of Creation seriously is in fact to see it not as ancillary to Redemption or the backdrop for Redemption, but as a motif in its own right as exhibited particularly by Second Isaiah and the Priestly Writer. The motif of Creation, especially in the way Second Isaiah uses it, bears witness to the fact that the Creator God can do the radically new thing in history. From this perspective, it would be possible to understand theologically the radical breaks in church history which Song notes as well as the new breaks of the people (minjung) of Asia for liberation and new possibilities. In this theological context, it would be possible to re-appropriate past traditions and re-interpret them so that the "old" speaks to the "new" and the "new" illumines the "old." The motif of Creation also permits us to view other traditions as witnessing to the manifold wisdom of the Creator God so that these speak in their own terms without our imposing a Christian or biblical principle of selection. Other faith traditions too have to be re-interpreted so that they speak meaningfully to the present, for these contain the experiences of our people, both their hopes and their fears. Theology in Asia, therefore, would have to be a shared enterprise and not just a Christian activity.

It must be noted that neither Song nor I argued that the motif of Creation become a theological center or a primary concept or category for Asian theology. Our contention was that Creation, rather than Redemption, History narrowly understood in terms of the ideology of Christendom, should provide the basic framework and emphases for doing theology in Asia.

Jesus Christ in the Asian Revolution

An East Asia Christian Conference document states the basic thrust of this position in these words:

> The church must endeavor to discern how Christ is at work in the revolution of contemporary Asia, releasing new creative forces, judging idolatry and false gods, leading peoples to a decision for or against him, and gathering to himself those who respond in faith to him. . . . The church must not only discern Christ in the changing life but be there in it, responding to him and making his presence and lordship known.[14]

The attempt to discern the presence of the Cosmic Christ in the Asian revolutionary process, which began under colonialism through independence to building new national human communities, was essentially the work of M. M. Thomas. He states his post-Kraemer position in these words:

> My own entry into the realm of theology has been through politics and the concern for political and social justice. Therefore, while agreeing with Kraemer that the gospel is from God and should ever remain centred in the Christ of God, some of us began to affirm with Arend Van Leeuven the other side of the medal, namely, that the gospel is "for men." Therefore Divine Truth should not be divorced from human values and social ideology. A Christ-centred Humanism is integral to the gospel and has its own evangelistic dimension. If theology is Christologically oriented, it need not be opposed to anthropology.[15]

From the perspective of the Asian revolutionary process aiming at the building of societies which realize the highest possible quality of human life,

Thomas viewed other religions not in terms of their "religiosity" but in terms of their potential for transforming and building human communities. He was interested in them as renascent religions within which one may discern "a partial acknowledgement of Christ." Thomas viewed not only religions but also secular ideologies, which are concerned with the task of building truly human communities, as expressions, albeit with distortions, of the activity of the Cosmic Christ. He held "that the common humanity and the self-transcendence within it, more especially the common response to the problems of humanisation of existence in the modern world rather than any common religiosity, or common sense of the Divine, is the most fruitful point of entry for a meeting of faiths at spiritual depth in our time."[16] He could therefore argue that "the Struggle for Human Dignity is a Preparation for the gospel,"[17] since in the basic quest and struggle of people for their humanity Christ is present in spite of the distortions that are present in any revolutionary movement. He describes the ethos or ideology of the Asian struggle as an "integral humanism, spiritually informed by the insights of the prophetic Christian faith and by the humanism of Asia's indigenous religions and cultures."[18]

I have quoted at length from Thomas because it was his theological leadership, expressed especially through the Church and Society Committee of the East Asia Christian Conference (EACC, now CCA), coupled with the ecumenical vision of D. T. Niles, that brought about the next stage for theological construction in Asia: a stage in which the three trends or thrusts outlined above are going through a crisis and being transformed to play a more energetic role in theological construction and ecclesial practice.

In a prophetic way, an EACC document, reflecting a debate with confessional families, states:

It is out of the contemporary necessity to confess the faith that there arises the task of theology for the churches in Asia. Theology is a living thing, having to do with our very existence as Christians and as churches. We cannot conceive of it in static or neatly defined final terms. A living theology must speak to the actual questions men in Asia are asking in the midst of their dilemmas; their hopes, aspirations and achievements; their doubts, despair and suffering. It must also speak in relation to the answers that are being given by Asian religions and philosophies, both in their classical form and in new forms created by the impact on them of western thought, secularism and science. Christian theology will fulfil its task in Asia only as the Asian churches, as servants of God's Word and revelation in Jesus Christ, speak to the Asian situation and from involvement in it. Dogmatic theological statements from a church that stands on the side-lines as spectator or even interpreter of what God is doing in Asia can carry no conviction. A living theology is born out of the meeting of a living church and its world.[19]

This statement admirably captures the ethos of the stage we are in now, and within which minjung theology and other Asian theologies are being articulated.

We will indicate the characteristics of the situation we are in and some of the causes leading to it rather than attempt a systematic description of it which may have to be done after several Asian theologies have emerged and we are more able to perceive larger collocations of theological accents and trends.

As a way of leading into the situation in which we are, let me quote the words of D. T. Niles expressing a vision which led to new paths of obedience, new adventures, crises, and now hopefully new or renewed beginnings. Speaking of the function of the EACC/CCA, he said that it would be

> . . . in building up within the life of each church and country a group of men and women, both older and younger, who are willing to probe the frontiers of the Christian enterprise . . . to venture into unchartered territory, whether of thought or action or organization, and to risk the mistakes that this kind of adventure demands. To give to these frontier people a sense of solidarity, encouragement and sharpened insight is a prime concern for such an organization as the EACC.[20]

The comprehensive vision within which D. T. Niles projected the function of the EACC/CCA was articulated in the words "the Christian Community within the Human Community." It was a time when Asian nations were coming out of the colonial period of their history. Nationalism and nation-building were the demands of the hour. Many Christians participated in the freedom struggle and in the process of nation building. There was the renaissance of indigenous religions which, under the impact of both Christianity and secular ideologies, were concerned to work towards the building of a truly human community. For the churches in Asia, the basic challenge was "what does it mean to be a missionary church in our own lands?" Historically, it was a time of rising expectations and great aspirations within which and in conversation with which Christian hope could be expressed.

In the early 1970s, the secular mood changed from one of expectation to despair and a great measure of pessimism. Independence had not meant the alleviation of the suffering of the masses. A few had much and many had little; and the direction of both human and economic development tended to favor the few. Neither did independence mean the coming into being of national human communities. Rather, what we see in Asia today is a certain ideological and/or religious crystallization with a corresponding sense of the communal element. Communities are in conflict with one another as each asserts its identity apart from and over against other communities. This situation of conflict is exploited by the many military dictatorships in Asia to stay in power.

Those who moved to the frontiers of the Christian enterprise experienced the deep contradictions in this general situation because they were now with "the people"—the ones who have to bear the heavier burdens. In this situation, there were not only social, economic, and political analyses, but a profound understanding of the people (the minjung) themselves—so that fundamental questions were raised about the role of both theology and ideology.[21] In essence, the criticism was that as elites we tend to articulate *for* the people, whether it be in terms of ideology, religious spirituality, or theology and not take into account the historical experiences and perceptions of the people themselves.[22]

The shifts in realizations and emphases in Asian Christian thinking over the years are evident in the EACC/CCA Assembly themes: The Christian Community within the Human Community (1968); Christian Action in the Asian Struggle (1973); Jesus Christ in Asian Suffering and Hope (1977); Living in Christ with People (1981).

Far from expressing despair and pessimism in the midst of the massive suppression of human rights, growing militarism, and tight technocratic control, and the displacement and destruction of people, there is a new mood of hope. There are unmistakable evidences of the awakening of the people themselves. Hence, basic to the new theological stance is the affirmation that not the rulers but the people are the subjects of history—a stance evident in the following affirmation:

> The wealth of Asia is in its people. Over half the world's population is in Asia. The wealth of people is not in numbers alone. People in Asia have a long history and a rich culture which spans thousands of years. Many of the world's greatest religious movements started in Asia. Many of the finest expressions of the creative human spirit are in Asia.
>
> The discovery of the wealth of people is in many ways new. Up to now people have been taken for granted. The abundance of their tradition and culture has often been ignored. The reason for this is that we tend to see the people through the eyes of the rulers and empire builders. History is often written from the perspective of the rulers and their boastful claims to fame.
>
> We seldom realise that it is the work of the people that has made it possible for rulers to do the things they claim. Time and again the traditions and the wealth of the people are used by the rulers for their own purposes. There is the need to discover people in their own terms.
>
> A new mood is emerging in Asia—an awakening of the people themselves. A new history is being written in our time. No longer are the victories and exploits of the powerful the central points for an understanding of history. Now the deep movements of the human spirit and the growing solidarity of the people are the reference points for a perception of history. Empires rise and fall, kingdoms come and go, but the people remain as the permanent reality of history.
>
> Jesus lived with people and ministered to them. It was in living with

people that Jesus understood the shape and purpose of his own ministry. He put the outcasts, dispossessed, and victimized at the very centre of his teaching and proclamation of the Kingdom of God. It is from this perspective that we must view the deep aspirations of the people to be the subjects of their own history.[23]

The challenge posed by the new situation has led to a re-understanding of the initial insight of Chenchiah in relating the two stories. It would no longer be possible to look at the story of the people from a Christian perspective. Instead, the Christian story would have to be looked at from the perspective of the people. As Kim Yong-bock once stated sharply in a debate, ''I am not really concerned with the mission of the church that derives its impetus from within the church. Rather, I am fundamentally concerned with the mission of the people to the church—their cries and their sufferings, their aspirations and their demands which should elicit from the churches not a 'churchy' response but a people 'response.'''

In other words, the emphasis of M. M. Thomas on the creation of a new humanity in Christ is being deepened in two ways.

First, the process of forming a new humanity in Christ is seen to be not just in the modern Asian revolution but as a continuous historical process coming from the past. It is discernible not in the history perceived and written by the rulers but in the history experienced and recounted by the people. Thus, a broadening of the theological base to include other religions and the formation of the new humanity through the present revolutionary processes has been extended to encompass the history of the people. As Hyun Young-hak states, ''We do not believe in an invalid God who was carried piggy-back to Korea by the first missionary. He was here working in our history before the missionaries came.''

Second, in the process of the interaction of the two stories, primary weightage is being given to the perceptions and modes of expression of the people with an honest recognition of the distortions within them, so that the tasks for theology emerge from within the people themselves. This approach is evident throughout the present volume, but particularly in Suh Nam-dong's ''Towards a Theology of *Han*.'' The same plea is being voiced also in other national theological contexts. In essence, new languages and modes of expression are emerging or being created for theological articulation.

The essays in this volume illustrate both these processes.

As indicated earlier, the essay of David Suh provides an introduction to the major themes in this volume. His essay, however, was written in the context of a particular dialogue and hence shows the sequence of that dialogue. The present volume has its own sequence and logic which are indicated in the section headings.

This book has no written conclusion. There are two reasons for this. *One*, the debate and clarifications are continuing in Korea; and in many ways, this volume is only the tip of the iceberg. It is a theology that is being lived and practised and can have no real conclusion except in the Messianic Kingdom. *Two*, minjung theology, as the Korean theologians themselves say, "is not for export." It is a highly contextualized theology and the reader must write his/her conclusion or rather derive from it emphases and motifs that speak to one's own situation. One such response from the black theologian James Cone is included in this volume.

Many of the issues raised in this volume will continue to be probed and clarified not only in Korea but also in other Asian contexts where they are being raised in slightly different ways. Paramount among these would be the question of a relevant ecclesiology for Asia and the issue of the shape of our political vision—a statement of penultimate goals and the shape of the society to which we should move that is between the "now" and the "not yet" of the Messianic Kingdom.[24]

A complicated history lies behind the production of this volume. Between the original papers, which were delivered at the Korean theological dialogue, and the final versions printed here, many of the authors were caught up in the turmoil following President Park Chung-hee's assassination. Some were in prison, others were in hiding for a while, and almost all of them lost their jobs. Only the firm conviction and the unwavering commitment that minjung theology must be heard outside Korea have made it possible to finish this project.

There has been a complicated process of translation, re-translation, editing, and sometimes even counter-editing to bring out a readable and authentic statement of Korean theology. Also, several new articles had to be written for this volume.

At the end of all of these difficulties, minjung theology makes its humble, but by no means tentative, appearance to an English-reading public.

NOTES

1. See my report to the Commission on Theological Concerns of the CCA on "The Role of the Theologian," *CTC Bulletin,* vol. 1 no. 2, pp. 16–19. See also *CTC Bulletin (Hayyim)*, vol. 1, no. 1.

2. See my report to the Commission on Theological Concerns of the CCA, *CTC Bulletin*, vol. 2, nos. 1–2, p. 10. This issue of the CTC Bulletin, *Some Emerging Theological Trends in Asia,* should be read in conjunction with the introduction to the present volume for a fuller picture of the theological ferment in Asia. See also my article, "Christian Mission and the Peoples of Asia," *CTC Bulletin*, vol. 3, no. 1, pp. 34–48.

3. M. M. Thomas, "Christ-centred syncretism," *Varieties of Witness*, ed. Niles and Thomas (Singapore: CCA, 1980), pp. 9–19, restates and clarifies the essential stand of Kraemer.

4. P. D. Devanandan, *The Gospel and Renascent Hinduism* (London: SCM, 1959), p. 47.

5. See Robin Boyd, *An Introduction to Indian Christian Theology* (Madras: CLS Press, 1975), pp. 37–52.

6. Robin Boyd, *Khristadvaita: A Theology for India* (Madras: CLS Press, 1977).

7. Lynn de Silva, "Theological Construction in a Buddhist Context, " *Asian Voices in Christian Theology,* ed. G. H. Anderson (Maryknoll, N.Y.: Orbis Books, 1976), pp. 37–52. See also "The Problem of the Self in Buddhism and Christianity," *What Asian Christians Are Thinking,* ed. Douglas J. Elwood (Quezon City, Philippines: New Day Publishers, 1976), pp. 105–118.

8. Khin Maung Din, "Some Problems and Possibilities for Burmese Christian Theology," *What Asian Christians Are Thinking,* pp. 87–104.

9. Aloysius Pieris, "Towards an Asian Theology of Liberation," *Varieties of Witness,* pp. 21–42.

10. Lakshman Wickremesinghe, "Living in Christ with People," D. T. Niles Memorial Lecture at Seventh CCA Assembly, Bangalore. See *A Vulnerable Discipleship* (Singapore: CCA, 1981), pp. 25–49.

11. Choan-seng Song, *Christian Mission in Reconstruction—An Asian Attempt,* (Madras: CLS Press, 1975; Maryknoll, N.Y.: Orbis Books, 1977).

12. Choan-seng Song, "From Israel to Asia—A Theological Leap," *Theology* (March 1976), p. 91.

13. D. Preman Niles, "Toward a Framework for Doing Theology in Asia," in *Asian Theological Reflection on Suffering and Hope,* ed. Yap Kim-heo (Singapore: CCA, 1977), and in *The Human and the Holy,* ed. E. P. Nacpil and D. J. Elwood (Quezon City: New Day Publishers, 1978; Maryknoll, N.Y.: Orbis Books, 1980), pp. 267–288. See also Song—Niles—West debate in *Occasional Bulletin,* vol. 1, no. 3 (July 1977), pp. 9–15

14. *Witnesses Together,* ed. U Kyaw Than (Rangoon, 1959), p. 60.

15. M. M. Thomas, "Christ-centred syncretism," p. 13.

16. M. M. Thomas, *Man and the Universe of Faith* (Madras: CLS Press, 1975), p. vi.

17. M. M. Thomas, "The Struggle for Human Dignity as a Preparation for the Gospel," *What Asian Christians Are Thinking,* pp. 267–276.

18. M. M. Thomas, "Christian Action in the Asian Struggle," *What Asian Christians Are Thinking,* p. 451.

19. "Confessional Families and the Churches in Asia," an EACC Statement (Kandy, Ceylon, Dec. 6–8, 1975), p. 21.

20. D. T. Niles, *Ideas and Services* (EACC, 1968), pp. 7–8.

21. See "Towards an Ideology and Theology of People—A URM-CTC Dialogue," *CTC Bulletin,* vol. 2, no. 3, pp. 13–21. See also *Theology and Ideology—A URM Discussion,* CCA-URM, 1980, and *Towards a Theology of People,* CCA-URM, 1977. For analyses of the Asian situation see *People Toiling under Pharaoh,* CCA-URM, 1976.

22. Reynaldo C. Ileto, "The Idiom of Change in Colonial Philippines: A People's Perspective," *Church, State and People—the Philippines in the '80s,* ed. Feliciano V. Carino (CTC-CCA Publication, 1981), pp. 47–59. See also his *Pasyon and Revolution, Popular Movements in the Philippines, 1840–1910* (Quezon City: Ateneo de Manila University Press, 1979).

23. Statement from a CCA staff writing team for the Seventh CCA Assembly.

24. See in particular Feliciano V. Carino, "The Philippine Dialogue: An Interpretative Report," *Church, State and People,* pp. 63–74, and his statement accepted by the CCA Seventh Assembly, section IV, sub-section 2. Carino argues for the necessity of a political vision that would enable us "to give an account of our hope" taking into account not only the struggles of the people but also the politicized expressions of Asian religions and the messianic claims of ideologies in Asia.

SECTION ONE:
MINJUNG AND THEOLOGY
IN KOREA

Chapter I

A Biographical Sketch of an Asian Theological Consultation

SUH KWANG-SUN DAVID

Setting the Stage

"The People of God and the Mission of the Church." That was the general theme of the first theological consultation organized by the Theological Commission of the National Council of Churches in Korea, which was held in Seoul, October 22–24, 1979. Seventeen Asians whose countries ranged from India to Japan came to participate in the consultation. Their being able to attend was, we thought, a miracle considering the tight control during those days over foreigners entering Korea. For the Koreans to attend this meeting was an act of courage and commitment. Some twenty-four of us participated in the meeting. (Perhaps it may not be inappropriate here to note that two nights after the consultation, President Park Chung-hee was assassinated by his own KCIA chief, bringing to an end his powerful eighteen-year-old regime. This event made us humble as we realized our ignorance and unbelief about the future and the *eschaton* of history.)

The theme "The People of God and the Mission of the Church" was actually a cover name for the consultation in order *not* to attract too much attention from the authorities who would keep an eye on most of the Korean participants. "The People of God" is church jargon; and for the authorities "mission" is a harmless cliché. Thus, the authorities were not too alarmed about the meeting.

Actually, the theme of the consultation was "minjung" and the recent theological development in Korea of the category of "minjung." "Minjung" is a dangerous word. In many ways, the whole purpose of the consultation was to delineate the danger implied in this word. "Minjung" is a Korean word, but it is a combination of two Chinese characters "min" and "jung." "Min" may be translated as "people" and "jung" as "the mass." Thus "minjung" means "the mass of the people, or mass, or just the people." But when we try to translate it into English, "mass" is not adequate for our theological purpose; and "the people" is politically dangerous in anti-Communist Korea, because it has become a Communist word. Although "the people of God" may seem to be the most safe and perhaps a neutral expression both in Korean and English, theologically and politically "minjung" cannot be translated into "the people of God."

Minjung theology is a Korean theology. "Minjung" is a term which grew out of the Christian experiences in the political struggle for justice over the last ten or more years. Theology of minjung or minjung theology is an accumulation and articulation of theological reflections on the political experiences of Christian students, laborers, the press, professors, farmers, writers, and intellectuals as well as theologians in Korea in the 1970s. It is a theology of the oppressed in the Korean political situation, a theological response to the oppressors, and it is the response of the oppressed to the Korean church and its mission. Theology of minjung is a creation of those Christians who were forced to reflect upon their Christian discipleship in basement interrogation rooms, in trials, facing court-martial tribunals, hearing the allegations of prosecutors, and in making their own final defense. They reflected on their Christian commitment in prison cells, in their letters from prison to families and friends, in their readings of books sent by friends all over the world, in their unemployment, in their stay at home under house arrest, while subject to a twenty-four-hour watch over their activities, and during visits with their friends. Theology of minjung is a socio-political biography of Korean Christians in the 1970s. This is the way in which Korean Christians have lived and acted, prayed and participated in the Lord's Supper. Thus the main purpose and objective of the consultation was to tell the story of Korean Christians—about what we have experienced. And out of that suffering and struggling but nevertheless victorious experience, we wanted to speak of what we have learned and about what we have reflected upon theologically, and share this with friends who in their own social and political milieu are searching for a relevant theology in Asia. It was a search for a contextual theology in Asia.

Having heard the theology of minjung described as a reflection of Christians about their experiences in a struggle, one may suspect that the recent development of the so-called Korean theology is but a Korean expression either of liberation theology imported from Latin America or of theological writings coming from West European and North American communities. This kind of suspicion has often been expressed both by Koreans and international visitors to Korea. On the one hand, if it is viewed as an imported theology from Latin America, one can easily dismiss the theology of minjung as a Korean version of a Latin American revolutionary theology inspired by Marxist ideology. Such a theology would be politically an anathema in South

Korea. On the other hand, if it is seen as an imported product of Western theological writings, then it would be a theology understood only by those who can read Western theology in foreign languages. Such a theology would have nothing in common with the experiences and thinking either of the people on the street or of the average Korean churchgoer.

While dissociating ourselves from imported models, we cannot in fact claim that minjung theology is *the* Korean theology, if by Korean theology we mean what is acceptable to the majority of Korean churchgoers and theologians. Although it is rapidly making inroads into the Christian community, beginning with the marginal elements, it is still a Korean theology in the making. It is *a* Korean theology for the future and of the future which is emerging out of the reflections on experiences of the Korean reality at this particular time in history.

While affirming that minjung theology is a Korean theology, those who are working on a theology of minjung would agree that it is a political hermeneutics of the Gospel and a political interpretation of Korean Christian experiences. The theology of minjung is in the general theological area of Bonhoeffer's "worldly interpretation of the Bible" and the "secular meaning of the Gospel." It is a development of the "political hermeneutics of the Gospel" in terms of the Korean reality. It is our effort to provide a framework of political theology which takes into consideration the socio-economic and political history of Korea and the socio-political biography of the Christian koinonia in Korea.

We must admit the fact that the "political hermeneutics of the Gospel" has opened up for us an entirely new horizon enabling us to look at the Korean Christian experience in terms of a new framework. In other words, in the light of political theology, we have discovered that throughout the history of the Korean church we have indeed been doing political theology. People's struggle for political and economic justice in the rapidly industrializing Korea of the 1970s and Christian participation in the struggle were triggered neither by the foreign ideology of Marxism nor by an imported theology of human rights or politics. Rather, it was a rediscovery of a tradition which was there from the beginning of the Christian church in Korea. That is to say that along with its spiritual growth, Korean Christianity has also matured politically and socially. It is this factor that gives Korean Christianity its distinctive character. We now find that the theology of minjung is a further articulation of the theological consciousness of the Korean Christian experience. It is an articulation which comes from the experience of Korean Christians who are suffering in the political and social struggles for justice and humanity. The methodology of political theology, which has been developed in the Western world, has helped us to understand more sharply the unique character of Korean Christianity and to reappropriate our heritage as we move into a further stage in the expression of Korean theology, namely a theology of minjung which has as its focus of concern the suffering of the oppressed people in Korea.

Usually, books about the history of Korean Christianity, nearly two hundred years old for the Catholic Church and one hundred for the Protestants, have been written by missionaries as a part of the history of Western mission in Korea. A Protestant mission history written by a Korean was published in the 1920s, but it was in English.[1] However, in 1972 a history of the Protestant churches in Korea written by a Korean in Korean was published.[2] This publication should be seen as part of a wider Korean Christian consciousness.

In the 1970s, looking toward the centennial year of Protestant mission in Korea, which will be in 1984, denominational churches have been organizing various activities and setting several goals for the celebration of the centennial year. Of course, many of these goals and activities are aimed at the numerical expansion of denominational churches. But many of these organizational meetings have also included historical reflections on the character of Korean Christianity. In the 1970s it was almost a theological fad to look back on the traditions of the Korean church. The historical reflection, or the examination of our traditional background, was not just about Christian mission activities and their characteristics. Rather, it was more or less directed to the religious and cultural background of Korean Christianity. In what kind of religious or cultural soil were the Christian seeds sown? And what kind of Christian fruits are we bearing? What kind of Christianity do we have now? How is Korean Christianity different from Western Christianity? Under the rubric of "theology of indigenization," these questions were carried over from the 1960s. As a result of such research into our past, we now have Christian-Buddhist dialogue, Christian-Confucian dialogue, or the Christian understanding of Korean Shamanism and of Korean Buddhism.[3]

Another consequence of the search for the roots of Christianity in Korea was that some Christians turned more toward political and social issues. This radical change of direction had already started in the indigenization theology of the 1960s. The shift was there in its national consciousness. Theological emphasis was given to the Korean character, the Korean people, those who received and nourished the Gospel in Korean soil, thereby recognizing the people not as an object for mission but as the subject of mission.

The first church history of Korea by a Korean author in the Korean language has the sub-title, Development of a *National* Church in Korea.[4] His thesis is that, from the beginning, the Korean church was nationalistic in its purpose and direction and had the dynamic to develop into a national church. It is not too clear as to what he means by nationalistic. He might have meant a national organization of the church without any institutional connections with foreign mission agencies, or a united national church without American denominational divisions, or a church working for the development of national politics and theology. In a way, he must have intended to include all of these aspects. For the growth of the Korean church may be characterized as the development of a national church, independent of the influence of missionaries, which served as a hotbed for a national consciousness which was asserting itself over against Japanese colonialism in the Korean peninsula. The author of the first Korean church history written in Korean perceives the history of the Korean church in relation to the growth and development of Korean nationalism. The impact of his discovery of the roots of the Korean church has been such that subsequent studies of the history of church growth and development in Korea have taken seriously the role of this heightened nationalistic consciousness in the church.

To be both bold and simple, in order that we may have a clear grasp of the background of minjung theology, we could say that from the beginning of the Christian mission in Korea, Christianity in Korea has been political. In Korea, Christianity has been a center for the politics of nationalism, so that today too we cannot really understand the character of Korean Christianity apart from the politics of Korean nationalism in the history of twentieth-century Korea. Korean Christianity has grown as the religion of the oppressed nation or race or the people. We may, therefore, say that Korean Christianity has grown in the context of the politics of nationalism and the politics of the oppressed people, since Christians in Korea took the essence of the Christian gospel to be political. We have intuitively grasped the fact that the Christian gospel is for the release of the people and for political liberation from foreign domination.

The Character of Korean Christianity

The consultation began with Professor Choo Chai-yong's paper, "A Brief Sketch of Korean Christian History from the Minjung Perspective," which gave the non-Korean participants a broad background of minjung theology.

Protestant Christianity was introduced by American missionaries in the 1880s when the old "hermit" kingdom of Korea was forced to open its doors to the West. From then on, Protestant missionaries were very much among the Korean people, in the royal court and in the newly-introduced modern schools and hospitals. It was a time when the Japanese and Chinese were claiming colonial rights on the peninsula and moving their soldiers on to our shores. American missionaries were right in the middle of the bloodshed caused by the *coup d'etat* of young Korean radicals for a modernized Korea in the 1890s. And Korean Christians had to witness the brutal assassination of Queen Min by the Japanese soldiers who invaded the already defenseless royal court in 1895. During ten years of mission work in Korea, between 1895 and 1905, the missionaries witnessed the social and political turmoil, confusion, and bloodshed which finally led to the fateful imposition of Japanese colonial rule in 1905 when Korea was declared a protectorate of Japan.

In this milieu of national political crisis, the people of Korea responded to the Christian message; and the Christian koinonia interpreted the Christian message politically. The reason for such a response was the possible reform of the social and political structure of the country. Arthur Brown of the Federal Council of Foreign Mission Boards in the U.S.A. wrote about the situation as follows:

Poverty, oppression and distress, resulting from excessive taxation and the corrupt administration of justice, had begotten in many minds a longing for relief, and a hope that the missionary could secure it for them. A Methodist missionary told me that most of those who came to the missionary for the first time were influenced by this motive. Beyond any other people that I saw in Asia, the Koreans influenced me as pathetically stretching out their hands for help and guidance out of bitter bondage.[5]

It was not that the people of Korea looked to the missionaries personally for relief from social and political misery, but rather that they looked to the Christian religion and its gospel for their national salvation as a people and as a nation. Some people even saw in Christianity the training ground and resources for national rejuvenation and reform and national independence from the domination of foreign powers such as Japan. This was because of the social and political impact that Christianity had on Koreans through the opening of modern schools for young men and women and the opening of new types of hospitals for the sick. This happened in spite of the fact that it was not the conscious purpose of the Christian mission in Korea. Regardless of the religious intentions of the Christian mission, people in Korea responded to the Christian message as embodying a social and political hope for liberation.[6]

The intensity of the Korean Christian experience of national crisis and national humiliation, enhanced by a strong anti-Japanese feeling, alarmed the missionaries. They were unsure about their mission work in Korea. The missionaries realized the hopelessness of any political action undertaken by the Koreans in general and Christians in particular. They also foresaw the danger of making the young Christian church a political agency. This was the general sentiment of the missionaries as Korean Christians faced the national crisis. "We (missionaries) felt that the Korean church needed not only to repent for hating the Japanese, but a clear vision of all sin against God. . . . We felt . . . that embittered souls needed to have their personal relation with the Master."[7] Ever since, missionaries have attempted to depoliticize the Christian message and Christian activities. Such an effort was made in the following years in the Great Revival movement in Korea; and it seems to have succeeded.

The revival meetings were designed to be a search for purely religious experiences. The main features of the mass meetings were the public confessions of sin which followed emotional sermons and prayers convicting the people for their sins. Missionaries viewed the Great Revival of 1907 as the outpouring of the Holy Spirit and emphasized the spiritual and theological dimension of the mass experience. The reports of the missionaries about the mass revival meetings give their impressions of the spirituality of such a revival movement. And when they mention the public confessions of sin, it is apparent that the sin they have in mind is limited to immoral acts. There is no mention of how people in the revival meetings felt about their national tragedy or the collective sin of the people as a nation. But the Korean church historian George Paik saw that this revival was due to three factors: (1) a sense of failure, (2) the message from the outside, and (3) the definite attempt of the missionaries to bring about a revival. The attempt of the missionaries was to spiritualize the Christian message and thus to depoliticize and even denationalize Korean Christianity. Apparently, the missionaries were quite successful in leading the majority of Korean Christians away from political involvement. The revival meetings set the subsequent tone of Christianity in Korea as emotional, conservative, individualistic, and other-worldly. Until today, the average churchgoer follows the fetishistic belief that Christianity is a mere religion for material success in this world *and* for spiritual success in the other world. This is due not only to the success of the missionary effort, but also to the harsh political and religious suppression of the Koreans by the Japanese. Such a religion also has its roots in Korean shamanism.

However, in the face of the Korean people's loss of their nation and the Japanese suppression of the people, including the nonviolent Christian Patriotic movement, the attempt of the missionaries to depoliticize Christians was not wholly successful. Although successful in depoliticizing the Christians, they were not wholly successful in denationalizing them. Perhaps one could say that the great gatherings at revival meetings served to bring about a greater sense of nationalism together with a sense of political koinonia among the Korean Christians. The numerical growth of the Korean church made it possible for this sense of political koinonia to penetrate many areas of Korean life. The March First Independence movement of 1919 was the culmination of the political awakening of Korean Christians which exploded in their active participation in the national liberation and independence movement of the time.

Although the missionaries were alarmed about the apparent politicization of the Korean Christians and attempted to depoliticize them, we now find that the so-called politicization of Korean Christians was not a conscious process. The nature of the gospel interacting with a people in a particular situation produced this result. Perhaps it was indeed a result of the Holy Spirit working in our history.

Although the missionaries were not involved in the so-called politicization of Korean Christians, one of the things they did led directly to this process. When they translated the Bible into Korean they did *not* use Chinese characters, which were used by the Korean literati and the learned men of the time, but into the vernacular Korean script. The vernacular script was looked down upon by the Chinese-reading intellectuals and aristocrats as the language of the common people, the illiterate, women, and children. Thus, the Bible was translated into the language of the common and oppressed people. It was the national language of the Korean people—of the minjung. The language was further denigrated when the Japanese forbade the use of the vernacular script at public and private schools and even in services of worship. As long as the

Bible was read in the Korean national language of the vernacular script, it was extremely difficult for the rulers and the missionaries to control the national and political consciousness of the Christians in Korea.

Not only was the medium of the Christian message the language of the oppressed nation, but the content of the Bible was full of the language of salvation and liberation of oppressed people. The people in the Bible spoke the same kind of language as the vernacular script users in Korea. Those who speak the vernacular Korean have difficulty understanding the abstract and metaphysical language of theology. Common Korean expressions are good for analogies, stories, metaphor, and concrete happenings and facts. Reading the Bible in the Korean vernacular script made the Bible stories come alive in the historical experiences of the oppressed Korean people. The historical experiences in the Bible were identified with Korean Christian experiences and transformed immediately into the religious language of the Korean people. The historical language of the Bible therefore became the historical language of the Korean people.

For the preachers and Sunday school teachers, the story of Moses and Israel's exodus from Egypt were favorite political stories which were told and retold to raise the national and political consciousness of the hearers for liberation. Inevitably they mixed this story with the story of the Korean people who were suffering under the bondage of a foreign power. Neither the preacher nor the teacher would speak directly about the Korean people under the Japanese rule. They only spoke of the people of Israel under the rule of Egypt, but the hearers of the story knew what was meant.[8]

The Book of Exodus was translated and published in 1909; it was printed by Fukuin Printing Company in Yokohama, Japan. Not surprisingly, the Old Testament and more particularly the Book of Exodus and the Book of Daniel were most disliked by the Japanese authorities and were later banned from the church. The story of Moses and the Exodus was too vividly related to the national destiny of the Korean people. The story exerted its strong spiritual power when it was told in the light of the political fate of the Korean people. The spiritual character of the story would have been meaningless, had it not been told and heard in the light of the historical situation of the time.

Along with the simplicity of the Korean vernacular script and its literary characteristics, observers of Korean Christianity often note the most conservative character, if not fundamentalistic features, of Korean Christianity. Along with the parabolization of the stories, there seems to have been a literal understanding of the biblical stories such as the story of Moses and the Exodus. Korean Christians understood the story of Moses not only as a *literal* event in the history of *Israel* but also as a *literal* event in the history of the oppressed people of *Korea*. This identification, evident in the development of the language of the Christian church in Korea, led to the subsequent resistance against the Japanese. In the 1930s, when the Japanese authorities ordered Korean Christians to pay obeisance to the Japanese emperor at the

Shinto shrines, Korean Christians expressly refused as an act of loyalty to God in keeping with the Second Commandment. It looked to many—Japanese as well as Koreans—to be a narrow and literal interpretation of the Ten Commandments. But, for many Christians who refused to obey the Japanese order, it was in essence a political decision. It was a political action, and an expression of the nationalistic commitment of the church. Korean Christians understood the Second Commandment not only literally and religiously, but also politically. Korean Christians obeyed the Second Commandment not merely as a religious commandment but as a political commandment. As the persecution of Korean Christians became more severe, they understood their own resistance and plight in the light of the suffering of the early Christians under the rule of Rome. It was in this context that they read the letters of Paul and the other New Testament writers.

(The political as well as ideological resistance of the Korean Christians was maintained even under the Russian and North Korean Communist regime immediately following the liberation of Korea in 1945. As communist persecution increased from harassment to arrest and detention without proper trials, and even to murder, Korean Christians came to realize that Communism is no ideology for the oppressed. It is just another way of oppressing the oppressed. Again from church pulpits, the Christian hope of an exodus for liberation from the Communist oppression and for the reunification of a divided nation was told and retold.)

Han and the Mask Dance of the Minjung

In his paper on "Historical References for a Theology of Minjung," Suh Nam-dong argues that the present theology of minjung is a continuation of this earlier history which provides a historical paradigm for the present. He says in his paper:

> It is not too much to say that today's struggle for human rights hears the outcry and the protest of persons who participated in the March First movement and the April 1960 Revolution. For it is evident that those who participate in the human rights struggle see their genealogy beginning with the Donghak movement and coming down through the Independence Association movement, the March First movement, and the April 1960 movement.[9]

In a way, the concern of the consultation was to outline the genealogy of minjung theology.

To most of the participants it became apparent that the present discussion of minjung theology is born out of the early experiences of Korean Christianity and in the political and social situation of the late nineteenth century. It was also clear that minjung theology has developed out of the Korean Christians' intuitive and acute awareness of the essence of the Christian message as both political and religious—as the good news and hope for liberation of the oppressed people. From the beginning, Korean Christians understood the biblical language historically and spiritually. In brief, minjung theology has its roots in the political theology of the early Korean Christian koinonias.

Given this fact some participants in the consultation felt that minjung theology is another name for a Korean theology of liberation, or a development of political theology in the Korean church. To an extent this way of summarizing the present discussion of minjung theology is quite appropriate. It puts this theology in the wider perspective of international theological discussions. However, as Suh Nam-dong puts it, "The historical consciousness which has this genealogy of the minjung movement needs to be manifested and realized as an appropriate political hermeneutic for today. . . . The events in the history of the minjung movement, however, must be seen only as stepping stones to the onward movement of Korean minjung history." Suh views the theology of minjung as a further realization and articulation of the historical experiences of Korean Christians.

There is perhaps another reason why the present discussion of minjung theology cannot be confined within the rubric of "Korean theology of liberation" or "the development of a political theology in the Korean church." It takes its paradigm, as Suh puts it, from the social biography of the minjung. Thus, minjung theology moves out of the confines of biblical theological language which has been filtered through Western civilization. Theology of minjung comes out of the political consciousness and culture of the oppressed minjung of Korea. This factor is taken into account in the method Suh proposes for theology in Korea. He says,

> The limitations in the situation of the minjung, who are to be contrasted with the ruling regime, may be clarified when we use the approach of socio-economic history. Once we clarify the history of the minjung through this approach, we can then see through the *social biography of the minjung* their corporate spirit, their consciousness and their aspirations, by using the method of the sociology of literature.

What he has tried to do is to first read the social biography of the minjung as manifested in their literature, their feelings, and their plays, and out of these shape a moving picture of the history of the minjung.

According to Suh, the most important element in the political consciousness of the minjung which appears in the social biography of the oppressed people of Korea is *han*. Most of the discussions at the consultation were around this word and its meaning. In terms of its etymology, *han* is a psychological word. It is a term that denotes the feeling of suffering of a person which has been repressed either by himself or through the oppression of others. According to Suh, such a feeling of helpless suffering and oppression is at the heart of the biography of the individual Korean person. And this feeling of *han,* the suffering and hopelessness of the oppressed, is a collective feeling in the collective social biography of the oppressed minjung of Korea. Suh's translator renders the Korean word *"han"* into the English phrase "righteous indignation," but participants at the consultation agreed that the rendering was not quite accurate. One bilingual American participant suggested that it be translated "a feeling of unresolved resentment against unjustifiable suffering." A footnote to the present text of Suh's paper, "Towards a Theology of *Han*," gives another rendering, "just indignation," and adds that *"han* is a deep feeling that rises out of the unjust experience of the people." "Just indignation" may be a close translation of *han,* but it evokes a refined emotion yearning for justice to be done. However, to put it more boldly, *han* is a deep awareness of the contradictions in a situation and of the unjust treatment meted out to the people or a person by the powerful. And this feeling of *han* is not just a one-time psychological response to a situation but is an accumulation of such feelings and experiences.

Some psychoanalysts view this feeling of *han* as the psychosomatic sickness of most Korean individuals. According to these, schizophrenia and other personal sicknesses stem from this feeling of *han. Han* could also be a socially caused situation and disease. As Suh observes, "Under Confucianism's strict imposition of laws and customs discriminating against women, the existence of women was *han* itself." It is the kind of feeling a woman has when she cannot produce a male child for the family and thus has to agree, against her will, to her husband bringing in another woman for childbearing, or when she has to obey her mother-in-law even though the order is absolutely unreasonable. It is an awareness of the structural injustice which a Confucian society imposes on women. *Han* is a psychosocial term which appears inevitably in the biography of Korean women and in their stories, novels, poems, and plays.

But the feeling of *han* is not just an individual feeling of repression. This is not just a sickness that can be cured by psychotherapy. This is a collective feeling of the oppressed. This sickness of *han* can be cured only when the total structure of the oppressed society and culture is changed. Suh describes the psychosocial element of this word very eloquently: "At a certain point in Korean history, about half of the population were registered as hereditary slaves, and were treated as property rather than as people of the nation. These thought of their lives as *han. "* The feeling of *han* is a feeling of helplessness. It is the feeling of slaves in the face of their social fate experiencing the contradictions in society. When people realize that they have been oppressed by foreign powers, and their sense of national independence has to be repressed, the feeling of *han* rises up to the level of psychopolitical anger, frustration, and indignation. The feeling of *han* is an awareness both at an individual psychological level as well as at a social and political level.

The feeling of *han,* however, also has a negative element. It is a repressed murmuring, unexpressed in words or actions. It does not change anything. It might arouse a sense of revenge at most. But mostly it would be submission or resignation to fate. As Suh admits, "It is a dominant feeling of defeat, resignation, and nothingness." An existentialist might say that *han* is a predicament of personal existence in the world. And theologically this is the state of sin from which one would cry out for religious help. For *han* may be regarded as the state of fallen man, and the metaphysical reality of human beings as they are.

But Suh refuses to view the feeling of *han* simply as an abstract metaphysical human state or as the existential sin of alienation. He sees the feeling of *han* as the essence of the social biography of the oppressed people of Korea. Furthermore, he does not see it merely in the negative sense of resignation to fate or to political oppression. He also sees a transforming, dynamic element in *han*. He says that "it is a feeling with a tenacity of will for life which comes to weaker beings," and this aspect "can often be used as the energy for a revolution or rebellion." Certainly for him, *han* is the tenacity of life of the oppressed spirit; it is a tendency for social revolution as expressed in the March First movement and the April 19th Student Revolution of 1960.

Suh then introduces very interesting and provocative contemporary Korean novels to illustrate the positive element which might emerge out of the accumulation of the collective *han* of the oppressed minjung. According to Suh, one of the most powerful stories depicting the transformation of *han* into a revolutionary consciousness is "The Story of the Sound" by poet Kim Chi Ha, published in 1972. This poem is now banned from circulation. The story is about "very strange bumping sounds" which "if people with money and power heard would tremble like aspen leaves and break out in a cold sweat." The whole story is about the origin of a bumping noise. A bumping sound is heard coming from a deep prison cell. A poor prisoner named Ando is expressing his deepest *han* over his unjust and cruel treatment in prison. His head and legs were chopped off; and the trunk of his body keeps rolling and bumping against the prison walls. This is the noise. The *han* of the oppressed people and the *han*-cry of the unjustly-treated people will accumulate to make the noise of revolution. Revolution is the explosion and culmination of the oppressed people's noise and shouts of *han*. Therefore, according to the poet Kim, the work of a poet is to transmit the *han* of the people in his/her poetry as an act of political imagination: "This little peninsula is filled with the clamor of aggrieved ghosts. It is filled with the mourning noise of the *han* of those who died from foreign invasions, wars, tyranny, rebellion, malignant diseases, and starvation. I want my poems to be the womb or bearer of these sounds, to be the transmitter of the *han* and to communicate a sharp awareness of our historical tragedy."

In his paper, Suh mentions the Korean mask dance as a minjung drama which depicts *han* as the tenacity of purpose for life. In various ways the Korean mask dances portray the pathetic life of the oppressed people and their deep sense of *han*. In many ways, the mask dances are the vehicles for transmitting the *han* of the oppressed people. With dramatic eloquence Hyun Young-hak presented a paper describing a typical form of the mask dance popular among the people of rural Korea and among university students.[10]

The students themselves have recreated some of these traditional performing art forms. In the mask dance, the actors, who are common people, are hidden behind the masks. Their identity is not known. The dance movements are bold and athletic rather than the refined movement in aristocratic court dances. The language used in the performance is coarse and satirical, full of vulgar expressions "with a great deal of sex-related dirty words." Most of the mask dances are community affairs, i.e., the performers and the audience are from the village—composed of ordinary people from the farms and peddlers from the market.

Most mask dances in Korea are composed not only of music and dance but also dialogue. These have a simple plot. Through the mask dance, the people make fun of the ruling class of the old Korean society. In the mask dance, the performers and the audience together ridicule the corrupt Buddhist monks and the Confucian aristocrats and make these the butt-end of their jokes. Through the playful laughter and jokes directed at the powerful segment of their society, the people release their accumulated repressed feelings of *han*. People's laughter, jokes, dances, and shouts are themselves expressions of "the tenacity of purpose for life"; and therefore they find newness and a revival of the spirit to persist even though they continue living the wretched life of the oppressed minjung. In their laughter, they are able to nurture a critical sense of resistance, revolt, and a hope for a better future.

In the evening, following Hyun's presentation, a group of university students who had been studying the traditional mask dance visited the consultation to stage a performance. It was most interesting and illuminating particularly to the international participants who had never seen and participated in a Korean mask dance. The performance was quite meaningful since the participants were able to reflect on it in the light of Hyun's paper. When the performers, as is usual, invited the participants to join in the group dance, all of them leaped up to join in the vigorous dance keeping time to the rhythmic Korean music. The sense of koinonia with the oppressed minjung was heightened, in spite of the political situation at the time which cast a threatening shadow over the place. Participants reported to me later that they thought they had experienced the gist of minjung theology with their bodies, although their minds had not yet grasped all the implications of minjung theology.

It is important to note an attempt of Hyun to draw a theological implication from the Korean mask dance which he thinks contains an important element of minjung theology. It is more than just a political interpretation of the mask dance or a political understanding of the collective *han* of the oppressed minjung. Hyun feels that the people in the mask dance "find themselves standing over and beyond the entire world which includes not only the rulers and leaders but also themselves." In their laughter the minjung in the mask dance experience and express "a critical transcendence" over this world and over themselves. It is only a depiction of the minjung's own life experience, and therefore, the stance of critical transcendence is provided within the minjung's own life. It is, according to Hyun, this-worldly, mundane, and secular, for it is not "given by some gods out there or by some objectively existing reality in 'the other world.' " When the mask dance is being performed, the suppressed feelings of *han* explode into reality, and according to Hyun, "the minjung get conscientized and are provided with a stance of critical transcendence." In other words, when the feeling of *han* explodes in the mask dance play, this stance of critical transcendence is acquired. And then and there, it is said that the minjung's *han* is "resolved."

At the performance there was a feeling or a hunch about what Hyun might mean by "critical transcendence." But the participants demanded a further critical delineation of such a term as it is extremely important in formulating a possible theology of minjung. Where does the God of Christianity or any deity come into this sense of transcendence? How can it be tied to the religious experience of Christian koinonia? The consultation was not able to solve these problems, and it is perhaps too early to evaluate Hyun's recent suggestion. But he has a hunch that this is the way and the area in which God works in human history, and perhaps this is the way the oppressed people, the minjung, communicate with God. Hyun feels that because of this stance of critical transcendence, Korean history bears witness to the fact that the people would not give up, they would not become cynical as did some of the learned, and they would not despair as some of the religious leaders did. Instead, they could laugh at themselves, while retaining a sharp and critical awareness of their reality and their world. Because they saw the world and history from another dimension, i.e., the dimension of worldly transcendence, they could continue fighting for a better world. There is this element of faith and trust in the human spirit that people can transcend the present history. In a word, Hyun seems to see some elements of faith and trust and even worship in the performances of the Korean mask dances. This is the reason why, Hyun feels, the mask dance ends with the cry: "Children, awake! The dawn is approaching from the east and the south."

Hyun notes that the experience of critical transcendence in the mask dance is something like what Paul Tillich calls "God above God." The mention of Paul Tillich here could be misleading. Tillich's God above God comes from the existential anxiety of the alienated Western man. But what Hyun describes in the mask dance is not an individual sense of transcendence; rather, it comes from the collective, accumulated feeling of *han* which explodes and is resolved in the community's performance of the mask dances. It is not an existentialist sense of transcendence, "deep down there," but is a social, political, and historical transcendence, "over the horizon of history." In other words, it comes from the sociopolitical biography of the oppressed minjung, and not from the existential biography of an alienated individual.

Historical Transcendence in Messianic Politics

In his provocative paper, "Messiah and Minjung: Discerning Messianic Politics over against Political Messianism,"[11] Kim Yong-bock explores further the theme of the self-transcendence of the minjung.

The minjung are the permanent reality of history. Kingdoms, dynasties, and states rise and fall; but the minjung remain as a concrete reality in history, experiencing the comings and goings of political powers. Although the minjung understand themselves in relation to the power which is in command, they are not confined by that power. The minjung transcend the power structures which attempt to confine them through the unfolding of their stories. Power has its basis in the minjung. But power as it expresses itself in political powers does not belong to the minjung.

Thus far we have tried to see the roots of the theology of minjung in the historical experiences and development of the Christian koinonia in Korea and in the deep feeling of the collective *han,* which expresses the pathos of the minjung and out of which various minjung art forms, such as novels, poetry, and mask dances have appeared. These may be considered the roots of a theology of minjung, but perhaps not, properly speaking, a theology. Or, these may be thought of as presenting a way of doing theology, but not as theology proper. This issue was raised at the consultation. Although the participants realized the importance of the issue, they did not seem to want to spend their time debating the frustrating question of "then what is theology after all?" Instead, these theologians took upon themselves the task of retelling and reflecting on the stories and the social biography of the minjung and the hopes and aspirations of the minjung in the world and in history.

In which case, after describing the *han* of the minjung and its expression in their stories and in the bodily movement of the mask dance, what more can theologians do? Where do we go from here? Once the stories have been told, what action do we take as theologians on the basis of the stories of the minjung? If the theology of minjung is to bring about change, what course of action should we take and in what direction? What are some of the concrete actions which are prompted by the social biography of the minjung? The answer seems to be in seeking the social biography of the *future* or the new story of the minjung.

In other words, a recognition of the stance of critical transcendence in the consciousness of the minjung requires that it also find expression as a historical transcendence of the minjung in relation to power. This is the essential relationship between Hyun's presentation of the mask dance and Kim's discussion of messianic politics. Thus, Kim's paper may be considered to be an attempt to delineate the minjung's social biography of the *future* or the political theology of the minjung. For Kim, there is nothing new in relating messianic politics to the social biography of the minjung, for messianic politics is already implied in the social biography. He says, "The minjung suffers these limitations (socioeconomic) in reality; yet the minjung as historical subject transcends the socioeconomic determination of history, and unfolds its stories beyond mere historical possibilities to historical novelty—a new drama beyond the present history to a new and transformed history."

Kim traces the messianic politics of the minjung from the Donghak

Peasant Rebellion of 1895 to the March First Independence movement of 1919 and on to the confrontation between Korean Christians and the Japanese imperial authority in the 1930s over the issue of Shinto worship. He considers the Korean Christians' political struggles to be messianic politics. As a false alternative to the messianic politics of the minjung, Kim delineates three forms of political messianism in Korea during the last fifty years: (1) Japanese ultra-nationalism in the form of colonialism; (2) the North Korean Communist movement; and (3) the emerging technocracy in Korea. He characterizes the whole recent history of Korea, in which Christianity has grown, as a battle between *messianic politics* and *political messianism*. He sees the fight as one between Jesus the Messiah and the secular messiahs of modern ideologies. To use more sociological terms, it is a fight between the minjung consciousness and the false consciousness of modern ideologies.

Kim's paper was well-received for it delineates clearly the false claims of the political messianisms manifested both in the North Korean Communist rule and in the South Korean technocratic regime. He reveals North Korea's Kim Il Sung as typical of the false messiahs imposed on the people. He says, "Communism is a secularized form of messianism. Its messianic role, understood in terms of the dictatorship of the proletariat, is in fact assumed by the political leader, and finds expression in a totalitarian political structure." According to Kim, the messianic politics of the minjung should oppose such expressions of political messianism, although "the constituency of the minjung is the poor, the suppressed, and the alienated." Furthermore, the idea of *"minjung"* is different from the Maoist notion of *"inmin,"* for the Maoist notion upholds the supremacy and dictatorship of the proletariat and it believes in total dictatorship. The notions of the dictatorship of the proletariat and totalitarianism are both foreign and antagonistic to the idea of the messianic politics of the minjung.

Instead, both Suh Nam-dong and Kim Yong-bock advocate the subjecthood of the minjung over against the idea of the dictatorship of the proletariat. In the words of Kim, "The minjung is the protagonist in the historical drama. It is the subject; and its socio-political biography is the predicate." In the Korean context the theme of the subjecthood of the people has generally been viewed as belonging to the North Korean political ideology. But Kim states the idea of the subjecthood of the minjung is different from that of the North Korean understanding. He views the North Korean notion as "the autonomy of the national totalitarian dictatorship which uses the name of the proletariat." The North Korean Communists assert, though falsely, that the people are the subjects of history and that their subjecthood has been realized. According to Kim, however, the minjung are in between the times of the "not yet" and the "already," that is, they are not yet fully the subjects of history.

Kim analyzes the South Korean type of political messianism and asserts that it is another form of national messianism with a false faith which proclaims that "technology and science, organized into the capitalist system, can solve all the problems of the Korean people.'' This is a messianism not *of* or *by* the people, but allegedly *for* them. Modern technocracy with its totalitarianism forces the people to recognize it as legitimate and as necessary for rapid economic growth and for securing the welfare of the people. In making this claim the regime elevates itself above all law and criticism and crushes down all the needs and demands of the minjung. Modern technocracy with its political messianic claims has turned out to be not for the minjung but for itself, and is even opposed to the minjung. Under its sway the people are reduced to nothing, and out of such an awareness the messianic politics of the minjung arises. Kim makes this point precisely and powerfully:

> These so-called radical reforms—all in the name of an earthly millennium—are undertaken with a great deal of social and political cost which have to be borne by the minjung. Indeed, the sufferings of the Korean people under these three political messianisms were and are extreme. The free subjectivity of the people is reduced to nothing in history. Socio-economic and cultural analyses of the Korean people's suffering under these conditions bear witness to the fact that political messianism is antagonistic to the people (the minjung). They experience it as a contradiction.
>
> Therefore, besides making and maintaining false claims to messianism, political messianism sets itself up against the minjung who face it as a contradiction.

It needs to be added that the messianic politics of the minjung also confronts *religious messianism*. Religious messianism is a false ideology deeply rooted in Christian millennialistic thinking. When the people are exhausted with their daily struggles for life, justice, and humanity, and when their feelings of *han* have reached a peak and they feel desperate and hopeless, they are tempted to place their hope in an other-worldly messianic kingdom. Religious messianism is a weakening of the minjung; and when it consorts with political messianism, it becomes a faithful servant of the existing political and social system. It makes the people totally subservient to the ruling power. Through the influence of missionaries Christian millennialism grew strong during the struggle of the people against the political messianism of the Japanese. It is a form of messianism which has a strong appeal for Christians and for the minjung who are suffering in this world. But it stands over against the minjung, just as political messianism stands against the messianic politics of the minjung. Furthermore, it is religiously both fundamentalistic and dogmatic. This is how religion sometimes stands over against the Jesus messianism of the minjung.

Returning to Kim's paper, the question that arises is, what is the shape or the blueprint of the messianic politics of the minjung? Can we translate the messianism of Jesus into an ideology of the minjung? Kim refuses to do this. At most, he is willing to view a participatory democracy and the national unification of Korea as historical components for such a messianism. However, it became apparent that what is important is a process of messianic politics rather than its end result. Kim refused to give any ideological indicators or landmarks to show the direction of the messianic politics of the minjung. The participants were rather dissatisfied with the position of Kim and the theologians of minjung as well. The real hard question they felt was: What is the messianic vision of the minjung when expressed in secular terms and in concrete political options?

There were objections not only to the mixing of political and religious language but also as a participant put it, "to applying the concept of political messianism to ideologies with a secular self-understanding." Furthermore, he felt that "to call socialism a political messianism is certainly no help for all those who—by necessity or choice—try to gain a working relationship with Marxism." He noted rather sharply, "The epithet 'messianic' forces Christians into a battle position against Marxism which may suit South Koreans but which would be disastrous for Christians living in a socialist country." But what Kim and other Korean participants wanted to say was that socialism does not follow the same course as minjung theology. The reasons for rejecting an identification of minjung theology with socialism is not just that we have to survive under an anti-Communist regime. Rather, as Kim states, the theology of minjung finds in Communism and in experiences under Communist regimes elements which are against the historical destiny of the minjung.

Those who complained about the mixing of political and religious language in Kim's paper seem to have missed the point. The basic problem with his paper, as it is with the theology of minjung in general, is that political language is not used more freely and concretely. Kim uses religiously loaded language when he attempts to delineate the messianic politics of the minjung in concrete terms, i.e., vis-à-vis secular ideologies and political systems. The reason for this is perhaps his conviction that the subjecthood of the minjung will never be fully realized until the end of the world. Thus, the religious language of the ultimate character of the messianic politics of the minjung comes into play in the delineation of penultimate goals. According to Kim, "The focal point of messianism is the general *resurrection* of all the people (minjung) . . . ," but the general resurrection of all the people is "a concrete vision of history in which the people realize their corporate subjectivity in participating in the messianic kingdom." It sounds as if our messianic politics has become a kind of religious messianism. However, he asserts that the content of the messianic kingdom is to be realized historically as justice, koinonia, and shalom. Borrowing from Tillich's dictum about God, this may be an ideology *above* ideology.

In the present situation, Kim Yong-bock proposes the following tasks for messianic politics in the Korean context: (1) "to *expose* the long history of political messianism which has enslaved us and to *struggle* against it," (2) "to rediscover the popular messianic traditions inherent in Maitreya messianic

Buddhism and the Donghak religion both through a research of extant literature and through dialogue with Buddhist and Donghak leaders who have
concerns similar to ours," and (3) to evolve in a concrete way "a Christian
political perspective" based on the ideas of the general resurrection of the
people, shalom in relation to the unification of Korea, and koinonia (participation) and justice in relation to the social and political development of the
Korean people.

Finally, he raises the question of the use of power in a political struggle. He
believes in the powerlessness of Jesus and the powerlessness of status of the
Messiah and the people. He believes that the essence of the messianic
kingdom lies in its powerlessness. Thus, messianic politics has to be carried
out without recourse to power, or better, violence. Perhaps we should begin a
political theology of the minjung in terms of a politics of powerlessness, or
perhaps in terms of the transformation of and the transfiguration of politics
in the process of realizing the messianic politics of the minjung. In this connection we can say that the Korean Christian struggle for human rights over
the last decade has been an exercise of the *powerless* messianic politics of the
minjung over against the exercise of *power* by the political messianism of the
state. We have accepted and stood firm on the principle, Kim Yong-bock
notes, that "the (powerless) Suffering Servant provides the two messianic
qualities of identification with the suffering people and functioning as servant to the aspiration of the people for liberation."

'Apiru and *Ochlos:* Identity of Minjung

As a basis for these theological and sociopolitical discussions on minjung
theology, two biblical research papers were presented at the consultation.
Here, the fundamental question is: What are the biblical bases for a theology
of minjung? This question having been raised, other questions suggest themselves. Over and beyond a political understanding of the Exodus stories, are
there other biblical understandings of the minjung? Do we find the minjung
in the Bible? Is the entire Bible *about* and *for* and even *by* and *of* the minjung?
Could we formulate a biblical theology around the notion of minjung? All
these questions were not answered at the consultation, since it was only a
beginning in attempting to answer these questions. One such attempt was
made by Moon Hee-suk Cyris who focused on Genesis 1:26f. in his paper
"An Old Testament Understanding of Minjung."[12] He attempted to draw
out an Old Testament theology of human rights on the basis of this passage
and viewed the Exodus as an attempt to have these restored to a people.
Professor Ahn Byung-mu presented a paper on "Jesus and the Minjung in
the Gospel of Mark,"[13] in which he probed the term *"ochlos"* (crowd) in the
Gospel according to Mark as a way of understanding the minjung in relation
to Jesus.

In discussing these two papers, I shall confine myself to the question "who
are the minjung?" because this question was brought up time and again in the

consultation. Moon considers the "essence of the Old Testament to be the history of faith arising from and concerning the liberation movement of the minjung (the Exodus event) and the creation of humanity." From the beginning of creation, God has blessed people and put them in charge of his creation; and in exercising this responsibility they become the subjects of history: "God blessed them and said to them: 'Be fruitful and multiply, and fill the earth and subdue it; and have dominion over all other living things.' " Therefore, according to Cyris Moon, minjung are those who "form human history by subduing and ruling the earth, and thus fulfilling God's purpose for creation." In being oppressed the minjung are denied their God-given blessing and right to be the masters of the world and history. Thus, the history of the Exodus is a history of the restoration to human beings of their God-given rights. Cyris Moon does not agree with recent Old Testament scholarship which identifies the minjung or the people with *'apiru* who had no national identity, were without legal protection and considered "outlaws." He seems to imply that though the minjung may be *'apiru* or *'am ha'aretz* sociologically speaking, theologically the minjung are the masters of the world and history. In terms of Kim Yong-bock's thesis, the messianic vision is already implied in the creation story of Genesis.

But the problem with Moon's identification of minjung with God's blessing is that the blessing in Genesis is understood generally in a *universalistic* sense and not in a *particularistic* one. In other words, the blessing is not believed to be limited to a particular group of people such as the minjung.

He makes this problem more acute by introducing the notion of "my people" which appears in the prophet Micah. For Micah, according to Moon, "my people" is none other than the minjung. "My people" is not *all* the people or humanity in general, but is the minjung over against and in conflict with the rulers and the enemy of God. Moon says, "In a word, 'my people' for Micah were the have-nots and 'my people' must be understood in socio-economic terms." Thus, sociologically speaking, "my people" of Micah are the have-nots, the oppressed, the alienated, and perhaps *'apiru* and *'am ha'aretz*. But theologically speaking, he seems to say that only "my people" are blessed by God. God is only on the side of "my people"—the minjung—standing over against "this people," which according to Micah, are the enemy of "my people."

If Cyris Moon intends to use the term "minjung" exclusively and imply that only the minjung is called the people of God, i.e., "my people," and only the minjung are recipients of the divine blessing of creation, then he will have to abandon his interpretation of Genesis 1 as signifying the universal blessing of all humanity. In other words, he does not argue clearly for a connection between the concept of people in Genesis I and in Micah.

Ahn Byung-mu's "Jesus and the Minjung in the Gospel of Mark" makes a sharper presentation of the notion of minjung in terms of Mark's use of the word *"ochlos"* as opposed to the word *"laos."* For him the minjung is definitely *ochlos* rather than *laos*. In his paper, Ahn contrasts *ochlos* with *laos*. His conclusion is that Mark does not define *ochlos* in a deterministic way, but rather describes the *ochlos* and uses the term in referring to a social historical class. On the other hand, the term *laos* refers to a national and religious group. He says that "Mark called Jesus' minjung the *ochlos*." By quoting the characteristic saying of Mark (2:17b), "I came not to call the righteous, but sinners," Ahn calls attention to the partiality that Jesus showed in expressing his love. Ahn states, "He loved people with partiality. Whatever the situation he always stood on the side of the oppressed, the aggrieved, and the weak."

But who are the *ochlos,* the minjung of Jesus, according to the Gospel of Mark? The minjung are the sinners, the tax collectors, the sick, those who opposed the powers in Jerusalem, the despised people of Galilee, prostitutes, etc. Understood in this way, the question of our relationship with the *ochlos* or minjung arises quite sharply because we have to do theology not *about* the minjung, but a theology that is *of* and *by* the minjung.

Participants asked each other this question. Just because one happens to be born a woman, is she automatically to be identified as minjung? Just because one was born in a colonial country, is he an *ochlos* of Jesus? In our society who is the minjung? Someone in the consultation attempted to make a distinction between the minjung "in-itself" and the minjung "for-itself." In other words, there are minjung who do not think of themselves as minjung even though they were born in that socio-economic group. This type of minjung "in-itself" are not aware of their lot; and they may be manipulated easily by the rulers. But the minjung "for-itself" is the one which is conscious of its lot, and in suffering under oppression opposes it, and tries to overcome it. This is minjung with self-awareness. The true minjung is the latter type, and this is the *ochlos* who might be saved by the grace of God. This is an interesting borrowing from Hegel. The minjung "for-itself" may be the "true" and conscious minjung, but perhaps the real minjung who need liberation might be the minjung "in-itself" who do not even know what their lot is and who are the sheep without a shepherd.

Finally we came to a tentative conclusion concerning who are the minjung. First, "minjung" is *not* a concept or object which can easily be defined or pointed at, for it is a living reality which is dynamic and changing, and it has to define itself as a subject. The minjung can talk about itself only through its social and political biography. Thus, besides the biblical references for minjung theology, the sociopolitical biography of the minjung is the key historical frame of reference for a minjung theology. Second, the minjung has to be differentiated from the proletariat so that the theology of minjung cannot be a theology of the proletariat using the false consciousness of Marxist ideologies.

The minjung is present where there is sociocultural alienation, economic exploitation, and political suppression. Therefore, a woman is a minjung when she is dominated by man, by the family, or by sociocultural structures and factors. An ethnic group is a minjung group when it is politically and economically discriminated against by another ethnic group. A race is minjung when it is dominated by another powerful ruling race as is the case in a colonial situation. When intellectuals are suppressed for using their creative and critical abilities against rulers on behalf of the oppressed, then they too belong to the minjung. Workers and farmers are minjung when they are exploited, their needs and demands are ignored, and they are crushed down by the ruling powers.

Concluding Remarks

As it is, this report is a sort of biographical sketch of the consultation itself. It attempts to interpret the papers. It does not really do justice to the dynamic exchange of ideas among the participants. Neither does it reflect adequately the critical comments made by the Asians who participated fully in the consultation. (Unfortunately, during the months of chaos following the death of President Park, the tapes, which recorded the entire proceedings of the consultation, disappeared mysteriously from the office of the National Council of Churches.) A full report should also take into consideration the views of other Korean research on minjung from sociological and historical standpoints; and it should also include some description of the Urban Industrial Mission and the human rights struggle. The next chapter attempts to fill some part of these lacunae.

As a summary of the present report, let me state the following: (1) The minjung theologians are not just academic theologians teaching in theological seminaries but are persons who have been actively involved for the last decade in Urban Industrial Mission and in the human rights movement; and they have been reflecting on their experiences. (2) They have reflected upon their experiences, interpreted them theologically, not only by looking back on the history of the Korean church, but on the entire history of Korea from a socioeconomic perspective. (3) We have tried to listen to and learn from the minjung and to see reality from the minjung's perspective. In this way we have tried to understand the working of the Holy Spirit in the history of Korea, particularly in the history of the struggle of the minjung. (4) We have not, however, dealt fully with all the theological problems that have been thrown up by this approach. Yet, we feel that we have come up with fresh ideas while groping for new ways of doing theology in a Third World situation: a situation in which a process of rapid industrialization clashing with long and deep-rooted traditions has produced forces of dehumanization.

As I have already indicated in the review of the papers, the question "What is theology?" has not been answered. In attempting to understand the historical reality from the minjung's perspective we have suggested some answers. Perhaps a more cogent theology from the minjung's perspective might emerge as we continue to clarify our thinking. This is something we look forward to with great expectation. We hope that it will also be a result of the common endeavor of all those who identify themselves with the minjung of the world.

With this expectation, the consultation closed with a love-feast *(apapē)* as an expression of our koinonia and as a covenant to continue the search for a living and relevant theology in Asia.

NOTES

1. L. George Paik, *The History of Protestant Missions in Korea, 1832–1910* (Pyongyang, Korea: Union Christian College Press, 1927).

2. Min Kyung-bae, *The Church History of Korea* (in Korean) (Seoul, Korea: The Christian Literature Society of Korea, 1972).

3. For example, Ryu Tong-shik, *The Christian Faith Encounters the Religions of Korea* (in Korean) (Seoul, Korea: The Christian Literature Society of Korea, 1965).

4. Min Kyung-bae, *The Church History of Korea.*

5. Arthur Brown, *Mastery of the Far East* (New York: Charles Scribner, 1919), p. 517.

6. See further chapter VI of this book.

7. L. G. Paik's quote from W. M. Blair, *History,* p. 369.

8. See W. L. Swallen, *Sunday School Lessons on the Book of Exodus* (Seoul Religious Tract Society, 1907), p. 4

9. See chapter IX of this book.

10. See chapter III of this book.

11. See chapter X of this book.

12. See chapter VII of this book.

13. See chapter VIII of this book.

Chapter II

Korean Theological Development in the 1970s

SUH KWANG-SUN DAVID

Christian Involvement in the Life of the Minjung

In the early 1960s, Industrial Mission groups were organized primarily for industrial evangelism. As these mission groups began to work among the laborers, it became evident that the traditional type of evangelism would not be effective. The evangelist was too far removed from the situation and experiences of the workers to be able to communicate the gospel to them. After much reflection and self-criticism, the industrial missioners decided to work as laborers. Anyone who wished to work in Industrial Mission had to become a laborer for six months to a year so that there would be a somatic identification with the life of the worker. Without such involvement the missioner could not share in the emotional and perceptual experiences of the workers—their fatigue, pain, and anger. Without such an experience of sharing, there could be no real communication between the missioner and the worker. This somatic incarnational experience of the industrial missioners changed the purpose of the work of Industrial Mission from that of a traditional type of evangelism to "finding the body of Jesus Christ among the workers themselves."

The role of the industrial missioner was now seen not in terms of distributing gospel tracts but in terms of being a servant to the workers, taking up issues that affect their lives. Thus, the issues of fighting for the rights of workers, of forming labor unions, of improving working conditions, and of struggling for social justice became integral to the expression of the servanthood of Industrial Mission. The Industrial Mission workers formed a small koinonia to share their experiences as they witnessed to the gospel of Jesus Christ in working with those who are most exploited during the period of the so-called rapid economic growth. This shift in the purpose and style of Industrial Mission which began in the 1960s was established more firmly in the 1970s.

The Urban Industrial Mission groups which were formed in the late 1960s were mostly in the Seoul metropolitan area. From the beginning, Urban Industrial Mission was forward-looking. It was concerned to organize power at the grassroots level to enable the urban poor to recover their rights and protect their interests. In so doing, it introduced the concept of the democratic power of the people (minjung), i.e., the urban poor. It was a kind of grassroots democracy which at the level of the self-understanding of the people was a recognition of their power over against that of the powerful and at the level of organization was a means of asserting and obtaining their rights and needs such as clean water and a garbage collection service from the municipality.

Another experience, similar to that of the Industrial Mission, was of the Student Development Service Corps (SDSC) organized by the Korean Student Christian Federation. The basic concern of this student mission was to be physically involved in the situation of the workers, farmers, and the urban poor. The students worked in a factory for a given period of time. They lived with the farmers or the urban poor and were involved in community organization. During this period the students would keep a daily diary and hold weekly discussions on the social reality that they were experiencing in living with the minjung. The exposure of the students to the living and working conditions of the poor minjung created in the body and life of the students a perception and awareness of the social reality of Korea. This experience conscientized them to act for justice and social transformation; and this action became a dynamic thrust not only for the SDSC but for the Korean Christian student movement as a whole. The experience of the SDSC also influenced secular student movements, so that they too became historically and socially conscientized and followed the SDSC model of action for social justice.

In addition to the emergence of Christian koinonias among the minjung in response to the task of mission, there were also some changes in the attitude of the Korean ecumenical movement. The Korean church stood up and opposed the unfair negotiations between the Park Chung-hee government and the Japanese government that went into the normalization treaty. Convinced that the treaty negotiation did not deal fairly with the terms of the settlement, the church issued statements and held protest prayer meetings. Many of the Christian protestors were expelled from their positions, especially the professors who led the protests. Although this was a brief episode, it was by no means insignificant. It was the first time since the liberation of Korea in 1945 that the church wholeheartedly took up a political issue. Consequently, the churches had to face a government that was increasingly becoming hostile to them.

During the period 1960–70, the Park regime began its drive for economic growth at all costs. The social problems began to intensify, and the political regime became repressive. Being unsure of his political future, Park began to carry out measures to prolong his rule, notably the constitutional amendments of 1969. At this time, some of the leaders of the Presbyterian Church of the Republic of Korea actively opposed the constitutional amendments; and the people began to respond favorably to the opposition political party. In the 1971 presidential election, the opposition candidate almost won.

In spite of all these involvements, the theological orientation of the Korean Christian movement did not show any clear development. Although there were intensive discussions on the issues of indigenization and the social implications of the gospel, these did not as yet produce many significant results. Towards the end of the 1960s, *The Christian Thought* magazine and a newly published small monthly theological magazine called *Jesamil* (The Third Day) played an important role in carrying forward discussions on the social implications of the gospel.

The Development of Christian Koinonias

In the early 1970s, Christian koinonias (mission groups) emerged as a new thrust in the Korean Christian ecumenical movement. Some of these were the Urban Industrial Mission groups (Inchon, Yongdongpo, Seoul Metropolitan Mission, and Korea Christian Action Organization for Urban and Industrial Mission which is a coordinating body for the UIM), the Christian student koinonia, which is the national network of the Korean Student Christian Federation, the Christian Ecumenical Youth Council, which is the national network of denominational youth groups, the Christian Faculty Fellowship, the families of political prisoners, and Church Women United. The National Council of Churches in Korea (then led by General Secretary Rev. Kim Kwan-suk) provided overall leadership and co-ordination for the Korean ecumenical movement. These koinonia groups often met at Thursday (and Friday) Prayer Meetings. At these weekly gatherings of the movement, the experience of prayer and prophetic witness emerged very forcibly.

There were also Roman Catholic koinonia groups like the Priests Corps for the Realization of Justice, the Catholic Young Workers Organization (JOC), the Catholic Farmers Association, and the Justice and Peace Commission.

These Christian koinonias engaged in mission work to protect the human rights of the workers, the farmers, and the urban poor, and to fight for the justice and freedom of writers and university teachers. The human rights movement, loosely co-ordinated by the Human Rights Commission of the National Council of Churches, also spread into the provincial cities of Pusan, Chonju, Kwangju, Kunsan, Chongju, and Inchon.

The Christian human rights movement also has its secular counterparts, namely, the secular student movements in university campuses, the organizations of writers and poets, journalists, professors, and politicians. These groups have worked closely with the Christian human rights movement. At one point there was organized a Coalition of Human Rights Movements to coordinate the whole area of human rights concerns and work.

The human rights movement in Korea has encountered several setbacks and has been treated very harshly. Yet, in it there has been generated the experience of koinonia and joy in the midst of sufferings, imprisonments, and even deaths. The human rights movement was essentially concerned to resist the "Yushin (revitalization) Political Reform" in which Park Chung-hee received almost unlimited dictatorial powers.

In 1973, at the Easter Sunrise Service at Namsan Mountain in the center of Seoul, a voice was raised: "The resurrection of Jesus Christ is the resurrection of democracy." This action was led by the Seoul Metropolitan Mission group. The people involved were charged with plotting to overthrow the government. This small incident, which was blown up by the authorities, was a symbol of the church's prophetic witness against the new Yushin System. Among the many dramatic events which followed were the famous so-called People's Revolutionary party case, in which ecumenical leaders and student leaders were charged under anti-communist and treason laws, and the March 1, 1976, Declaration at Myongdong Cathedral, for which the signers were tried and given heavy prison sentences. It was the human rights movement, Christian and secular, and the experiences of koinonia within it which provided the historical context for theological reflection in Korea.

Theological Development

For quite some time, theological discussions in Korea were concerned with issues like indigenization, the thesis of secularization, the scope of political theology, etc. In the early 1970s the theme of minjung (the downtrodden people) became a concern of Korean theology when theologians were invited to speak at minjung mission groups such as the Urban Industrial Mission. The theologians began to learn and reflect upon the experiences of mission work at the grassroots level. The theologians Ahn Byung-mu and Suh Nam-dong wrote several important articles in the early 1970s on the theme of the minjung. In his writings, Ahn differentiated the idea of minjung from that of minjok (national people); and Suh began to explore church history for treatments on the theme of minjung.

However, it was in the latter half of the 1970s that there was a concerted effort to articulate minjung theology. Several articles were written on the theme of minjung and published in various journals. Not all of these were theological. Quite a few were historical inquiries; and others were sociological studies. There were also studies of minjung literature, drama, and art. Consequently, there were lively interactions between theological reflections on the minjung and secular intellectual efforts to articulate the reality of the minjung.

The Asian Theological Consultation, held in October 1979, sponsored by the Commission on Theological Concerns of the Christian Conference of Asia and the Korean National Council of Churches, was a high water-mark in the development of minjung theology. At this meeting, Korean theologians, in dialogue with other Asian theologians, were able to clarify and push further the concerns of minjung theology.

There is an ongoing informal discussion group on minjung theology involving about two dozen people from various theological disciplines. Frequently there are dialogues between theologians and scholars of other disciplines such as sociologists, economists, and political scientists. Quite often these dialogues also include journalists, artists, and poets. These conversations have inspired many books and articles on the theme of the minjung.

Some Important Emphases in Minjung Theology

Those working with the theme of minjung have often been under pressure to define the term "minjung" very clearly in sociological terms. But, there has been a certain resistance to defining or conceptualizing the term. There are two reasons for this: (1) Attempts to define the people especially in terms of "the proletariat" have not really served the minjung. Such understandings are connected far too closely to the totalitarian political ideology which operates in our own context. (2) A scientific definition would be an objectification of the minjung on the epistemological level, thus making the people an object for study and reflection.

Instead of attempting to define the concept of minjung, theologians and others have tried to clarify the minjung in historical terms. In these attempts, the social biography (story) of the minjung has been an important point of reference. In other words, the social history of the minjung liberation and messianic movements, the minjung religious traditions (both Buddhist and Donghak), and the past and the present cultural expressions of the minjung are all being studied as one of the two important reference points for minjung theology.

The other important reference point for minjung theology is the Bible and Christian theology. Minjung theologians are keen to discover the socio-economic background of the biblical texts so that these may be studied from a minjung perspective. Of particular interest in the area of biblical studies are the theme of the *ochlos* in the new Testament, the poor in the covenant Code and prophetic traditions in the Old Testament, and other related themes like the *'am ha'aretz* and the people of God. In the area of theology, special attention is being given among others to studies on theodicy, apocalyptic, the Suffering Servant, and the Messianic Spirit (Holy Spirit).

The essential concern of minjung theologians in using these two reference points is to interweave the Korean minjung story and the biblical story. In fact, Korean church history is being looked at again for evidences of the meeting together and interweaving of the two stories.

A short list of recent writings, besides those found in the present volume, may give some idea of the contents of minjung theology. Many of these articles have been published in the Korean book, *Minjung and Theology in Korea*.

Ham Sok-hon, "The True Meaning of *Ssial* (Minjung)."

Hyun Young-hak, "To Be Incarnated among the Minjung."

Ahn Byung-mu, "The National People, the Minjung and the Church."

Kim Chung-choon, "The Old Testament Basis for Minjung Theology."

Sye In-suk, "Law is the Rights of the Poor."

Park Joon-suh, "Yahweh of the Hebrews."

Min Young-jin, "The Meaning of the Year of Jubilee."

Whang Song-kyu, "Understanding Galilee in Terms of St. Mark's Gospel."

Suh Kwang-sun, "The Minjung and the Holy Spirit."

Kim Yong-bock, "The Social Biography of the Minjung and Theology."

Kim Sung-jae, "The Methodology of Minjung Education."

Hyun Young-hak, "Theology as Rumor-Mongering."

Suh Nam-dong, "The Interweaving of Two Stories."

Increasingly, minjung theology has become a subject of debate in Korean society as well as in the Korean church. This fact is in itself evidence of the seriousness with which Koreans view Christian involvement in the life—the pain and aspirations—of the minjung who, we believe, will be the co-rulers with the Messiah in the Messianic Kingdom.

SECTION TWO:
THE MINJUNG REALITY

Chapter III

A Theological Look at the Mask Dance in Korea

HYUN YOUNG-HAK

The Mask Dance

The mask dance has its roots in an old village festival. Once or twice a year, usually before the 15th of January (lunar calendar), the villagers would perform various religious ceremonies asking for the blessing of the gods for better crops for the year. These were either followed or preceded by a variety of entertainment in which the people gradually included satirical portrayals of aristocrats. By the 1700s the commercial class began to appear, and cities were coming into existence. With the support of the rising commercial class the mask dance came into its own. It was later performed on festival days in April or May instead of in January. The satirical content of the mask dance became more audacious. The village ceremonies which were performed in order to pacify the gods became instead the play for the suppressed ordinary folks, i.e., the minjung's play ridiculing and thus criticizing their oppressors. The 1800s saw not only the performance of a bolder type of mask dance but also the creation and increase of various new forms of artistic expressions like the novel, Pansori (a dramatic solo performance with songs and jokes), and paintings, which were all expressive of the minjung consciousness.

The mask dance is composed not only of dance but also rhythmic instrumental music, songs, and dialogue between the performers and the musicians and between the performers and the audience. The dance movements are dynamic and bold compared to those of the aristocratic dance, which are graceful and elegant. The mask dance is full of humor, satire, and vulgar expressions with a great deal of sex-related dirty words. It is a play and festivity with a great deal of improvisation and much disorder. Originally the masks depicted gods. In the mask dance, however, they depict the characters that the performers represent. They also help people slip into the world of dream, fantasy, and vision. This happens especially when the masks become more grotesque with the rapid play of the flickering light of the bonfires on them as the actors dance.

The mask dance consists of eleven scenes. Five scenes relate the three main stories that will be the major concern of this paper. The remaining five scenes are related to the former, introducing or commenting on the stories.

The Nojang (Old Buddhist Monk) Scenes

A group of young monks lead in an old monk, Nojang. The old monk disappears. When they find him crouched in a corner, they take him for a collection of goods or a huge monster of a snake, and have difficulty in recognizing him. The young monks sing into his ears popular songs he used to like. He begins to stir. They then lead him by his stick. He disappears again. Again they look for him. Finding him lying down so quiet, they think he is dead. They sing a requiem mass. He begins to move again.

The young monks then bring in a pretty young girl. The old monk takes a look at her and begins to move. He courts her and gives her his string of beads, which is a symbol of his status; and they dance together. When a travelling shoe salesman appears, the monk buys her a pair of shoes.

A playboy called Chipali comes into the scene. Chipali defeats the monk, and with his money buys the affection of the young woman. She begets for him a baby boy; and he happily places his hope for the future on the baby.

Monks are supposed to give up worldly pleasures,[1] so that they may meditate and pray for the good of the people in the world. This they are supposed to do in a secluded place, usually in the mountains. But the old monk succumbs to the temptation of the flesh. However, he turns out to be too old, impotent, and unproductive. On the other hand, Chipali is young, virile, potent, productive, and naturally happy as a man. This Nojang represents a senile spirituality and a metaphysical religion that is separated from this world and thus is unproductive. As such, the value and leadership of this so-called "higher" religion is the target of jokes, satire, and laughter.

The Three Yangban (Aristocrats) Scenes

Three yangban brothers are brought in by Maltugi, their servant. Maltugi announces the arrival of the yangban by saying, "Yangbans are coming! But don't think these yangbans are scholars or are civil servants holding high government posts." He degrades the word "yangban" by punning on it to mean all kinds of derogatory things. When the oldest yangban brother protests, Maltugi corrects himself by saying that he referred to them as those who have been in high government service and are very respectable. The yangban accepts his explanation. Later, this yangban calls for him. Maltugi replies, "I looked for you all over the world but could not find you. I went to your home and found your wife alone. I did it again and again. As I was leaving after a sumptuous feast she gave me a penis as a gift.'' To the protest of the yangban, he corrects himself by saying that she gave him a stick of dried fish.[2] Again the yangban is deceived. Later Maltugi defeats the yangbans in a poetry contest—a favorite pastime of the yangbans in which they are supposed to be quite skilled. In this sport Maltugi proves to be far more able and makes fun of the literati's so-called "learned" words.

The yangban class is the ruling elite. They are supposed to be scholarly, respectable, and removed from the mundane world of ordinary folks. Thus, they do not hear what Maltugi is saying, but accept his explanations at face value. They do not see what is happening around them. They are so preoccupied with their own world and the existing system in which they hold very prestigious and privileged positions. This preoccupation makes them blind to the reality of the world. The audience however hears everything and sees everything. They laugh heartily. Maltugi, knowing the reality, dramatizes the situation and caricatures the aristocrats and thus exposes the incongruities in the establishment.

The Miyal Halmi (Old Woman Miyal) Scene

Miyal halmi comes into the scene looking for her husband. She was separated from him many years ago when there was a war on the Cheju Island where they used to live. Then an old man comes in searching for his long separated wife. These two stage a reunion and happily engage in sexual intercourse. Nothing happens. They begin to tell each other all the troubles they have been through. The husband suffered hunger, trouble with tax collectors, beatings from monks for raping a nun, etc. The old woman tells him how their children were carried away by a tiger when they went to the mountains to gather wood for fuel. Their lives were miserable. Then the old woman discovers that her husband has a young concubine. They fight with each other; and they try to negotiate a divorce. But the husband will not give her any alimony. In the fight the old woman gets killed. A village elder comes in and calls for a shamanistic ritual for the purpose of committing the dead woman's soul to heaven.

The minjung audience participates in the sad story. This is their lot in this world. In a world where the aristocrats rule, it is the minjung who suffer hunger, separation, exploitation, beatings, etc. No help comes from the so-called respectable religion. Even nature (tiger) seems to be against them. They also have trouble among themselves. There is no exit! And yet both the performers and the audience participate in the story-telling with jokes and laughter. Their conditions and they themselves are laughable. Also laughable is their own religion which is the only source of consolation in this weary world. The whole world is laughable.[3] Both the performers and the audience weep and laugh at the same time.

At the end of the scene, which is also the end of the whole mask dance, a village elder's advice, "Children, awake! The dawn is approaching from the east and the south," is often added. Dream-time and phantasy are over. One has to go back to the world of everyday life.

Experience of Critical Transcendence

In and through the mask dance, the minjung, the ordinary folks, experience and express a critical transcendence over this world and laugh at its absurdity. By satirizing the aristocrats they stand over against the aristocrats. By laughing at the old monk they stand above him. The concern of the younger generation in Korea, who are fond of and participate in the performance of the mask dance, is centered around these two stories. But I feel that the most important and significant one is the Miyal halmi scene. In this scene the minjung lament their lot, but they do it with humor. They laugh at and make fun of their own fate in this world, thereby transcending their own conditions. They find themselves standing over and beyond the entire world which includes not only the rulers and leaders but also themselves and their own religion.[4] They not only see correctly the reality of the world, which neither the rulers nor leaders can see because of their obsession with or separation from the world, but also envision another reality over against and beyond this one which neither the rulers nor leaders can see either.

The stance of critical transcendence is not given by some gods out there or by some objectively existing reality in "the other world." It is provided by the minjung's own life experience. Every time they lie in bed looking for restful sleep after a long day of back-breaking work, they would reflect upon their lot. Why is it that some are born into aristocratic families? Why is it that some are so fortunate that they don't have to work? Why is it that we have to work so hard like slaves? Why is it that heaven is so mindless? But they would immediately suppress these thoughts and fall asleep. Or they are too tired or too scared to play with such ideas. During short periods of rest between hard labor they would sit together and casually engage in rumor exchange. A certain aristocrat did such and such. I just don't understand. He is silly. Others would join in fulminating or laughing. Then another one will give a joking jibe. Who the hell do you think you are? Do you think you (or we) are any better? Aren't we just as silly? Then they would all laugh loudly expressing their agreement. When they find some leisure hours in the evening, especially with children around, they would also engage in innocent story telling. Stories such as how the hare outwitted the tiger in saving a man's life. The feelings behind these activities cannot be expressed openly. At least in public they would have to be suppressed. In the mask dance, these suppressed feelings explode into reality. The minjung are conscientized and are provided with a stance of critical transcendence. In other words, the stance of critical transcendence comes out of the accumulated suppressed feelings of the minjung's everyday life.⁵ The accumulated minjung's *han* (a Korean word for a kind of unresolved sense of resentment against the injustice suffered) is resolved.

The Subject of Transcendence

Sociologically speaking, the subject is, of course, the minjung. The ruling class, the better-to-do people, are the privileged class. They get most of the benefits out of the existing system and consider this the best world. They have vested interests in this world and are anxious to maintain it. They tend to rationalize and manipulate this world. On the other hand, the minjung, the ruled ones, get the worst possible deals in this world. Whenever there are changes such as price hikes or disasters, both natural and human, it is the minjung who suffer first and the most. They are the ones who are the most vulnerable and sensitive to what happens in the world. At the same time, without vested interests in the existing world, they are freer than those who are politically, economically, socially, and culturally in the upper echelon of the society.

Philosophically speaking, the subject of critical transcendence is the life that is lived by a person in response to physical needs. Because of the social conditions of the world, the minjung is forced to live with, by, and for the body. Bodily life produces bodily responses to reality in the form of feeling. This feeling is the total human response to the whole of reality.⁶ It is raw and concrete, not refined or abstract. It is honest, authentic, and truthful. On the other hand, the ruling class grasps the reality second hand, that is, through reflection. The brain as the organ of reflection can and does rationalize and manipulate things in the process. This is not to romanticize the minjung, for their nature is just as perfect or imperfect and just as good or bad as that of the aristocrats. As human beings, morally there is no difference between them. The difference between them, between the visceral and the cerebral, is created by social conditions. Because of their status in society, the minjung can with their bodily feeling not only grasp the unreasonableness of society but also see a vision of what it ought to be, though that vision is presented negatively as a critique of the present. For the society to be transformed and humanized, the cerebral elements always have to be faithful to and learn from the visceral elements, especially in times of radical changes.

The Social Role of Transcendence

The effect of the experience of transcendence can be either negative or positive. When oppressive measures become extreme the minjung may explode and rebel, but do so without envisioning possibilities for structural changes in the society. In order to prevent rebellions, clever rulers usually manipulate and brain-wash the minjung. They permit and even help the minjung to have festivals and to perform mask dances as a means of diffusing the pent-up feelings of the minjung. They also spiritualize the minjung's vision so that the realization of the vision may be in "the other world" rather than in this world. Catharsis may happen, but there would be no changes in the concrete everyday life. The minjung thus become fatalistic.

The experience of transcendence can also produce positive effects. First, it creates among the minjung the wisdom and the power to survive. Becoming sure of the fact that the existing world is a fallen one and that they are standing over against and beyond it, they are able to bear the hardships of the world with good humor. This is especially true in times when there seems to be no exit, no possibility for effective change. Without such wisdom they could not survive as human beings with dignity in a world where their dignity is not recognized. It is because of the experience of critical transcendence that they can continue to live with humor and without falling into despair.

Second, the experience provides the minjung with the courage to fight for change and freedom. Either due to the inner power struggles within the ruling class, or because of the minjung's revolts against the corruption of rulers and their exploitative policies, there appear times when the establishment becomes unstable. Sensing with their bodily feeling that something is happening and knowing that this world is not the ultimate one, the minjung perceive the desirability and seize the possibility for a successful fight, and become active. This fact has been demonstrated in a series of peasant revolts and the Donghak Revolution of the nineteenth century. The minjung feel the power welling up from their guts. The experience of transcendence gives the minjung both the wisdom to survive and the courage to fight. And that happens without much self-righteousness, for this experience of critical transcendence places them not only over against others who oppress the minjung but also over against the minjung themselves. Self-transcendence rather than self-righteousness makes it possible for the minjung to insert a wedge (grace) into the vicious circle of the ruled becoming the same kind of oppressive rulers by seeking revenge. Thus, one sees the capacity of the minjung both to be involved in political revolutionary activities and to transcend them at the same time.

Incidentally, here we see three types of minjung. The first type is those who have been brain-washed by the intellectual apparatus of the system and the rulers. Generally the peasants belong to this type. They are subservient, conservative, and reactionary. They are the ones whom those who work for the minjung consider to be "headaches." The second type is those who see and know what is really happening. They can in turn be subdivided into two groups. One is those who become opportunistic and serve the rulers, and the other is those who become clowns and only pretend to serve the rulers. The urban poor tend to belong to this second type. Those who work for human rights do not know how to relate to this type. The third type is those who are conscious of what is happening and are ready to act when the occasion calls for it. They become activists and revolutionaries. The factory workers generally belong to this type. It is usually this third type that the intellectuals consider to be the real minjung. However, these three types do not exist as separate entities. They exist all at once as a mixture both within the individual and in the minjung as a whole. They are all integral parts of the minjung of Korea.

A Reflection and Witness

For nearly one hundred years, from the time when the "Hermit Kingdom" opened its doors to foreigners till now, it has been very difficult for Koreans to study seriously Korean history and culture. The modernizers, especially the Christians, respect the so-called superior Western culture so much that they tend to despise Korean culture and consider it backward, vulgar, and superstitious. The Japanese, who ruled Korea for thirty-six years (1910–1945), being anxious to prevent Korean nationalistic sentiment from being maintained or activated, prohibited studies of anything Korean except for the purpose of downgrading it. After the national liberation of 1945 we were free to study Korean history and culture. But the disastrous war of 1950 forced us to waste many more years.

In recent years, younger scholars of Korean history have successfully liberated themselves from the Japanese colonialist interpretation of Korean history which pictured Koreans as lazy, divisive, and, therefore, incapable of self-rule. They have also begun to take a new look at Korean history, that is, Korean history not as the history of rulers such as kings, generals, and aristocrats, but as the history of the minjung, who are the majority of the population. The minjung are correctly seen as those who bear the main burden of the national history, and yet, as those who died and disappeared without leaving their names in history. Similar attempts have been made in other areas of study such as literature, music, dance, and painting.

The Christian intellectuals, especially the theologians (a small minority of them), are the latest to come into this vigorously active movement. Yet the theological task is urgent and enormous. Has God been working in our history? If not, what does God have to do with us? If yes, was God working only in the history of rulers? If yes, was God indifferent to men and women who compose the minjung, the majority of the population? As Christians we have to start with the premise that God, as the Lord of History, has worked in and through our history and that God, as revealed in the life, death, and resurrection of Jesus Christ, has a special concern for the underdogs, namely, the minjung. Otherwise, the Christian God would have no place in our history, in the events of our time, or for that matter in the future.

As one of the latecomers to this theological movement, I was attracted to the mask dance, among other art forms, and decided to study it with the help of specialists in the field. Often, I also participated in performances by dancing with the performers at the end as the audience usually does. What I have presented here is not much more than a hunch or "a pop theology." But, at least on my part, it was a serious attempt to grasp the meaning of the mask dance not only for the minjung but also for the whole people who create and form the history of Korea. Instead of starting with theological categories and propositions (which were formulated mostly in different historical contexts) I have tried to begin with the mask dance as a secular event that happened here in Korea at a particular period in history. Of course, it does not mean that I made myself completely free of theological presuppositions. It is impossible for me to do so, for I am already deeply immersed in the Western theological currents. As anyone can see, there are many theological currents[7] hidden in my presentation. What is significant for me is that in the course of study I have found my theological concepts strongly challenged and modified.

For instance, my understanding of transcendence had to be modified. Transcendence is not movement into some metaphysical world out there or into "Spirit," but is deeply rooted in the historical experience of the human. The idea of transcendence as a dichotomy between metaphysical and physical categories had to be re-examined. My understanding of God's incarnation was deepened in more concrete and existential terms. God is working and revealing his will in and through the minjung of Korea, especially the minjung's history and culture. God was not carried piggy-back to Korea by the first missionary. The minjung as the "cultural proletariat" has a messianic significance and role in Korea's history. Beginning to do theology in such a way is exciting, for you feel theology with your body and dance with it before you think it.

NOTES

1. Buddhism had been suppressed for nearly 500 years during the Yi dynasty. The Yi dynasty replaced Buddhism with Confucianism as the state religion. Buddhism removed itself from the center of everyday life to the mountains for meditation and prayer.
2. The vulgar expressions in Korean for both "penis" and "stick of dry fish" sound nearly the same.
3. Visitors to Korea are often surprised at the happy mood of Koreans in spite of their suffering. The ability to laugh in spite of their suffering comes from the minjung tradition which is epitomized in the mask dance.
4. Here they seem to experience what Paul Tillich calls "God above God."
5. Viewed as such, transcendence is not merely spatial. It is also temporal.
6. Charles Davis, *Body as Spirit: The Nature of Religious Feeling* (New York: Seabury, 1976). Esp. Ch. 1, "Feeling as the Human Response to Reality."
7. "The currents" include, among others, theologies of secularization, of politics, of liberation, of *missio dei*, and especially of laughter, play, and festivity.

Chapter IV

Towards a Theology of Han

SUH NAM-DONG

Sometime ago two incidents happened in relation to the mission of Korean churches. One was in the Y. H. Company, in which the Protestant Urban Industrial Mission (UIM) was involved. The other concerned a Mr. Oh Won-chun and the Catholic Farmers' Association. In connection with these incidents, church leaders, ministers and priests, and several lay persons were arrested, charged, and sentenced to prison terms, thus increasing the number of prisoners of conscience. I want to begin with these events which, I believe, indicate the nature of God's intervention in our history and then move on to a discussion of the problem of *han*[1] which both events raise in a crucial way in terms of the life and history of Korean people.

In both these events, the clergy who were arrested became involved somewhere in the middle of the proceedings. The core persons (workers and farmers), who were involved from the very beginning and were the initiators, were people (minjung) with a firm Christian faith.

In 1966 Mr. Chang Young-ho started the Y. H. Trading Company to produce wigs. At first there were only ten employees, but it grew to be a big business. Within four years with 4,000 employees it became the fifteenth largest export company in the nation. In the year 1970, the company's net profit was 1.3 billion won. In the same year the president, Chang Young-ho, shifted most of the company's assets to New York and started running a department store there. He did not pay off the 1.5 billion won debt of the Y. H. Company. The Y. H. Company received bank loans of W632,550,000 in 1974, W1,691,000,000 in 1975, W3,173,570,000 in 1977 and in 1979, W4,050,000,000 (total assets of 2.3 billion won); and the number of employees was reduced to 1,800. The daily wage for a female worker was 220 won in 1975. Some of the typical characteristics of modern Korean export businesses are special provisions for bank loans, tax exemptions, rapid expansion, low wages paid to workers, and the smuggling of capital out of the country.

The employees of Y. H. Trading Company learned the meaning and worth of struggle for human rights and justice in accomplishing two things. First, they successfully organized in May 1975 the Y. H. Trade Union as a branch of the National Textile Trade Union. This involved much sacrifice and struggle. Second, as a consequence of their actions and struggle they received their first 50 percent bonus on their pay. However, the harassment of the trade union increased; and the membership of the union decreased to 500 in 1978. When the chief of the union was taken by the Korean CIA on March 25, 1979, the union protested for her release by demonstrating for three days. Then the company announced that the factory would be closed down by the end of April. The workers rose up again from April 13 to 17 to fight not just for a raise in wages but this time for their very survival. That was the beginning of the Y. H. event.

The trade union faced various difficulties in the process of the fight, and finally, after experiencing many failures, on August 9, 200 women workers went to the New Democratic Party building to appeal to the government party to work out a fair solution. It was reported that a few leaders of the Korean civil rights movement and UIM intervened just before the workers went to the NDP building. Finally, at 2 a.m. on August 11, during a forced dispersal of the workers by a 1,000 strong police force, Miss Kim Kyong-suk (twenty-one years old) was killed. The police sent the rest of the trade union members to their homes in the countryside.

Miss Kim was an executive committee member of the Y. H. Trade Union and was a leader in initiating the demonstrations and rallies, composing and reading statements and appeals. According to the letter she left for her mother and younger brother, in her eight years of experience as a factory worker, she had had innumerable nosebleeds from exhaustion, and she sometimes worked three months without being paid. She had to live on, struggling with near-starvation, inadequate clothing, no heat in winter; and often she had only small thirty-won cakes to eat for a meal. Feeling very frustrated at being unable to attend church services on Sunday, she recommended regular church attendance, Bible reading, and theology as important for her brother; and she pleaded with her mother to believe in the power of the labor movement.

In the death of Miss Kim were concentrated not only the various contradictions of political and economic structures, but hers seems to be a death which embodies the *han* of eight million Korean workers.

Several times the Korean Christian Action Organization of the UIM and the Special Committee for the Kim Kyong-suk Case planned for and advertised a memorial service—once in the Yongdongpo UIM Center, then the Dongdaemun Catholic Church, and finally the Christian Building. But every time the police prevented the holding of the service.

Mr. Oh Won-chun was a board member of the Andong Diocese Federation of the Catholic Farmers' Association. He was active in the farmers' rights movement, notably the campaign for the refund of damages to sweet potato farming. He was seized by "a certain authority" on May 5, 1979, was beaten up severely, and then taken by boat to Ullung-do Island on May 6 and kept there until May 21. The priests in Andong Diocese attempted to contact the police to find out the truth about Mr. Oh.

On May 26, thirty plainclothes police broke into the headquarters of the diocese and forcibly took Fr. Chung Ho-kyong, who is a supervisory priest for the Farmers' Association, as if they were capturing and taking a dangerous animal. Such was the brutality. In reaction, continuous national movements were organized, including special prayer meetings. There were reports on the incident to refute false statements published by the police through the mass media and in all the schools. Oh himself is alleged to have admitted, no doubt under pressure and torture, to the prosecutor that he had lied about his kidnapping, thus denying the Declaration of Conscience he had written earlier.

This is seemingly a small event from a far-away country place. Yet, it shows all the structural contradictions and crises present in an agricultural society.

Brother Oh Won-chun is in solitary confinement, which affects him both physically and psychologically. He cannot talk about his situation, not even to his priest. This is his *han*.

The statement made in the middle of Mr. Oh's case by the Korean Catholic Farmers' Association and the National Supervisory Priests for the Catholic Farmers' Association states, "The movement to recover the inalienable rights of the farmers, who are now alienated and oppressed in the present distorted industrial structure, is an activity of the Christian spirit and the historical mission of Christians. However, the activities, which we were to carry out as the mission of a Hyonjang church[2] in a rural society, have been severely repressed particularly with the accusation of the authorities that we are pro-communist." In his sermon, Cardinal Stephen Kim also reaffirmed the description of the Catholic Farmers' Association as a Hyonjang church. If this is so, then various UIMs, the rural activities of the Korea Christian Academy, the National Council of Churches' Human Rights Committee, Friday Prayer Meetings, Thursday Prayer Meetings, and Galilee Church would all be new Hyonjang churches which have appeared in the present-day Korean situation. I think this Hyonjang church is a third form of the church, besides the Catholic and the Protestant churches; and it is similar to the people's church referred to by Gutiérrez and Moltmann.

Several theologians working for the Institute for Mission-Education have been involved in the above-mentioned events and have made theological reflections on these cases. These are indeed theology in praxis or theology in the actual context. I firmly believe that theological activities do not end with the exposition of biblical texts on the salvation or liberation of man by God. In the Bible, the Exodus, the activities of the prophets, and the event of the

Cross offer new insights, but these texts ought to be rediscovered and re-interpreted in the context of the human struggle for historical and political liberation today.

The suffering of Korean workers and farmers is concentrated in the suffering of the late Miss Kim Kyong-suk and Brother Oh Won-chun. The structural contradictions in the Korean economic and political systems are an inseparable part of the two stories. In addition, Korean Christians are aware that God himself asserts his own cause when his justice is invaded. So the acts of faith to be in solidarity with the sufferings of these people and the acts of commitment to solve these contradictions often start with special prayer meetings like the Friday Prayer Meetings. Almost always, the prayers plead with God to resolve our suppressed *han*. There is no more urgent prayer than this. Every agony and all contradictions are included in the words "suppressed *han*," and everyone prays with the same intent and with one mind, so that these words adequately express everyone's prayer.

The meaning of the prayer of Korean Christians is like that of Luke 18:3, "Vindicate me against my adversary," and Prov. 31:9, "Open your mouth, judge righteously, maintain the rights of the poor and the needy." In the new translation of the Korean Bible, "I will vindicate . . ." is translated "I will resolve your suppressed *han*."

(1) Koreans have suffered numerous invasions by surrounding powerful nations so that the very existence of the Korean nation has come to be understood as *han*. (2) Koreans have continually suffered the tyranny of the rulers so that they think of their existence as *baeksong*.[3] (3) Also, under Confucianism's strict imposition of laws and customs discriminating against women, the existence of women was *han* itself. (4) At a certain point in Korean history, about half of the population were registered as hereditary slaves and were treated as property rather than as people of the nation. These thought of their lives as *han*. These four may be called the fourfold *han* of Korean people. Indeed, as the poet Ko Eun exclaims, "We Koreans were born from the womb of *han* and brought up in the womb of *han*."

Han is an underlying feeling of Korean people. On the one hand, it is a dominant feeling of defeat, resignation, and nothingness. On the other, it is a feeling with a tenacity of will for life which comes to weaker beings. The first aspect can sometimes be sublimated to great artistic expressions and the second aspect could erupt as the energy for a revolution or rebellion. Hwangchoga (17 B.C.),[4] Kongmudohaga (second century A.D.)[5] of old Korean poetry, and Chungupsa,[6] Kasiri,[7] Chungsanpyulgok[8] of Koryo poetry, and such arts as Pansori[9] and Mask Dances[10] of the Yi dynasty are all artistic sublimations of *han* which the powerless and the frustrated experience as renunciation. However, in Pansori and Mask Dance, it is more than renunciation. An awareness of the moral contradiction in the ruling class, a growing social consciousness and self-criticism of the oppressed people can be felt and experienced. On the other hand, *han* is the tenacity for life of oppressed spirits; it is a tendency for social revolution as expressed in Kungye[11] and Kyonhwon's[12] rebellion, Mangyi and Mangsoyi's[13] rebellion, Manchuk's[14] rebellion, Hong Kyung-rae[15] and Imsul[16] People's Rebellion, the Donghak Rebellion,[17] the struggle of Hwalbindang,[18] the March First movement,[19] and the April "Student Revolution."[20]

Instead of exploring the etymology of *han,* which may not be helpful in understanding living expressions of *han,* let me introduce some works of contemporary writers and poets which, I consider, are more appropriate for an understanding of *han.*

Let us first look at a novel called *Changma* (Rainy Season) by Yun Hyong-kil. In a small farmhouse there lived an old woman, her older son and his wife, and their ten-year-old son. They lived in the inner part of the house. In the outer part of the house there lived the daughter-in-law's mother and her other daughter. These in-laws living in the outer part of the house were from the same village, but had moved later to Seoul for the children's education. During the war they had returned to take refuge in the village. The son of the outer house was a university graduate and a South Korean army officer. He was killed during the war by guerrillas. The younger son of the owner of the house was a farmer with middle school education, who was now with communist guerrillas in the mountains. These two young men had been friends.

During the war, the old mother of the inner part of the house always worried about her younger son in the mountains, while the old woman living in the outer part of the house prayed that in the rainy season lightning should strike and kill the armed guerrillas in the mountains. Because of this situation, the two old women quarrelled and became enemies.

Tired of waiting, the woman of the inner part of the house goes to a fortune-teller to ask what will happen to her son and the answer is that he will come back home. So she has her older son and daughter-in-law prepare food to welcome him home.

On the day he is supposed to come, a huge snake is seen heading towards the house, followed by a group of children with stones in their hands. At this sight, the mother faints and the snake climbs a persimmon tree in the middle of the yard and stays there with its tongue out. In this state of chaos, only the woman of the outer part of the house keeps calm. She drives away the children and sets a ceremonial table with food in front of the snake and speaks to it: "Not forgetting the families, you have come all this way. For many days, your mother prepared all this food for you. Although you can't eat it, just enjoy the sight of it, and then go your way. Your older brother has everything under control. So don't worry. Go your way as soon as possible. You shouldn't be lingering around here. Take good care of yourself." Being talked to like this, the snake comes down from the tree and vanishes into the bamboo forest behind the house. A doctor is summoned to treat the mother. She recovers consciousness; and the first thing she asks is, "Has it gone?" When she is told that the snake has disappeared, she thanks the other woman and is reconciled with her. However, she dies a few days later and the story ends.

Reading the novel, I was greatly moved by the vivid imaginative description of *han* which is symbolized by the huge snake. The *han* which took the form of the huge snake is the *han* of the young farmer who fled into the mountain and became a member of one of the guerrilla bands. At the same time it is the *han* occasioned by the division of the country which longs for the unification of the nation. By the snake coming and vanishing, the *han* is imaged and resolved, and the two in-laws, who had confronted each other like enemies, are reconciled and unity is restored. Here, the *han* of national suffering and the contradictions in our society are rooted in the tragedy of our divided nation.

Next we will look at "The Story of the Sound" (1972) by the poet Kim Chi-ha. Some time ago in Seoul, very strange bumping sounds could often be heard. When people with money and power heard the sound they would tremble like aspen leaves and break out into a cold sweat. The sound originated in the following manner. There was a fellow called Ando. He came as an aspiring young man to the city. He lived in a rented room of a shanty on the bank of Chongryang Chon (river) in Chongryang-ri (part of Seoul). Unfortunately, nothing he did was ever successful. It is not known whether it was bad fortune related to his previous birth or his ill fortune to have an evil spirit. When he attempted to stand up with his two feet on the ground, immediately he would be bombarded with endless visions of crimes no one had ever heard, seen, or thought of, so he could not help but run all the time, day and night, all the year round. Even if he earned 10 won, he would lose 100 won; if he borrowed 100 won, 1,000 won would be taken away; he would be robbed and stepped on by various rascals until at last his fare to go back to the country, which was kept inside his underwear, was also lost. Going around from east to west to south to north, he became tired. He was starving and near crazy. So, on an evening when there was a beautiful sunset, he stood up with his two feet on the ground and said, "Damn! This is a doglike world!"

Because of this word of damnation about the world, he was immediately taken away, beaten up, then taken to the court and found guilty of having spread a false rumor and of slandering the regime. His head and legs were chopped off, so that only the trunk of his body was left. It was put into a cell for a five-hundred-year imprisonment.

"Why, what is this? I didn't say a word even though I was naked, starving, being worked to death, beaten, and oppressed. What is this? You will know my mind, you flying wild goose. Ah! Mother! I'm coming home. I'm going home through the wall, over the wall. I'm going home over the red brick wall as a grieving ghost."

He would hit the walls of the cell by rolling the trunk of his body, shouting in a soundless cry. Every time he did it, it made a bumping sound which made people shiver, and those with money and power tremble.

This is the false rumor, and the wind without sound, the *han* of the suppressed people (minjung). This rumor accords with the modern expressions of the supernatural, as Peter Berger describes it in *A Rumor of Angels*.

Furthermore, it belongs to the category of Psalm 19:3,4: "There is no speech, nor are there words; their voice is not heard; yet their voice goes out through all the earth, and their words to the end of the world."

In his poem "Hwangto" (1970), Kim Chi-ha talks of himself as a transmitter of *han:* "This little peninsula is filled with the clamor of aggrieved ghosts. It is filled with the mourning noise of the *han* of those who died from foreign invasions, wars, tyranny, rebellion, malignant diseases and starvation. I want my poems to be the womb or bearer of these sounds, to be the transmitter of the *han* and to communicate a sharp awareness of our historical tragedy." Like the prophets of the Old Testament, who felt that they would be cursed and consumed with fire if they did not proclaim the word of God, this poet of *han* sees himself as chosen to be a medium of the sound of the *han.*

The third work is the novel *Shingung* (God's Bow) (1977) by Chon Seung-se. His major works deal with *han* in depth, and in many ways he is as great a transmitter of *han* as Kim Chi-ha. *Nakwoldo Island*, *Scream of a Yellow Dog*, and the play *Mansun* are masterpieces which have *han* as their theme. *Shingung*, could be taken as one of the best literary works about *han.* The story itself is not very complicated, but the heavy use of dialect and its satirical style make a summary difficult.

It is a story of a shaman living in a fishing village in Changsungpo, an island off the southwest coast. The heroine Wangnyon is a famous shaman; her mother-in-law was a shaman and her daughter-in-law too is a shaman. After ten years of practicing her shaman rites Wangnyon made quite a lot of money and was able to buy a fishing boat for her husband. However, because of three years of bad fishing which followed and through the wicked trick of a usurer called Pansu, the boat is taken away to cover their debts. Even worse, while now working as a fisherman for this immoral rich man, Pansu, her husband, Oksu, is killed in a storm. Wangnyon develops a deep grudge *(han)* against Pansu because of this, and goes into a deep depression during which she performs no shamanistic rites. She depends on her daughter-in-law's insufficient income. Then she receives a strong request from Pansu to perform a shaman's rite for good fishing. At first she refuses, but suddenly experiences ecstasy with the spirits calling down to her. So, she begins the shaman's rites. In the middle of the rites, she puts a bowl on Pansu's head and shoots the poisoned arrow from God's bow and kills him, thus resolving the *han.*

Even among the oppressed minjung, the heroine of this story is a very demeaned person. She is a symbol of the *han* of the common people, the oppressed minjung. At the same time, she is a great artist and a heroic person who takes care of the *han* of the minjung. Traditionally, Koreans depend on the rites of the shaman to release grievances from various causes. But this contemporary storyteller makes the shaman resolve her *han* through more than a shaman's rite. She resolves her *han* through an act of vindication. Also, this work portrays, more vividly than do most other works, that the

cause of *han* is not nature or fate but is human greed and social contradictions.

In this novel, Chon Seung-se makes a valid criticism of the basic dogma of
Haewonkongsa (Work of Resolving Han) of Jeungsankyo (an indigenous
religious sect) and, in addition, indicates the limitations of shamanistic rites.
Han is a common dominant feeling of powerless Korean people. It is the
feeling of women, despised slaves, common people, etc., all of whom com-
monly resort to shamanistic rites. The shaman thus becomes a kind of national priest. The rites for resolving *han* are based on the thought that the
suffering of people is caused by those who died with *han*. Therefore, the
object of the rite is limited to dealing with *han* on the personal level. The
Jeungsankyo hold the theory that nationwide historical *han* also can be resolved through a disciplined spiritual power, called "Youngryuk," which
can be obtained by Zen. This is called "Haewonkongsa," and when it is
extended worldwide it is called "Chunjikongsa."[21] The rites of shamanism
and Haewonkongsa of Jeungsankyo are limited to releasing the *han* of the
dead; and they are carried out as a religious ceremony. While it is alleged that
they have universal significance, in effect they function as an anesthesia,
offered by the rulers to the people, to de-politicize the minjung and to distance the oppressed people with their longings from reality. In opposition to
this, the contemporary writers mentioned above aim at post-shamanization
or the politicization of shamanistic exorcism by viewing and describing the
han of the minjung in and through historical and realistic events.

Fourth, there are many poems with the theme of *han*. Among them, Yang
Song-wu's *Slave Diary* contains many traditional and typical expressions
about *han*. His view is that the *han* which has been absorbed into the bones
and muscles of the people of the country for 5,000 years is still breathing in
the roots of the grass which covers the graves of the dead. The last stanza of
the epic is worth quoting:

> Even though you survive for a million years
> like worms in dying petals;
> I will look down, waving my hands in the air,
> being torn like a rag.
> Even though you vanish as dew on a sword
> the blood scattered when you rolled and rolled;
> I will wet the scars of the swords, the gunshot wounds,
> wet your stained hearts
> as a shower falling down in May.
> Even though you thrash without stopping
> like the sleet in mid-winter;
> I will shout out
> breathing as roots of grass
> which sleep not under the ground. . . .

Do you hear, you poets,
the thick voice which echoes to the end of the earth
hitting the air with fists,
fists from inside graves,
sorrowful graves of 5,000 years?

This is a persistent sort of *han*—insistent strong voices and the sobbings of grieving ghosts—which is captured well in this poem. The poet, Yang Song-wu, thinks that the mission of a poet is to be a medium of the *han* of the people.

The person who has done most to develop *han* as a theme of Christian theology is Kim Chi-ha. The idea that consistently underlies Kim's poetry is the theme of *han*. However, it was in his memos written in prison that he began expressing the belief that *han* can be sublimated in dynamic form as the energy for revolution. The memos were written over the period November 1974 to February 15, 1975, when he was freed for a short while. There are 500 sheets of manuscript paper on this subject. In these papers, there are also several poems, theories of poetry, thoughts on training for life, deep and moving statements of commitment to the Catholic faith, observations on prisoners and self-identification with them (which he refers to as identification with *han* and the Abyss). But much of the space in these papers is devoted to sketches of literary works. Four major works are outlined: *Sacred Place*, *Famous Mountain*, and *Malttuk* (all plays), and *Chang Il-dam* (an epic poem).

Famous Mountain portrays the life and activities of Shin Dol-sok, a volunteer army officer. *Sacred Place* is Kim's allegorical poem in which there is heavy use of parody about the prison and prison life. Malttuk is the name of a servant who appears in the Pong San mask dance. In the sketches for *Sacred Place* and *Malttuk* the theme of *han* is presented more dynamically through a modernization of traditional dialogue forms. A similar development of *han* is found also in "The Identification of God with Revolution" which is his exposition of Catholic theology. His clearest and perhaps most powerful statement of the theme of *han* is in *Chang Il-dam*. In fact, his heroes Malttuk and more so Chang Il-dam are incarnations of *han*. If his first book of poems, *Hwangto*, may be taken as announcing the birth of a poet for the minjung, *Malttuk*, *Chang Il-dam*, "The Identification of *Han* with the Abyss," and "The Identification of God with Revolution" may be taken as heralding the second birth of a Catholic poet Kim Chi-ha as a minjung poet.

Chang Il-dam is an admirable attempt to reconcile Korean folk tradition and Christian tradition by telling the gospel story of Jesus in the form of the traditional Pansori (narrative drama).

Let us first see how *han* was sublimated dynamically in the sketches of *Sacred Place* and *Malttuk*, works to which he refers as examples of the art of political imagination, before we turn to *Chang Il-dam*. The term "Sacred

Place" is more than simply a paradoxical word for prison. Kim Chi-ha believes that the prison is a real place with a potential for revolution (Exodus) and that true humanity can be found among the prisoners. "A prison is an oppression of oppressions and a contradiction of reality itself. At the same time one finds collective *han* expressing itself spatially in 'Sacred Place'. This massive *han* shines in a tension of silence like a shadow which is waiting to explode. Its symbolic place of manifestation is the prison."

Malttuk, who is a servant-slave, appears in traditional mask dances as the embodiment of satire, jocularity, and humor. These expressions also function as protests against the yangban, the ruling class. Therefore, Kim sees them as pervasive phenomena of *han*.

Being beaten by the yangban, Malttuk finally gets his revenge by beating the yangban with his quick wit and brave actions. This leads to an ecstasy of dances and songs where real humanity, i.e., koinonia, is realized, which the author calls "God's involvement in history."

Han is an accumulation of suppressed and condensed experiences of oppression. Thus "accumulated *han* is inherited and transmitted, boiling in the blood of the people," which is also defined as the "emotional core of anti-regime action." This is the genesis of *han;* and the author goes further to grasp and express the structure, contents, development, and explosion of *han*. He ends with a climactic description of *han as a people-eating monster*.

In *Sacred Place   han* appears as a metal-eating ghostly creature who rules prisoners; and in *Malttuk han* appears as Imae (yangban-eating creature in Hahoe Mask Dance). The metal-eating creature in *Sacred Place* is conceived like this in the memo. *"Han,* separating itself from human emotion, becomes substantial and grows into a ghostly creature. It appears as a concrete substance with enormous ugly and evil energy and rules and commands all the prisoners. It is a hero, ghost, and leader of a religious faction; how can I describe all this?"

How can we overcome the *han* which becomes a monster that rules prisoners and is the Imae of nightmares? The author's plots for *Sacred Place* and *Malttuk* have peaks coming one after another leading to triumphs, ecstasy, and koinonia.

Let us also consider Kim Chi-ha's memos on "The Philosophy of *Dan,"* "The Priesthood of *Han,"* and "Church Resolving the *Han* of the Minjung" which will help to illumine the author's conception of Chang Il-dam.

Dan is the poet's self-denial. To start with, "I separate my body and mind from every comfort and easy life, circles of petit bourgeois dreams, and secular swamps without depth. This is the total content of my faith—I know that only vigorous self-denial is my way. Let us leave as a wayfarer, leaving everything behind. This is the revolution which I have to show and realize with my life itself. The delusion is finished, 'Ah, a sad and painful act of a spider which goes up in a single line in the air. . . .' "

Dan also has in view a social dimension of the people. "Cutting the chain of the circulation of *han: dan* is for the transformation of the secular world and secular attachments. Accumulated *han* being met with continuous *dan*. On the one hand, there is the fearful *han* which can kill, cause revenge, destroy, and hate endlessly, and on the other, there is the repetition of *dan* to suppress the explosion which can break out of the vicious circle, so that *han* can be sublimated as higher spiritual power. The opening of the total dimension of the minjung with a dialectical unification of the complicated *han* and *dan:* that is the decisive basis of my artistic effort. *Dan* is to overcome *han*. Personally, it is self-denial. Collectively, it is to cut the vicious circle of revenge.''

About the dialectic between and unification of *han* and *dan,* Kim Chi-ha wrote in his ''Declaration of Conscience'' as follows:

People's *han* and rage ought to be liberated from its masochistic exercise to be a great and fervent clamor asking for God's justice. If needed, it ought to be developed into a decisive and organized explosion. This miraculous transition lies in religious commitment and in internal and spiritual transformation.

Kim Chi-ha declares himself as a priest of *han* with this philosophy of *dan*. He wants to be a priest of *han* who speaks for the *han* of the miserable victims of the third world, which goes through tyranny-division-fabrication-oppression as classically found in capitalistic colonialism.

Furthermore, despite the suppression of the human rights movement, he is determined to remain in the church and hopes the church can be for the minjung. ''The church ought to be the comforter to resolve the *han* of the minjung and to cut the vicious circle of violence and to change it into a progressive movement. For this purpose, churches ought to accept limited violence and ought to be a sanctuary for radicals and fighters who are progressing out of the dark.''

In his memos on *Famous Mountain, Sacred Place,* and *Malttuk,* he does not integrate his thoughts on *dan* philosophy and on being a priest of *han*. But in his more recent memo on *Chang Il-dam,* he has integrated these ideas completely in his hero. Although in this memo there is no separate explanation of *han,* all the above-mentioned elements are artistically intermingled in *Chang Il-dam* which may be taken as a theological exposition of *han*.

It is a history or biography of Chang Il-dam which portrays the overcoming of *han*. The memo starts like a preface to John's Gospel and is a contemplation on ''the word.'' The contemplation on ''the word'' is repeated in both the prophecy before the execution and in the resurrection and in the stories after that. So we can say that contemplation is the core of the Chang Il-dam story.

Chang Il-dam is not himself the word but a sad memory of the word. Through oppression the word has been reduced to silence. A rumor declares that the resurrection of the word will come like a storm. The storm is the people, the word is liberation and revolution; and it is prophesied that Chang Il-dam will be resurrected in a storm.

Let me attempt to interpret the memo. The basic theme is that human beings are originally the word (freedom). It is suppressed (silenced). Then *han* arises, comes up (resurrects) as a rumor, and then becomes a storm (the revolution of the minjung).

After the preface, the story goes thus: The starting point is a prison. Chang Il-dam escapes from prison, which is a contradiction of freedom. He depicts the path of his escape as that of a road travelled by a wayfarer who is going up to the top of heaven from the lowest bottom fighting against the dark stream of life. He perceives this journey as the reverse journey of the direction most of the unhappy minjung are forced to take. In the process of this journey one goes through dramatic experiences, meets various kinds of people, gains several insights into life and gradually understands the truth of the gospel more deeply. He then becomes the preacher of liberation, teaching disciples and training himself together with them and forms a community to realize koinonia. He proclaims Haedongkeugnak (Heaven on Earth), which is the coming of a new world.

The butcher Chang Il-dam is a wanted man. Having escaped from prison, he hides in a back street where prostitutes live. He happens to see one prostitute giving birth to a child. She is dying. Her body is rotting with venereal disease. She has tuberculosis; and she is also mentally ill. Yet she is giving birth to a child. At the sight of it, he says, "Ah, from a rotten body, new life is coming out! It is God who is coming out!" He learns the truth of the world. He kneels down and says, "Oh, my mother, God is in your womb. God is the very bottom." And he kisses her feet.

He becomes a preacher of liberation, although he is wanted by the police. He meets and argues with various Urban Industrial Mission pastors, Catholic priests, intellectuals, professors, trade union leaders, Buddhist monks, servicemen, and social workers, and criticizes their self-deception and easy life. However, he learns many things from this encounter which deepen his thoughts. His previous blunt and violent attitudes change into more flexible ideas; and they are sublimated into the philosophy of *dan* and the road of a wayfarer. Later, he leads his disciples who follow him into Kyeryong Mountain[22] and forms a community or koinonia. He teaches them the philosophy of *dan,* which is the self-denial that casts out the temptation of selfishness and comfort and is the revolution of cutting the vicious circle of revenge by following the eternal stranger's road which leads to heaven. He interprets the theory of Innaechon[23] as "food is heaven" and the bottom is heaven so that turning the bottom up is to realize the justice of heaven. He speaks of the unification of God and revolution; the unification of acts and prayers; and the unification of earthly food and heavenly food. He establishes a system of thought in which he unifies individual spiritual reformation and the reformation of social justice. (Kim confesses he discovered this synthesis in the Catholic faith). The first stage in this process is Shichonju (worshipping God in the mind), the second stage is Yangchonju (nurturing the body of God), the third stage is Haengchonju (practicing the struggle), and the fourth stage is Sangchonju[24] (transcending death and living as a single, bright resurrected fighter for the people). He teaches his disciples Chonju (reflection and effort). A few times he predicts his impending death and resurrection and the coming of the next world.

Finally, Chang Il-dam and his disciples begin a march to Seoul declaring Haedongkeugnak as a vision of the future. Haedongkeugnak is not a paradise for a few chosen bourgeois, but rather a millennium where the whole society is renewed and made righteous by the coming of the Messiah (Revolution). He invades Seoul, which is filled with devils and corruption. In the invasion there is a scene showing the march of starving farmers. It is a piece of poetic imagination in which there are recollections of the Donghak Movement, Exodus March, and the human rights movement which began in 1971 and still continues. As this big march gets near Seoul, the tyrannical power group becomes confused and frightened. A reward is offered for the capture of Chang Il-dam. As in the case of Jesus, Chang Il-dam is arrested with the help of a disciple who betrays him.

In his trial he says, "My paradise is not in this land. It is a single white road which is like a wind moved by time, passing Seoul towards the world, universe, and sky. This road is the paradise and I am a wayfarer who follows the road." He is sentenced to death; and his head is chopped off. Then a miracle happens. Chang Il-dam is resurrected three days after his death, but a very strange thing happens: Chang's head appears on the betrayer's body, and the betrayer's head is on Chang's body.

Kim Chi-ha says, "It is an expression of Chang's conflicting thought that this is revenge but at the same time also the salvation of vicious men." The head speaking justice and truth is bonded to the body carrying injustice and falsehood; and then the word of the resurrection becomes a storm (minjung) and spreads to every corner of the nation. The word is as follows:

> Food is heaven
> As you can't go to heaven by yourself
> Food is to be shared
> Food is heaven
> As you see the stars in heaven together
> Food is to be shared by everybody
> When the food goes into a mouth
> Heaven is worshipped in the mind
> Food is heaven
> Ah, ah, food is
> To be shared by everybody.

Chang Il-dam is a butcher and the son of a butcher. That is the symbol of killing the beast in human beings. Speaking of his lineage, three generations were killed during the Donghak upheaval and only a son by a prostitute survived, but was killed during the liberation movement in the Japanese period; a son of his, again begotten through a prostitute, survived. He was later killed, allegedly as a Communist during the Korean War. And again a son by a prostitute survived. This one is Chang Il-dam. A lineage of three generations of butchers and prostitutes. This is a symbol of *han* lineage. But in Chang Il-dam's spiritual lineage are included revolutionary rebels like Man-chuk, Yim Kok-chong, Park Chang-kak, Kal Chu-sa, Chang Kil-san, Hong Kyung-rae, Chon Bong-jun, Myo Chong, Samyongdang, Suwun, Manhae.[25] When Chang Il-dam is executed he is thirty-three years old. His birth and life as a priest of liberation, the betrayal by a disciple, trial and execution, prophecy and resurrection are all reproduced from the life of Jesus.

When Kim Chi-ha wrote this memo (1977), he was thirty-three years old. With Chang Il-dam the poet identifies the Korean minjung, Jesus Christ, and even himself in one composite image. In the story, he brings together the human rights movements of the Korean church and the exodus from bondage in Egypt. And finally he juxtaposes Jesus Christ with the *han* of the people. He sees the acts of Chang Il-dam as a repetition of the event of Jesus Christ so that when one commits oneself to these acts, salvation and liberation are actualized.

Let me conclude by making an appeal to my fellow theologians in Korea. Let us hold in abeyance discussions on doctrines and theories about sin which are heavily charged with the bias of the ruling class and are often nothing more than the labels the ruling class uses for the deprived. Instead, we should take *han* as our theme, which is indeed the language of the minjung and signifies the reality of their experience. If one does not hear the sighs of the *han* of the minjung, one cannot hear the voice of Christ knocking on our doors.

NOTES

1. *Han* is a deep feeling that rises out of the unjust experiences of the people. "Just indignation" may be a close translation of *han,* but it evokes a refined emotion yearning for justice to be done (translator). The author offers this explanation: *Han* is the suppressed, amassed, and condensed experience of oppression caused by mischief or misfortune so that it forms a kind of "lump" in one's spirit (editor).

2. Hyonjang Church is a Christian koinonia engaged in a social movement. The term may be translated as "field church" or "church on the spot."

3. *Baeksong:* individually or collectively, those under the rule and control of a sovereign. This term is nowadays used to mean "common people."

4. Hwangchoga: A love song composed by a king of Ancient Korea (17 B.C.), in yearning for his concubine who had fled because she could not endure the jealousy of the king's other concubine.

5. Kongmudohaga: A love song composed to commemorate a woman who died following her husband who was drowned in a river. One of the oldest Korean songs.

6. Chungupsa: An ancient love poem written by a woman who was waiting for the return of her merchant husband.

7. Kasiri: A song of the Koryo period (918–1392, A.D.) which expresses yearning for a departed lover.

8. Chungsanpyulgok: A love song of Koryo period. The writer expresses the *han* of one-way love.

9. Pansori: Folk opera of the stories of the people's life. From late Yi period in southern Korea.

10. Mask Dance: Korean folk mask dance, which dramatizes the lives of the people through social satire.

11. Kungye: Leader of an ancient Korean rebellion (A.D. 901) who claimed to be Maitreya Buddha (Messianic Buddha).

12. Kyonhwon: The first king of a short-lived kingdom in Korea (nineteenth century A.D.).

13. Mangyi and Mangsoyi were leaders of a peasant rebellion in the Koryo period (A.D. 1176).

14. Manchuk: A man using this name led a rebellion to free slaves (1198).

15. Hong Kyung-rae: Leader of a peasant rebellion in 1811.

16. Imsul: Title of the year 1862, when there was a rebellion.

17. Donghak Rebellion: The largest peasant rebellion at the end of the nineteenth century (1894–95).

18. Hwalbindang: Korean Robin Hoods of late Yi Korea (nineteenth century).

19. March First Movement: The 1919 Korean Independence Movement against the Japanese colonial regime.

20. April Student Revolution: The 1960 student revolt against the Syngman Rhee Dictatorship.

21. Ritual of Heaven and Earth.

22. Kyeryong is a legendary holy mountain in the middle of Korea.

23. Innaechon is Chondokyo doctrine, meaning humanity is heaven or heaven is in humanity.

24. Shichonju, Yangchonju, Haengchonju, and Sangchonju are religious doctrinal concepts of Chondokyo (Heavenly Way). Chonju means heavenly Lord—Korean Catholic designations for God.

25. Yim Kok-chong, Park Chang-kak, Kal Chu-sa, Chang Kil-san, Hong Kyung-rae, Chon Bong-jun, Myo Chong, Samyongdang were rebel leaders in recent Korean history. Suwun was a religious leader, the founder of Chondokyo; and Manhae was an Independence Movement leader.

SECTION THREE:
THE MINJUNG ROOTS
OF KOREAN CHRISTIANITY

Chapter V

A Brief Sketch of a Korean Christian History from the Minjung Perspective

CHOO CHAI-YONG

Introduction

In 1984 we will be celebrating the one-hundreth anniversary of Korean Protestant Christianity. In the year 1884 Dr. Horace N. Allen, a medical missionary of the Presbyterian Mission Board, entered this land and founded a church in Soras in Hwanghae Province. This one hundred years of history is no more than one-twentieth of the two-thousand-year history of Christianity. But for us it is an important period because it concerns the introduction and the role of Christianity in modern Korean history.

That is to say, the Christianity which was accepted in Korea developed within a particular milieu, namely, the continuous suffering of the common people (the minjung), and was affected by the uncertain and yet revolutionary tendencies in the history of the Korean minjung. To be sure, Korean Christianity was not always responsive to its context and thus sometimes lost its true identity in Korean history.

In this paper, we will sketch the reality of Korean Christianity from 1884 to the present. In facing this task, it will be necessary, as already indicated, to see Korean Christianity in relation to Korean history. When we analyze Korean Christianity, we will pay particular attention to the social consciousness of Korean Christians in the history of the struggle for justice, human rights, and independence. We will thus approach this history of Korean Christianity from the perspective of the minjung.

Analysis and Critique

The Period of Acceptance (1876–1896)

Christianity was introduced to Korea earlier than the year 1876. But there are two main reasons for considering the year 1876 as the first year of the period of acceptance of Christianity. First, in 1876 in Manchuria Yi Ung-chan, the Korean language teacher of John Ross and his fellow missionary, John MacIntyre, was baptized by MacIntyre. He was the first Protestant Korean Christian. Sixty years had passed since the Chinese Bible was distributed by Basil Hall to Koreans, and ten years had passed since Rev. R. J. Thomas was killed by Koreans on the banks of the Taedong river near Pyongyang. Second, in that year the Korean government signed the Byungja (the name of a chronological era) treaty of peace and amity with Japan. Although the treaty itself was an example of an unequal treaty with a foreign country, at least it was a break in the Korean government's policy of seclusion. It opened the ports of Korea to foreign influence; and a period of enlightenment began.

As we shall see, the period 1876–1896, when Christianity was accepted by Koreans and formed its identity, was an extremely complicated and uncertain period.

In 1896, the *Independence Newspaper* was published and the *Independence Association* was founded. The leaders of this movement were Su Chae-pil and Yun Chi-ho, who were Christians, and Yi Sang-jae, who then was not a Christian. The *Independence Newspaper* was published in Hangul, the Korean alphabet. Hangul was the language of the common people or lower classes (minjung). The Independence Association was one of the main movements led by the Korean Christians. Therefore, from the beginning, Korean Christianity was founded among an oppressed people, and Korean Christians played a leading role in the realization of a national consciousness for independence. Korean Christianity was not distant from the people in their sufferings.

During the period 1876–96, the Bible was translated into Korean (Hangul) and published in Japan and in Manchuria. Lee Su-jong, who fled to Japan to save his life during the restoration of the Taewongun in 1882, with the aid of Chinese and Japanese Bibles translated the Scriptures into Korean for the American Bible Society. His translation of the Gospel of Mark was published in 1884. Consequently the first ordained American missionaries who came to Korea through Japan had in their hands the Gospel of Mark in the Korean language. In Manchuria, the Bible was translated and published by John Ross and John MacIntyre assisted by Yi Ung-chan and some other Koreans. In 1882, the Gospel of Luke was published, the Gospel of Mark and Matthew in 1884, the First Letter to the Corinthians, the Epistle to the Galatians, and the Epistle to the Ephesians in 1885. In 1887, the whole New Testament was translated and published. It is called the "Ross Version." The fact that the Bible was translated into Hangul, the language of the minjung, meant that the minjung was the focus of attention and the subject of Korean Christianity from the beginning.

As already mentioned, in 1884 the first Korean church was founded in Sorae and in Manchuria by Koreans. In the same year, Dr. Allen entered Korea and played the role of a John the Baptist in the missionary work in Korea. He was appointed as the physician for the American, British, and other diplomatic missions in Seoul. When Min Yong-ik, nephew of the queen, was stabbed by an assassin and was lying at the point of death with several severed arteries and seven sword wounds on his head and body, Allen succeeded in bringing the prince back to health. It took three months of constant care, attended with much anxiety and peril. The reward was gratifying. Though the king soon knew that Allen was a missionary, he did not prevent Dr. Allen's mission work as a doctor. In 1885, H. G. Underwood (Presbyterian) and H. G. Appenzeller from the United States began to do missionary work. They were the first ordained Protestant missionaries appointed to Korea.

In 1893, the early missionaries adopted the mission policies embodied in the so-called "Nevius Method." The following were the main points: (1) It is better to work at the conversion of the working classes. (2) The conversion of women and the training of Christian girls should be a special aim. (3) Much could be effected in Christian education by maintaining elementary schools in country towns. (4) To translate and publish the Bible and Christian books in Hangul is a priority.

In order to illumine the context of early Christianity in Korea, let me list the main political events in that period and then comment on two of them. The main events were the Imo Military Revolt (1882). Korean and American Treaty of Amity (1882), the Kapsin Coup by the Independence Club (1884), the Kabo Reformation (1894), the Donghak Rebellion of the peasants (1894), the Sino-Japanese War (1895), Queen Min's death at the hands of a Japanese assassin (1895), and the founding of the Independence Association.

Two of these, which deserve special comment, are the Kapsin Coup and the Donghak Rebellion.

Kaspin Coup. On December 4, 1884, the radical leaders in the government of that time plotted a bloody revolution. The leaders of the revolution, of which Su Chae-pil was one, were imbued with a desire to overturn a corrupt and impotent government which was riddled with intrigue. They planned to assassinate the leading reactionary ministers. The time of the uprising was the banquet given on December 4, 1884, celebrating the opening of the first post office in Seoul. On that night Min Yong-ik was one of the reactionary ministers who was assassinated.

Donghak Rebellion. Under the pro-Chinese reactionaries, the selling and buying of government positions was a common practice. Anyone who purchased an official position would generally reimburse himself through extortion. Taxes and levies were increased by local and national governments until they reached three or four times the legal rate. Extravagance, licentiousness, and debauchery were the order of the day at the court. "Like the drips of the candle falling on the banquet table fell the tears of the people; and as music swelled in merry-making so increased the outcry of the discontented masses."

The suffering people could no longer remain silent. In 1894, the Donghaks rose in rebellion in the South. The Donghak movement has both a religious and a political significance. Because of the oppression of corrupt officials, the Donghak movement took a political direction. They were determined to resist unto death the corruption of the officials who oppressed the people.

After the eighteenth century, the Korean government was in the worst possible national financial crisis. The people, particularly the farmers, were in great distress and suffered with poverty and illness.

In 1860 there were many revolts of the people (peasants). For example, there were revolts in Chinju in 1862, in Cheju Island in 1862 by fishermen, and in Pyongan Province by Hong Kyong-rae.

By the end of the nineteenth century, Korea was faced with two tasks. One was to reform feudalism from inside, and the other was to maintain the land free from imperialistic invasion. Therefore, the preservation of civilization and independence was the national priority.

In this situation, Christianity was accepted by the Korean people in fighting for justice, equality, and human rights. American Christianity, which was a blend of pietism, evangelism, and conservatism, and was non-political in its orientation, planted itself in Korea. It should be noted, however, that the Korean people made that Christianity a politically oriented one. Christianity in Korea was a religion of hope and power for the oppressed and suffering people. American Christianity was contextualized in Korea.

The Formative Period of the Church of the Minjung (1896–1919)

During this period the main purpose of Korean Christianity was to achieve independence and human rights for the Korean people. The people were enlightened and inspired by the analyses of current situations and problems in the *Independence Newspaper* and were stirred up against the maladministration and illegal judgments of government officials.

Another important activity of the Independence Association was the "Common Meeting" of a cross section of the people with common concerns. The people of the lower classes, students, housewives, and even government officials attended these meetings and discussed common problems. For example, Park Song-chun, belonging to the lowest class of butchers, attended the meeting which was called for declaring the independence of the nation and to defend human rights. He had led the Butchers' Liberation movement from 1895 to 1898. He was one of the founding members of the Seungdong Presbyterian Church in Seoul.

In 1898, the meeting adopted the following resolutions: (1) to protest the economic advantages permitted to foreign countries, (2) to preserve Korea's independence vis-à-vis foreign powers, and (3) to protest the injustice, incompetence, and corruption of the government.

For passing these resolutions, the order was given to dissolve the Independence Association; leaders of the association were imprisoned in 1899. From then on, the government began to watch Christian movements; and Christian leaders were persecuted.

Confronted with this problem, the Presbyterian Mission Board recommended a policy of separating religion from politics, and, in this connection, requested the Koreans to read the following words from the Bible: Rom. 13:1–7; 1 Tim. 2:1–2; 1 Pet. 2:13–17; Matt. 22:15–21; 17:24–27; John 18:36, etc. All these texts enjoin obedience to authority. This effort of the missionaries was intended to stop the Korean church from confusing religion with politics and to save it from political repression. In fact, however, this policy created a gap between the Korean Christians and the missionaries.

From 1895 to 1905, there was a considerable increase in the number of Korean Christians. In 1905, the Japanese invasion of Korea became patent with the making of the Eulsa Protectorate Treaty. Japanese political and military control over Korea seems to have been the major reason for the common people joining the church, for they wanted to get power and protection especially from the jurisdiction of the prefect. They also wanted to escape from private inspectors and arrest.

Although Korean Christian movements were restricted by strong outside powers, they were reconstructed from within by the Revival movement in 1907. The main purpose of the movement was to bring about both the discipline of Christians and an increase of Christians in numbers. Both these concerns of the Revival movement made Korean Christianity strong. The Korean Christians' struggles for independence and human rights were persistent despite the regulation concerning security (1907), the regulation concerning meetings (1910), and the regulation of guns and explosives (1912). It was the struggle for independence and human rights of this period that became the spiritual backbone of the March First movement of 1918.

The leading people of the movement were the Chondokyo who were minjung Christians and had the tradition of the struggle of the farmers for liberation. Of the people who constituted the movement, farmers were 59 percent, Christians 22 percent, and men in their twenties 40 percent. The farmers were representative of the suffering people in that time. With 22 percent Christians, we may say that the Christian minjung provided much of the leadership of this movement.

The Depoliticization Period (1919–1932)

The Korean church moved into a new political situation in the 1920s. The Japanese governor general abandoned the use of the military police and began to practice a policy of appeasement. The governor general had already created a group of pro-Japanese Koreans in order to rule Korea more effectively. In so doing, he was infringing upon the human rights of the Koreans. During this period Korean tenant farmers increased from 37.6 percent in 1919 to 46.5 percent in 1930. The number of disputes involving tenant farming increased from 27 cases in 1921 to 667 cases in 1931. Labor disputes also increased from 36 cases in 1921 to 205 cases in 1931.

The Chosun (Korea) Communist party and the Communist Youth Association were organized in 1925. They were concerned with the sufferings of the workers, the farmers, and the students.

In this situation, however, Korean Christianity was losing its identity and forgetting its mission in Korean society. The Korean church did not share the sufferings of the farmers, who were the majority of the Korean population. It stayed aloof from the anti-Japanese movements of the students. Japanese imperialists called these movements "the impure power movements"; and the Korean church was not involved in these.

In the 1920s, the main characteristics of the Korean church were the following: (1) sectarian Protestant movements which lacked a historical consciousness, (2) church education programs which focused on children instead of the youth, and (3) the ghetto mentality of the Korean church which viewed Christianity essentially as a Sunday-centered religion. A famous novelist, Yi Kwang-su, said in criticism: "The Korean church looks down on modern culture, and curses the drivers and the soldiers who are working on Sundays. There is no difference between God's work and the work of this world. The merchants, industrialists, scholars, and workers are all doing the work of God. Our daily occupations serve God."

The Korean church was now facing a crisis. The attitude of the Korean people toward Christianity changed. Thus, when there was a general meeting of the Korea Sunday Schools in 1926 in Seoul, the Hanyang Youth Association held an anti-Christian meeting. This was the first public anti-Christian meeting.

The Period of the Babylonian Captivity (1932–1960)

During this period the Korean church was enslaved to authority and lost its subjective consciousness with the trials it faced and the confusion which set in. For example, (1) the Korean church yielded to the enforcement of worship at the Japanese Shrine (Shintoism), (2) the Korean church was under the sway of dogma and imported theology, and (3) the Korean church became a captive to those who were striving for ecclesiastical authority.

In this period, even Kim Chai-choon, who led the movement of new theological thought, was not interested in social problems outside the church. It was the young students who emerged to challenge the Korean church and set it on a new course.

The Period of Awakening (1960 to the Present)

I take the Students' Revolution of April 19, 1960, as the beginning of the period of awakening because this revolutionary movement was an heir to the spirit of the March First Independence movement of 1919 and to the historical traditions of the movements for freedom and human rights. With the emergence of the students' revolutionary movement, the Korean church once again began to see its mission.

On May 16, 1961, there was a military *coup d'etat*. The Korean National Council of Churches (KNCC) issued a statement in 1962 urging the military government to hand over its political power to civilians. In 1965 the KNCC also objected to the restoration of relationships between Korea and Japan. In the same year, 240 Korean Christian leaders had a meeting and made a statement opposing the ratification of the agreement between Korea and Japan. At the end of the statement, it said: "We resist all forms of dictatorship, injustice, irregularities, and corruption. We reject the impure influence of foreign powers on all aspects of economics, culture, ethics, and politics. We resolve to make a contribution to the historical development of our country with prayer and service led by the Holy Spirit." The mass media noted that this statement was the first political resolution of the whole Korean church since the March First Independence movement of 1919.

We also find new perspectives in the themes for Christian Youth meetings in 1965. For example, the theme of the Methodist Youth Conference was "Please Send Me." The Association of the Jesus Presbyterian Youth selected the theme "Christ Calls for Us," the theme of the PROK Youth Conference was "Korean Society and Christian Youth." Such themes did not appear during the period 1945–1960.

In 1969, Kim Chai-choon, a great Korean Christian leader, was elected the chairman of the committee for national opposition to the revision of the constitution in order to elect the president for a third term.

The Urban Industrial Mission in Korea developed during the period 1968–1973. Both Rev. Park Hyung-kyu's distribution of leaflets on Easter Sunday and the Korean Christian Declaration of 1973 made by leading clergymen of the Korean church show clearly the awakening of the Korean church. In its conclusion the 1973 Korean Christian Declaration states:

> Jesus the Messiah, our Lord, lived and dwelt among the oppressed, poverty-stricken, and sick in Judea. He boldly confronted Pontius Pilate, a representative of the Roman Empire, and he was crucified while witnessing to the truth. He has risen from the dead, releasing the power to transform and set the people free.
>
> We resolve that we will follow the footsteps of our Lord, living among our oppressed and poor people, standing against political oppression, and participating in the transformation of history, for this is the only way to the Messianic Kingdom.

Besides this declaration, "The Declaration of Human Rights in Korea" by KNCC (1974), "The Declaration of Conscience" by Bishop Daniel Tji (1974), "The Theological Statement of Korean Christians" signed by sixty-six leaders of churches and seminaries (1974), and "the Declaration for the Restoration of Democracy" (1976) signed by twelve church leaders, all show clearly that once again Korean Christianity has begun to see the mission of the church to be that of a church for and of the minjung.

Chapter VI

Korean Christianity as a Messianic Movement of the People

KIM YONG-BOCK

The theology of minjung is, relatively, a newcomer on the present-day Korean theological scene. It emerged largely as a result of the experiences of the people who were involved in the Korean human rights movement and in the mission of the church with the lower echelon of Korean society, namely, the minjung. However, the roots of this theology and experience lie further back in Korean history. Indeed, they lie as far back as the period of entry of Protestant Christianity into Korea.

At that time the missionaries preached, on the one hand, a form of Christianity which was continuous with doctrinal and dogmatic positions worked out in the West. Also, to avoid trouble with the Korean aristocracy and later the Japanese imperial authority, the missionaries tried to prevent any kind of political or historical application of the Christian message. On the other hand, the message as received by the people was historicized and became the religio-political language of an oppressed people. To be sure, this was not a thoroughgoing systematic process; neither was it always conscious and articulate. But, there is undeniable evidence of the internalization and historicization of the biblical message by the people in the lower echelon of Korean society.

In this chapter we shall review briefly the factors which gave rise to this process and look at the process as it unfolded itself in Korean history.[1] We will cover the period from the beginning of the Protestant Mission up to the eve of the March First Independence movement, which in many ways is a landmark in the history of the Korean church. Finally, we will look at a few examples of the use of the Christian message in the language of the Korean Christian koinonia in relation to political and historical processes in Korea.

Lower-Class Orientation of Protestant Mission in Korea

The policy of the Yi government toward the West had been that of Choksa Chongwi (Expel the Wrong and Defend the Right). This policy was followed with considerable consistency. Internally it was evident in a series of persecutions of the Catholics and externally in an uncompromising shutout of the proposals and gunboats of the Western powers.

After the forced opening of the door to Japan, the Yi government (led by the Min faction) could not pursue this policy because of pressures from international powers. However, the official ban on Western religions was not lifted.

The Korean-American treaty of 1882 did not allow Christian evangelism. Although religious propaganda was not allowed, American Protestantism followed the footsteps of its imperial power to East Asia. Calls were made for the Christian occupation of Korea from China and Japan by the missionaries and their colleagues.

The first Protestant missionary to come with the intention of evangelizing Korea was a medical doctor, Dr. H. N. Allen, of the Presbyterian Church in the U.S.A. He arrived in Korea in September 1884. He came in through the "back door" of the American legation, which appointed him the legation doctor. With his Western medical skills he gradually gained the favor of the royal family and laid a foundation for future evangelistic work. On April 5, 1885, Rev. M. G. Underwood, a Presbyterian missionary, and Henry Appenzeller, a Methodist missionary, and his wife joined Dr. Allen. As time passed, the missionary community grew and carried out a considerable amount of medical work.

The next breakthrough for the American mission was the opening of a girls' class or school and then a boys' school in 1885. The doors that the missionaries could open through education were for lower-class children. The sons of the yangban, the high class, were not attracted to these schools.

Since Christian evangelism was banned, the work of the mission had to be done among the lower-class people; and it had to be a secret and underground work. Like the teaching of Christianity, the baptism of adherents also had to be secret because these could be put to death. The first baptism of a Korean (Mr. No Toh-sa, an inquirer) took place on July 1, 1886. The missionaries pursued with determination their mission to make as many converts as possible in a discreet manner.

The main policy of the missionary community at the first stage of their work was to gain the favor of the government and to be very cautious and patient in doing their work of evangelism. They used philanthropic and educational work to gain the confidence of the government and the people in

Seoul. Thus, on the one hand, the missionary community was using the good offices of the American legation, including the favored nation clause, to approach the Korean court and, on the other, they were slowly penetrating the lower echelon of the Korean society.

However, the missionary community was very limited not only in terms of achieving their goals of evangelism, but also in terms of facilities and contacts with the people. The life of the Western missionaries was very different from that of Koreans. The people who came to Korea were well-educated elites, and the people that they were trying to convert were the common people who were totally ignorant. It was not only a gap between the East and the West, but it was also a gap between the Western upper class and the Korean lower class. They not only had a very limited understanding of Korean culture and customs, but also did not know the Korean language and had no really effective way of learning it. In this sense the missionary community was an island in Korean society, and a mission station was an extension of Western Christendom.

However, there was a major breakthrough, namely, the development of Christian literature in the Korean vernacular script, which was used by the common people. The significance of the translation and production of Christian literature into the Korean vernacular language was not merely in the mechanical sense of communication, but in the injection of Christian language into the language of the common people in Korea. This was achieved through the translation of the Bible and other simple Christian literature. It was done by the missionaries themselves with help from their language teachers. From then on the missionary work in Korea was almost exclusively in the Korean vernacular language.

The first Korean Protestant congregation was organized in Seoul on October 7, 1887. Missionaries began to make converts in Seoul and also began to itinerate throughout the local provinces; and by 1890 there was an extensive exploration and itineration of the country. At the same time denominational mission agencies from America, Britain, and Australia sent missionaries to Korea. From the close of 1889 to the end of 1897, eleven different missions entered the country; besides these came independent missionaries, and there were two missions that had come earlier. The occupation of the mission field by so many missions created not only organizational problems among the missionaries, but also a problem and limitation for the effective development of the Korean Christian koinonia. The organization of denominations, denominational theological and faith articles, and even the partition of the mission field into various areas according to missions, became fundamental limitations for the emerging Korean Christian koinonia.

The factor which to a large extent counteracted this situation was an important decision made by the missions in Korea to follow the general policy of mission in "mass line." This was based upon their practical experiences and was also due to the official ban on religious propagation in Korea. Four articles of the policy outline, adopted by the Council of Missions at its first meeting in January 1893, are important for our study.

1. It is better to aim at the conversion of the working classes than that of the higher classes.
2. The conversion of women and the training of Christian girls should be a special aim, since mothers exercise so important an influence over future generations.
3. The Word of God converts where man is without resources; therefore it is most important that we make every effort to place a clear translation of the Bible before the people as soon as possible.
4. The mass of Koreans must be led to Christ by their own fellow countrymen; therefore we shall thoroughly train a few as evangelists rather than preach to a multitude ourselves.

In Seoul, particularly after the Sino-Japanese War, missionary work made inroads into the outcaste class of butchers, who rode the tide of social reforms for class abolition. Reportedly, a large number of butchers became Christians. After the Donghak Revolutionary movement and its crushing by the government and Japanese forces, the countryside was wide open for missionary penetration. Missionaries went deep into the countryside and made contacts with the people who were associated with the Donghak movement.

L. G. Paik makes a comment on the relationship between mission work and political conditions of that time.

Political oppression was another cause for the increase of the believers. The people felt that they had reached the bottom of misery: There was no justice in the courts, cruelty, torture, and extortion were prevalent. This political maladministration and general poverty resulted in dissatisfaction. The splendid teachings of Confucius concerning state and society and fine traditions of the forefathers seemed a failure. The people were ready to accept any new religion and civilization. . . . By accepting Christianity the oppressed hoped to win lawsuits and secure justice from the tyrants and protection from the hands of extortioners.[2]

Besides, the missionaries were often seen as the bearers of the Western civilization and Western power; and the poor people sought temporary relief under their protection. In short, the mission work begun in a mass line connected the Christian message to the social dynamics of the oppressed people.

From the beginning, the message of Christianity was delivered to the common and lower-class people who were condemned to the social conditions of oppression and exploitation. This was one of the chief and persisting causes as to why there were favorable responses to a Western religion, namely, Protestant Christianity.

The Language of the People and Christian Mission

When missionaries came to Korea, they found the Hangul, the vernacular script, despised and neglected. They picked it up to study and learn it and to use it to communicate to the people of Korea. Thus, the medium of their message was the language of the lower-class people, although they found the Chinese language was the official written language of Korean officialdom and among the yangban class. This policy was in sharp contrast to the introduction of the Catholic message through Chinese books on Christianity. Christian books in Chinese had a certain advantage, because they were written in Chinese and they were read by the educated yangban Koreans. However, for the Protestant missionaries, the use of Chinese Christian books was very limited because they could not read them. Thus, the medium of Hangul encouraged and facilitated the contact of the Christian message and of its bearers—missionaries—with the common people in Korea. Consequently, missionaries spent considerable time and effort in the study of the Korean language through the vernacular script. This was the beginning of the process of rehabilitating the language of the Korean people.

The first great event was the translation of the Bible into the vernacular language. The New Testament was published by the British and foreign Bible societies in 1887. In Japan, Rijutei (Lee Su-jong) translated the Gospel of Mark into Korean in 1884 and the Gospel of Luke in 1885. By 1900 the Bible was translated into the Korean vernacular language.

Therefore, besides the general significance of the rehabilitation of the Korean script, the main significance of the translation of the Bible was the fact that it created a major language-event, introducing a messianic language to the common people of Korea, who were oppressed and exploited, and were suffering under social chaos and foreign threat. This translation of the Bible into the Korean vernacular became one of the most significant events in modern history, which went beyond its religious significance for the Christian church.

Other books and tracts were also published; and the circulation of these and the Bible became the most effective strategy of the missionaries in spreading Christianity. In 1889 the Korean Religious Tract Society was organized to publish and circulate Christian tracts and periodicals throughout Korea. The Society in its first year of establishment published 890,000 pages of tracts and leaflets; 32,600 books and tracts were planned to be published in the next year. Their sale reached 17,654 books and tracts.

With regard to the genre of literature that should be made available, J. S. Gale advances a most interesting thesis:

> The Oriental mind, whether possessed by literati or coolie, is cast in the same mould. They all think alike in figures, symbols, pictures. For this reason, I believe that allegory and suggestive literature must have a special place with them.[3]

Gale's observation was very perceptive especially about the common people. Although he underestimates the influence of the esoteric Chu Hsi Confucianism and of the rigid formalism of Chinese composition and literary style especially on the Korean literati, he is essentially right in recognizing the fact that the Korean vernacular, the discourse of the people, would not be at home with metaphysical notions and rigid formalism of thought. Rather, it would be at home with stories, symbols, parables, and allegories both from the Bible and other Christian literature, since it itself was full of symbolic and parabolic elements. Metaphysical language, whether Eastern or Western, was difficult for the people to grasp.

Although the Bible was the best form for presenting the message of the gospel, the missionaries had their own theological norms and notions concerning the Christian message which was to be presented. They emphasized the norms of Christianity as manifested in catechetical books such as the Westminster Catechism. However, these were not easily understood by the people. Therefore, the theological aspects of the message as understood by the missionaries were not always prominent in the minds of Korean Christians. They liked the Bible much better than the doctrinal teachings of Christianity. Here we begin to detect a fundamental split between missionary Christianity and Bible Christianity. Whereas missionary Christianity was limited by a set of rigid doctrines developed in and for the West, the biblical message was in stories and parables that could be easily understood by the common people of Korea.

The Organization of the Church and the Reception of the Christian Message

Once the policy to reach the lower working class people with the Christian message was decided upon, missionaries had to reach out into the countryside. Initially the visits to the outside were made upon invitations by indigenous Christians. Subsequently many trips to the north as well as to the south were made. The itineration was done not only by the missionaries, but also by colporteurs, Bible women, and evangelists.

As a result of this policy of itineration seventy-three percent of the Christians in Korea are in the villages. In the cities there are two hundred and twenty-five centers of work, and in the country, seven thousand.[4]

By establishing mission stations in the cities and substations and centers in the countryside and by itinerating from those centers and between centers, missionaries and their Korean fellow workers wove the nation with their network.

A local substation would usually be manned by an unpaid Korean leader; and the local group often set aside a man or two of their number who could preach and sent them out to teach unconverted neighbors or to itinerate. Bible women and colporteurs sometimes operated from substations. This was the process of extending the Christian koinonia. The mission stations in the major cities and centers were manned by Korean Christians under the leadership of missionaries. But the actual congregations and their operations and evangelical work were carried out by the Koreans themselves.

The missionaries gradually ceased to be pioneers and to do direct preaching to the people. Missionaries became the organizers or managers, directing and supervising the Korean Christians' missionary enterprise from mission stations. Missionaries would make occasional trips into the countryside, visiting churches and administering sacraments.

This type of organization meant that Korean Christians, leaders or not, stayed very close to their own congregations and to the people in the villages. Thus, the congregational life was a small koinonia among the poor people, existing like a cell organization. However, missionary control over the large mission network prevented the development of any strong links between Korean Christian koinonias although the congregations on the local level had developed a cohesive community life.

The local koinonia was first of all a Bible-centered community. The biblical language made the koinonia different from the surrounding community. The general importance of the Bible in the Korean Christian koinonia is pointed out as follows:

> The Bible itself has of course been pre-eminently the greatest factor in evangelization, as it is in all countries—but it has certainly occupied a rather unique position in the work in Korea, and the Korean church derives its power, its spirituality, its great faith in prayer, its liberality, from the fact that the whole church has been, as it were, saturated with a knowledge of the Bible. The Bible study and training classes constitute the most unique and most important factor in the development of the Korean church.[5]

The people in Korea responded to the Christian message. The motives and reasons for the response, in great measure, were to alleviate their social and political condition. This was true particularly after 1895. For example,

> When the Reform Era dawned, the butchers petitioned the government for liberation and equal treatment. The petition was granted and they were given an improved social and political status. The first convert among the butchers became an instrument for spreading Christian liberty as well as social freedom among his caste. It was reported that a large number of butchers became Christians.[6]

Perhaps the Christianity of the missionaries gave some hope to the outcasts. Political oppression was another cause for the increase in believers.

The people felt that they had reached the bottom of misery. Brown of the Federal Council of Foreign Mission Boards in the United States writes:

> Poverty, oppression and distress, resulting from excessive taxation and the corrupt administration of justice, had begotten in many minds a longing for relief, and a hope that the missionary could secure it for them. A Methodist missionary told me that most of those who came to the missionary for the first time were influenced by this motive. Beyond any other people that I saw in Asia, the Koreans impressed me as pathetically stretching out their hands for help and guidance out of bitter bondage.[7]

Even a Japanese editor stated that the chief motive of Christians for entering Christianity was relief from social and political oppression.

The people in some sections saw missionaries as the bearers of a new religion and a new civilization. When they began to realize that one of the reasons for the unrest, disorganization, and weakness of their nation was the factionalism of Confucian politics, they felt strongly that the only way to unite the people was to adopt some religious or unified political program. This was particularly true during the activities of the Independence Club, the first democratic progressive group, led by So Jai-pil (Philip Jaisohn). Robert Speer writes,

> The leading spirit in the Independence Movement is a Christian. Most of the patriotic demonstrations made while we were in Korea were by Christians. . . . One spoke on the text which describes the apostolic missionaries as men who were turning the world upside down and pointed out how in Korea men had been really standing on their heads in the mud. The missionaries have come to right things. Society must be turned upside down. There is no hope in the upper classes. Christianity begins at the bottom. . . . Christianity is essentially an emancipating religion and leads inevitably to the desire for free government and peace and popular institutions. These "progressive" Christians, though small in number, saw Christianity as the bearer of the new Western civilization. They believed: "The only hope of the country is in the churches. There is no moral character in Korea. It is being created in the churches. There is no company of men, however small, capable of acting together. The churches are raising up bands of men who know how to combine for a common object, who are quickened intellectually, and are full of character, courage and hope. To convert and educate the common people is the hope of the land."[8]

These Christian leaders of the Independence Club recognized that the only hope of the country lay in the power of Christianity and Christian education.

These men hoped that Christian mission would become the vehicle of national independence and social transformation.

Emergence of Christian Mass Movement in the Context of the National Crisis (1905)

The year 1905 was a fateful year for the Korean people. That year Korea lost its independence and sovereignty and became the protectorate of Japan. The Treaty of Protectorate robbed the Kingdom of Korea of its diplomatic rights to deal with foreign powers; and the Japanese established the office of governor general under the Korean king to control the Korean government.

The sense of crisis was very deep, and it was expressed in a newspaper editorial:

"We Mourn This Day"

. . . Alas, the so-called ministers of our government, who are less than dogs or pigs, cannot discern our national interests and tremble under threats, and they have sold out the nation without hesitation, and become national traitors. They "dedicated" our country of four thousand years and our dynasty of five hundred years to others and made twenty million living spirits into slaves. Park Che-sun, the Foreign Minister, and other ministers, who are less than dogs or pigs, can blame no one. Didn't the so-called Ch'amjong Taesun, who is the head of the government, only attempt to sign "no" to avoid blame and to leave his name untarnished? The tearing of books and mourning of Chongum Kim Sang-hon, too, and Tongkye Chong-on's committing suicide by *hwalpok* are impossible for us to follow. Now we still remain in this world; how can we face the Emperor and the other twenty million people? Alas, our hearts are about to burst open! Twenty million slaves, shall we live or die? Is it not the ruin and perishing of our national spirit that has been for four thousand years since the Kija and Tangun era in a matter of one night? It is painful, Brothers! It is aching, Brothers![9]

This editorial was written in response to Ito Hirobumi's strong-arm negotiation of the treaty of 1905 that made Korea the protectorate of Japan.

This event represents a decisive shift in the political situation of Korea after the Donghak Rebellion (1894). Around the time of the Donghak Rebellion, the political contradictions were characterized by the internal social contradictions of the disintegrating Yi society. Since then, the foreign powers such as Japan, China, Western nations, and Russia had thrust themselves into Korea very rapidly, with fierce competition among them. The Sino-Japanese and Russo-Japanese wars were the outcome of the international struggle for hegemony over the Korean peninsula. By 1905 Japan came out as victor over China and Russia and gained the diplomatic right to dominate Korea in negotiation with the Western powers (Portsmouth Agreement). Japan became the sole dominator in Korea; this was materialized in the 1905 Treaty of Protectorate.

For the Korean people this meant that their historical contradiction was no longer merely the internal social contradiction, but, in the main, it was the international political contradiction between the Korean people and the Japanese power. Independence and the expulsion of the Japanese power from Korea became the main concern of the Korean people. Thus, the event of 1905 shifted the attention of the Korean people from internal contradictions to external contradictions, from issues of internal reforms to the issues of national sovereignty and independence.

The king sent a secret mission to the Hague Peace Conference in 1907 to appeal to the nations of the world. The effort was futile, and a member of the secret delegation of the king, Lee Chun, committed suicide in the Hague.

There were a series of suicides of the Confucian patriotic officials to protest the treaty of 1905; and there were the Sangso statements of loyalty to the king from Confucian scholars in the provinces. However, the most powerful response was from the people themselves. It took the form of an armed struggle against Japan. This was the so-called Uibyong (Righteous Army) movement, which continued till 1911 when it was completely crushed by the Japanese forces.

The most celebrated leader of this movement was Ch'oi Ik-hyon. Ch'oi issued a declaration calling on the Confucian scholars to rise up in arms:

Alas! My heart is aching. The national affairs are in an unspeakable state. When the dynasty fell in ancient times, only the court was changed, but now when the nation falls, the people are destroyed with it. In olden times a nation invaded another nation in arms, but today it happens by treaty.

Alas! The incident of the Tenth Moon, 21st day, is unprecedented all over the world! We have neighboring countries, but we cannot communicate directly and instead someone else does it for us. This is the same as not having a nation. We have the land and the people; but we cannot be the Master, and someone else supervises us. This means that we do not have a King. Without nation and King, the people in the three thousand ri of land are all slaves and concubines—people of others. When we people are the slaves and concubines of others, living is worse than death. Moreover, they clearly try to exterminate our lives with treacherous deceits like those of a fox. Even if we volunteer to become slaves and concubines, our lives will not survive.[10]

The wave of the Righteous Army movement swept the whole country. The language and leadership came from Confucian scholars and the officers of the former royal army, and the people joined the uprising in fifties and hundreds. But the uprisings were scattered all over the country and scattered also in terms of time span, without forming national united fronts. Also this traditional type of volunteer army groups could not stand up to the well-trained and well-equipped Japanese army. The Righteous Army failed to achieve anything militarily or politically.

The uprising of the Righteous Army led by the Confucian literati did not mean the revival of the Confucian language and revitalization of Confucian ideas to meet the national crisis. Rather, it was a last desperate effort to express the frustration and humiliation of the Confucian order against the external enemy who are overrunning the country. In short, Confucianism was already too bankrupt to be an effective antithesis to the Japanese challenge.

In this situation of crisis, the existence of the Christian koinonia, though dominated by the missionaries, was bound to trigger some movement. It was almost inevitable that the great vitalization of the Christian koinonia and its biblical symbols took place and induced a mass movement on a very large scale. This was in sharp contrast to the course of the Uibyong movement.

Korean Christians were not exempt from a sense of national crisis and national humiliation and an intense anti-Japanese feeling. The missionaries also felt keenly the estrangement between the Korean people and the Japanese which seemed to presage a general uprising. There was every reason for the missionaries to avoid such an occurrence. They not only understood the hopelessness of fighting for a lost cause, but also foresaw the danger of making the young Christian church a political agency. Paik quotes from W. N. Blair of Pyongyang:

We (missionaries) felt that the Korean church needed not only to repent of hating the Japanese, but a clear vision of all sin against God, that many had come into the church sincerely believing in Jesus as their Savior and anxious to do God's will. . . . *We felt . . . that embittered souls needed to have their thoughts taken away from the national situation to their own personal relation with the Master.*[11]

It seems that missionaries were successful in de-politicizing the Korean Christians through mass revival meetings. The main features of the several revival meetings held in 1907 were the confession of sins after a sermon convicting the people for their sins, loud prayers, and various forms of collective emotional expressions. Here is a description of one:

The meetings begin at seven p.m. Last night's meeting closed at two a.m. One after another arose and confessed his sins—many of them suffering agony in the fighting with the devil. We could see the fight going on and we could see victories won. "Awful" is the only word that will express the feeling we had as we witnessed the struggle between God and His arch enemy yesterday evening. Some men confessed to having murdered fellowmen before they became Christians; many confessed to having broken every one of God's laws; church officers had stolen (taken what some call a legitimate squeeze), and there were jealousies, and hatreds confessed; an elder had been holding hatred in his heart for a missionary and publicly asked forgiveness for it. One man would cry out to another asking his forgiveness after having confessed the sin to God. Every man in the house was weeping. . . ."[12]

Paik sees three factors for the success of this revival: (1) A sense of failure, which created an acute sense of conflict ("divided soul"); (2) the message from the outside; and (3) the definite attempt of the missionaries to bring about a revival.

A Korean writer, Kim Yang-son, gives an explanation of why Korean Christians confessed their sins in such revival meetings:

There is no question that the progress of the Christian Movement was effective because of the eagerness and the training of those who undertook it. However, there was another reason. Christians fell into deep despair when, after its victory over Russia in 1904, Japan took over Korea. *The Christians prayed at home and at church for God's help and protection to recover their nation. They called themselves patriots.* However, God did not hear their prayers. When their prayers were not fulfilled, they confessed their own sins first, because they felt that the absence of God's blessings was not due to God, but due to their faults.[13]

Kim does not make a systematic and substantial link between the national crisis and the Great Revival. Materials produced by the Koreans themselves about their own personal experiences are hard to come by. Therefore it is difficult to know what Korean Christians were thinking in the process of that experience. However, it is most important to note the fact that the Christians were patriots who sought national reformation. Due to the loss of their nation, as well as the Japanese suppression of the Korean people, including suppression of the Righteous Army movement, the missionaries' attempt to depoliticize Korean Christians could not be wholly successful. Nevertheless, they had control over the religious language and the church organization on the central level.

This situation made it impossible to systematically and positively link the contradiction between the Japanese power and the Korean people on the political level and the contradiction between God and the devil on the religious level, even though Christians experienced these two contradictions at the same time.

In any case the Great Revival represents a pivotal change in the Christian consciousness in that Christians sought to resolve their inner contradictions on the personal level; and it was a collective experience. Paik points out that:

The great awakening marks the spiritual rebirth of the Korean church. The religious experience of the people gave to the Christian church in Korea a character which is its own. Following the revival, the new religious experience was severely tested, but it has survived as a moral and spiritual force. Korean Christians of today look back on the movement as the source of their spiritual life.[14]

The Great Revival of 1907 represents the first major stage in the internalizing of the Christian message in the Christian koinonia in Korea. There arose a deep sense of koinonia and fellowship among Christian communities; there was a moral transformation of individual lives. Besides the self-transformation in the Christian koinonia, the Great Revival movement produced a powerful messianic dynamic out of the Christian koinonia. This took the course of the Million Movement to convert a million Koreans into the Church.

The catch-phrase "the Million Movement" expresses the ambitiousness of the missionaries to "conquer the people with the Gospel." There were only eight thousand Protestant believers, including catechumens. Missionaries estimated that there were about two hundred thousand who were leading some form of Christian life. The entire missionary force was about two hundred at that time. To win one million converts in a year was beyond calculation. But the missionaries were shrewd in reading the political situation and conditions of the people. They knew that political and social conditions were ripe to exploit the despair and hopelessness of the people.

Never was an evangelistic movement more carefully planned; never were plans more systematically carried out. City districting, house-to-house canvassing, newspaper advertising, handbill and tract distributing, earnest preaching, personal work with individuals—all these were energetically and skillfully executed along the lines of the best revival meetings of the West. Every theater and public hall in Seoul was engaged for a month, so that no other public meetings and entertainments could be given to distract the attention of people. A column a day was secured in each of the six papers. Every family in the city was visited every day for six days.[15]

Yet, for all that was done, the expected response was not forthcoming. There were, it is true, greatly attended meetings and many people expressed a desire to become Christians, but the net result was not what had been expected. Certainly this was a blow to the missionaries' over-zealous ambition. Brown suggests that there had been a change of situation in Korea and points out several problems: (1) The waning of the initial missionary aura, (2) the Korean Christians' literal understanding of the Bible, (3) the problem of the missionary control of the Korean Church and the missionaries' relationship with the Korean Christians.[16]

This is certainly true; but a more fundamental reason may be the fact that the Christian message of evangelism was not geared to the social and national crisis of the Korean people, but was limited to the rigid and narrow definition of the salvation of the soul. The Korean Christians' aspiration for national "salvation" was completely ignored; and the missionaries' tight control of the Korean Christian community stifled the dynamic of the autonomous Christian koinonia which could have responded better to the historical predicament. Besides, the common ground between Christians and other Korean people was their chief aspiration for the independence of their nation. Korean Christians, even after their becoming Christians, always thought as other Koreans thought, namely, that the small self (the individual self) is less important than the great self (the nation).

The Outlook of the Christian Church in Korea

The Korean Christian community around 1910 may be described in the following manner.

In the first place, the Christian community was at the bottom of the Korean society. The new religion spread chiefly among the humble and poor. The oppressive social and political conditions drove the people to the new religion to seek relief and salvation.

Jesus himself was a man of the country, so his parables and discourses appealed to the farmers, and the life stories were very vivid to the uneducated rural farmers and urban poor. The Koreans understood the Gospels and Acts of the Apostles more readily than the subtle theology of the city man, Paul. So too, the biblical stories were more readily accepted than the theological arguments of missionaries. It was easier for Koreans to retell the stories of Jesus and the parables of the Gospels than to explicate the doctrines of Christianity. A typical church in Korea was a village church. The Christians lived among the poor and common people who lived in a situation of oppression both before and after the coming of the Japanese.

The Korean Christians lived in a village or city community which was rather like a religio-political cell. This formed the basic unit of Christian community life. The social environment was often hostile in the earlier stage; and later, the political environment was also hostile to the Christian group. The basic life of the community was in Sunday services, midweek prayer meetings, constant Bible study, Sunday schools and evangelistic enterprises, and sharing common problems among themselves like a mutual aid society. On the level of this lowest unit of Christian community were found the so-called doctrines of self-government, self-support, and self-propagation, which had been often talked about by missionaries. From this local center, the Bible women and evangelists operated; and from here religious tracts and handbills were distributed to people in the village and neighboring villages. Visitation attempting to reach every family was made from this local frontier.

The national organization of the Christian community was delayed until late. Even when they were organized, they were virtually under complete control by the missionaries. In each provincial center there were mission stations; and local Korean Christian communities were organized into circuits around the mission station which supervised and controlled them. The con-

trol was not only in administration, but also in theology, discipline, and programs.

Missionary Christianity lacked largeness of view and creative flexibility
and the recognition of the fact that believers of equal piety and loyalty to
Christ differ in their interpretation of the Bible and in the degree of liberty
that should be permitted in the matters that do not involve questions of right
or wrong but merely of Christian judgment and expediency. Another characteristic of the Korean Christian community under the missionary leadership
was other-worldliness. Brown describes the typical outlook of the missionary
as follows:

> The typical missionary of the first quarter century after the opening of
> the country was a man of puritan type. He kept the Sabbath as our New
> England forefathers did a century ago. He looked upon dancing, smok-
> ing, and card-playing as sins in which no true follower of Christ should
> indulge. In theology and biblical criticism he was strongly conservative,
> and he held as a vital truth the premillenarian view of the second coming
> of Christ. The higher criticism and liberal theology were deemed
> dangerous heresies.[17]

It would be gravely misleading, however, to conclude that Korean Christians copied missionary Christianity exactly. The biblical writings provided
the stories of Jesus and of Israel and the early Christian community rather
than any rigid doctrinal and confessional formulas. The language of the Bible
was Hangul, which brought out with great vividness the parables and stories
in the Bible. Therefore, it was not possible to completely control the minds of
the Korean people and Korean Christians and make them adhere strictly to
the teachings of the missionaries. In fact, as we shall see below, the exact
opposite occurred. The Christian message not only brought about the personal spiritual transformation of Korean Christians but also provided the
language to interpret the world and history; and thus it helped Korean Christians move far beyond the limits of the official doctrines and confessions.

The other major break of Korean Christians from the missionaries was on
the political level, especially after the Japanese domination of Korea. Even
before 1905 when Korea became the protectorate of Japan, the relatively
educated Christians sought in Christianity spiritual and moral resources that
would transform and regenerate their nation and their people. The aspirations of the people in Korea for national independence was no less than the
aspirations of the Korean Christians. Christianity for them represented an
intelligent, moral, and religious power that could transform the corrupt and
degenerate life of the people.

However, Christianity as the religion of the oppressed and of national regeneration was not articulated because of dominant missionary controlled
orthodoxy. Nonetheless, the Christian message remained messianic and powerful for the oppressed and suffering people in Korea, particularly on the

symbolic level; and it is on this level, as a Christian messianic symbol system, that the Christian community gave power and resources to the process of historical transformation.

Since missionary Christian orthodoxy prevented the power of the messianic message and its symbolic language from becoming more conscious and articulate, the creative interaction between the messianic message of the Gospel and the historical experience of the Korean people took place outside of missionary Christianity and the missionary dominated church.

Christian Koinonia and the Suffering of the Oppressed People

August 29, 1910, was a day of national humiliation for the Korean people. This was the day when Korea was formally annexed to Japan. The Korean people lost their country and became enslaved as subjects to the Japanese military rule. The Yi dynasty formally ended and the right of government was transferred to the Japanese Emperor.

The Japanese government appointed Terauchi as the resident general in Seoul. After the signature of the Annexation document on August 22, 1910, all the social and political organizations were dissolved, and all mass media were either closed down or under the tight control of the governor general.

As we have already noted, the Korean people, especially the Confucian yangban, chose suicide rather than a life of humiliation. Then there was the response of the Righteous Army movement. In the fall of 1909, the Japanese launched a systematic anti-guerrilla campaign for about two months (September and October). During this campaign the main forces of the Righteous Army were crushed, and after the Annexation the Righteous Army actions were scattered and small in size.[18]

Under these circumstances the Christian community and the people around it represented the single most powerful force confronting Japanese rule. There emerged a progressive force in Korea at the end of the nineteenth century, which was started and led by So Jai-pil (Philip Jaisohn), and subsequently by Christian progressive men such as Lee Sang-jai and Yun Chi-ho. In 1909 the progressive forces around the Christian community formed the semi-underground organization "New People's Association" (Sinminhoe), which was established nationwide. Their main activity was carrying out progressive Western education to train future leaders in Western knowledge, to develop national consciousness through a cultural movement, and to develop modern industry for national economic power. The goals of the New People's Association were: (1) to conscientize the people to the national cause and be independent of Japanese control in their thinking; (2) to organize comrades to build a national people's power; (3) to establish educational institutions to promote education of youth; (4) to promote the wealth of the people and finance commercial and industrial activities.

Associated with this New People's Association were the Youth and Student Association Taesong School, Taeguk Book Store, and a pottery factory.

But the most important spiritual and personal support came from the Christian churches and Christian educational institutions. At that time the Christian community was carrying out the "One Million Movement." According to the Northern Presbyterian Report, there were 962 mission schools, 500 congregations, and 25,000 Christians. Property was worth over one million dollars; and annually the total expenditures of the Christian community were over 25 million dollars. Also, the Christian community was under the "protection" of foreign (mostly American) missionaries, who numbered about 330.[19]

Furthermore, the language of the Korean Christian community was bound to have profound consequences. Paik comments:

> That is not all! When one looks at the language and deeds of Christians, they profess that the people of Israel under the oppression of Egypt succeeded in their exodus for national independence and liberation under God's help and under the leadership of Moses. They teach the biblical story that during war with another nation the people of Israel were vindicated by David, the Apostle of Justice who destroyed the giant Goliath. And whenever they congregate together, they sing hymns, "Believers are like soldiers of the Army!" and "The Army of the Cross." This language was easily construed to be rebellion-oriented, as Christian rulers now saw.[20]

No doubt the language of the Christian community had a powerful influence in shaping the national consciousness of the Christian people and of the people who were associated with them. Language like this was the language of the Christian community, but for Korean Christians the language was the language of Korean people. The identification of the people of Israel with the people of Korea as a whole is quite different from the identification of Israel with the church. For the Korean Christians, the Exodus was not just that of the church but of the whole people of Korea.

Obviously the existence of the Christian community was a formidable problem for the new military regime of Terauchi in Korea. The problem was complicated by the fact that the leadership of the Christian community was the Western missionaries, who were not subject to the rule of Japan, and it was very difficult to control, manipulate, or subvert a very cohesive group like the Christian community.

Although it tried, the Japanese regime could not Japanize the Korean Christian movement and get leading Christians to identify themselves with the new regime. The missionaries also took a position against the Japanization of the Korean Christian movement.[21]

The failure of the regime to get the Christian movement into their hands resulted in action to crack down on the Christian nationalist forces. Under the existing conditions in Korea, such an action was politically necessary.

In October 1911, about forty of the teachers and students of the Presbyterian Academy in Sinchon were arrested and brought to Seoul for imprisonment. Subsequently 157 persons were arrested and 123 among them were prosecuted. One hundred and five among the prosecuted were Christians, including Christian leaders such as Yun Chi-ho and Lee Sung-hun.

The charge was that the arrested had plotted to assassinate Terauchi, the governor general, on his way to the opening ceremony of Amrok-kang Bridge. The accused allegedly organized Sinminhoe—a secret society— and established a military school in Manchuria to carry out systematic terrorist activities. Later, as it turned out, the case was built on confessions extracted under extreme torture. A missionary position paper established the innocence of the arrested.

> It is admitted that the parties have been arrested upon suspicion and have been called upon to furnish evidence to convict themselves and one another. The strain of cross examination by unfriendly officials without the aid of counsel is in itself a terrible ordeal. Add to this what seems to be established, that physical torture is used, and we have a truly shameful and unfair method of procedure.

The position paper goes on to give evidence of testimony extracted under torture.[22]

The suffering of the Christians in the "Conspiracy Case" had a symbolic significance. To missionaries it represented a politically motivated religious persecution and violation of human rights. But for the Korean Christian community and to the Korean people it had more of a political significance in that the suffering was the outcome of the historical contradiction; and it symbolized the suffering of the people under the Japanese military rule. It was a bigger question than simply a legal human rights question or pure religious persecution. The act of the regime was first of all political oppression. That is, the Christians were inserted into the contradiction between the people of Korea and the oppressive Japanese regime. Christians were well aware of the fact that they suffered not just because they were Christians, but because they were Koreans. The Korean people also viewed the sufferings of the Christian people in these terms.

The Korean Christian community came to find a new identity in this experience of suffering. One of the arrested, Sonu Hun, termed the experience "The Suffering of the People" (Minjogui Sunan) in his personal memoir. He uses Christian language to recall and interpret his experiences during torture and in prison:

> Here I came to find God, by taking one step forward. When I felt despair in my heart, and dark thoughts covered my eyes, I read the Bible, which Mr. Shorrocks had brought to me, and prayed to keep my mind

in peace. I came to know that the death or life of man is in the hands of God. All things are done according to his providence. I only meditated on the sufferings that prophets and saints received and the life of the bygone patriots who lost their lives for the country . . . I decided to face death with firm resolve not to betray my brothers. In order to strengthen my resolve I prayed and read the Bible every day.

The Christian language of suffering was being related to the suffering of the people. This was indeed a beginning in the "historicalization" of the Christian symbol system. The same person directly relates his experience of torture, and the suffering of the people, the biblical stories of suffering, and Jesus' words:

Jesus marched on a donkey to Jerusalem, being hailed with "hurrah!" and he said, "Jerusalem! Jerusalem! You shed the blood of the righteous and killed the prophets who came to you, and now you are coming to kill me. You boast your grandeur now; but you will be ruined so that not one stone will be on top of another stone!" The blood of Min Young-whan turned to bamboo trees and the blood of Chong Mong-ju became a stream for five hundred years. The blood of the righteous lives forever and tolls a bell in the hearts of one hundred thousand people. . . . These thoughts went through in my head, while I was being exhausted due to tortures.[23]

These kinds of experiences were not isolated incidents, but for Korean Christians, whether in prison or out of prison, the biblical language was the language of the common historical experience of the Korean people. This fact was understood also by the Japanese regime. There were numerous incidents around the sermons and teachings of Christians, because of their political implications. Some examples:

As the Japanese police note the multitude of Christians flocking to the churches, they irritably wonder why these Christians meet so often and what they are doing . . . Their suspicions are roused as they hear the great congregations sing with fervor such hymns as "Onward, Christian Soldiers, Marching as to War!" "Stand Up, Stand Up for Jesus, Ye Soldiers of the Cross!" . . . and then listen to a stirring sermon which may personify the forces of evil in the heart, as Paul did, and summon the believer to cast them out. One of the missionaries, Mr. George S. McCune, . . . expounded the narrative of David and Goliath, emphasizing the conventional lesson that the weak man whose cause is just and whose heart is pure can overcome the strongest. This was promptly reported to the authorities as treasonable, since Mr. McCune must have intended to teach that David symbolized the weak Korean and Goliath the strong Japanese. One pastor is said to have been arrested because he preached about the Kingdom of Heaven; he was told that there was "only one Kingdom out here, and that is the Kingdom of Japan."[24]

The Conspiracy Case linked the Christian community and the suffering of the Korean people in a new way, that is, the Christians used the biblical stories to interpret the historical suffering of the people of Korea. The various stories and themes of suffering provided rich parables for the interpretation of history.

One could not avoid analogies between the experiences of the Korean people and the biblical stories of Exodus, the torture of Jesus under Pontius Pilate and the trial of Jesus in the court of Pilate, etc. Indeed the Bible was the book of parables and stories which provided rich symbolic resources for Korean Christians to understand and interpret the destiny of their people, not simply the destiny of the Christian church.

Korean Christian Koinonia and the Japanese Government

The Korean people never accepted the authority of Japan as legitimate. For the Korean Christians, political neutrality was not possible whether they were in the church or outside of it, whether they were Christians or not. Living under the oppressive Japanese rule was inevitably suffering for a powerless people, but the oppression was never accepted.

Anti-Japanese feeling in Korea had deep historical roots. Hideyoshi's invasion is the first historical reference; then the opening of the country by force; the suppression of the Donghak revolutionary movement; the forced reform of Kabo (1895); the murder of Queen Min; the Treaty of Protectorate (1905); the forced abdication of Emperor Kwangmu; and finally the Annexation of Korea (1910)—all these form a catalogue of the historical events that humiliated and oppressed the people of Korea. The main contradiction in Korean society was Japan's rule over Korea.

After the opening of the country (1876), the people of Korea—particularly the Confucian yangban literati in the countryside—vehemently protested the action of the government. The anti-Japanese sentiment was intense and swept over the whole country. The people rose up and attempted to correct the national situation (Donghak Revolution); the people attempted revolution, or *coup d'etat;* many committed suicide; others joined guerrilla movements and fought until death. Some others attempted reforms, politically and administratively; others devoted themselves to modern education.

To envision any political neutrality on the part of Christians is not possible. The opposite had occurred. Throughout the period of Japanese rule, Christians were more ardent and better nationalists than the average Koreans. Christians were more educated than their counterparts in society. They were champions of social and political reforms. They were educational and cultural leaders, in spite of the fact that they were largely from the poor and the lower class.

Especially after the incident of the Conspiracy Case, the Korean Christian koinonia was the vicarious symbol of the Cross for the entire Korean people. They were not bearing the Cross only because they were Christians, but because they were Christian *Koreans*. The people of Korea and the Korean Christians themselves understood the symbolic significance very clearly. Now events brought about the identification of the Korean Christian koinonia with the people of Korea and their cause. The koinonia was becoming that of the people of Korea whose chief aspiration was to be free from the Japanese oppression. Thus, already the Korean Christian koinonia, whether missionaries liked it or not, approved it or not, was deeply inserted into the historical contradiction between the people of Korea and the rule of Japan.

After the incident of the Conspiracy Case (1911–12), the political Christians and leaders of the National Independence Movement could not stay in Korea, and the independence fighters had to go into exile in Manchuria, China, and America, or they had to go underground. Often the church was a hiding place for those Christians who were explicitly committed to the national cause. The Japanese charged that "the Korean Christian church is honeycombed with sedition." But the policy of political neutrality of the missionaries made it very difficult to do anything from the Christian church as a base.

Korean Christians Under Korean Government

The first to express a political stance were those politically progressive Christians associated with the Independence Club. The political orientation of these Christians was very much influenced by Western ideas; and they believed that there should be a radical change in the political and social life of the people and the nation. This partially explains the reason for the rapid increase of Christians in spite of extreme difficulties.[25]

The *Independent* states:

. . . the cry of the poor answered; the meek inheriting the earth; every crushing burden loosed; every yoke of oppression broken; ignorance supplanted by the wisdom whose beginning is the fear of the Lord; lust cast into the bottomless pit; the idolatries and cruelties of paganism swept away, and its weak and sinful people made subject to the holy God, whose voice is in the thunder which rends the mountains, in the gentle breath of conscience and in the law which giveth wisdom to the simple. Under the leadership of Christ, and with His Gospel in our hands, we are charged to found the Kingdom of Heaven, everywhere and among all men, to supplant sin by holiness, ignorance by knowledge, hatred by love.[26]

Often missionaries and mission historians emphasize the spiritual reasons for the rapid acceptance of Christianity in Korea. But in fact the social reasons and even political reasons were the most important and strongest reasons for accepting the Christian message. To this extent Koreans accepted Christianity as a social and political religion. In Christianity they saw the hope of national regeneration and reformation, although the way in which Christianity was related to this task was understood in various ways. For Korean Christians, personal transformation, social reform, and national regeneration through education were not different things, but related aspects of one cause: the salvation of the people of Korea in their totality.

For Koreans, culturally and conceptually, the separation between individual and society was not desirable. In the Confucian setting the individual was a small self (Soa) and the society was the Great Self (Taea). The small self was often used in a pejorative sense. The salvation of Soa could not have an ultimate significance; and in fact the preoccupation with the Soa's welfare to the neglect of the Great Self (Taea) would be selfishness, immorality, and an unforgivable sin.

These Korean reformers were not merely concerned with the transformation of character in persons, which anyway they had been trained to accept from childhood. The Confucian ideal of self-cultivation was continuous with the missionaries' belief in character building in the church. In Confucianism and missionary teaching the transformation of individuals was the basis for social peace and improvement, although Confucians believed that the individual is a microcosm of the society, not an independent entity as missionaries believed. But these Christian reformers were concerned more directly with social transformation and reform.

On the last Sunday we were in Korea, another great mass meeting was held in a royal building, at which half a dozen spoke, and some of the speeches ran in the same fervent political strain. One spoke on the text which describes the apostolic missionaries as men who were turning the world upside down, and pointed out how in Korea men had been really standing on their heads in the mud. . . . "Society must be turned upside down. There is no hope in the upper classes. Christianity begins at the bottom. After all, a man's a man, be he king, noble or coolie." Then a voice in the crowd said, "What kind of talk is this?" "Christianity is no Donghak or rebellious doctrine," the speaker went on, "it teaches only to worship God, fear no man and do right." "Whom have we to fear?" asked the next speaker. "Who is there to trust except God? Great men? If you should stick a knife into them it would hurt just as it would hurt me. No, trust God only, and we shall win. Christ's Kingdom will prevail. Where is Alexander's Empire? Where are Greece and Rome? Gone utterly. And where is Christ? Ruling everywhere. It cannot end otherwise. Right and God and Christ will win." "There is no reason," he added, "why we should not expect to see a Christian King on the throne of Korea." Little of such free and stirring speech as this has been heard in Korea before.[27]

The political platform of the Independence Club shows this point more clearly, as it is expounded in the editorial pages of The *Independent* (Tongnip Shimmun), their official organ in Korean and English. Their ideals were oriented toward the Western political ideals of democracy. In the Confucian feudal society these democratic ideals were indeed radical and revolutionary.

McKenzie wrote about the demands of the Independents in a mass rally as follows:

> The Independents were determined to have genuine reform, and the mass of the people was still behind them. . . . The Conservatives, who opposed them, now controlled practically all official actions. The Independence Club started a popular agitation, and for months Seoul was in a ferment. Great meetings of the people continued day after day, the shops closing that all might attend. Even the women stirred from their retirement, and held meetings of their own to plead for change. . . . The Cabinet promised fair things, and various nominal reforms were outlined. The Independents' demands were, in the main, the absence of foreign control, care in granting foreign concessions, public trial of important offenders, honesty in state finance, and justice for all. In the end, another demand was added to these—that a popular representative tribunal should be elected.[28]

This was the beginning of the tradition of the Korean Christian koinonia for social and political reform. The National Independence Movement, for the Christians as well as for other progressives, meant a movement for social transformation and political reform. This ideal was maintained by Christians throughout Korean history. And yet it was not possible for them to realize the ideal due to their inexperience and due to a lack of practical political skills and understanding.

Korean Christian Koinonia Under the Japanese Power

The Treaty of Protectorate made Japan the virtual ruler of Korea, and this was actualized at the Annexation (1910). From 1905 the nation was boiling with a sense of shame and crisis. The Righteous Army guerrilla movement was sweeping the whole country, and Japanese forces were crushing the guerrilla forces. In this kind of political situation it was natural for the Christian Koreans to feel the same humiliation and indignation; and they felt in equal degree, if not more strongly, the crisis in the national destiny of their people. However, it was not possible to carry out their political actions openly, even if they had had a liberal political program. Rather, they devoted their ener-

gies to educational programs through various mission schools and established national schools to train the young for the future of the nation.
When a semi-underground organization such as Sinminhoe was organized
under Christian leaders with largely enlightenment programs, the Japanese
crushed them very harshly. There was virtually no possibility of organizing
the people, except under the umbrella of Christianity. The national feelings
of Christians ran very high; and something was bound to happen in the Christian koinonia, if it was not strictly controlled by the missionaries. The energy
of Korean Christians was not directed solely to the Revival movement. Clark
observes the political movements within the Christian church:

> About three years ago the movement known as the Chungyunhoi
> sprang up in the Methodist churches with headquarters in the Sandong
> Dong Methodist Church in Seoul. In three months there was a branch
> of it in every Methodist Church in the thirteen provinces. It was purely a
> political organization and the chairman of it was the Korean pastor of
> that Methodist Church. Worst of all they had appropriated the Korean
> name of the YMCA. We by hard work kept the movement out of more
> than nine-tenths of our churches and by putting pressure to bear on the
> Methodists, finally made them understand the danger and suppress the
> organization. That was the Epworth League movement Mr. Todd
> speaks of.[29]

The YMCA—a Christian organization that accepted non-Christians—
was an ideal organization for the Korean young people to enter, and in the
national crisis this was bound to have political implications. On this A. A.
Pieters gives some details:

> The YMCA, which included both Christian and non-Christian men
> and is under the leadership of Americans, has appealed to the people
> in a singular way. You know that the Koreans, while without much
> backbone individually, attach much power to organizations. The
> Donghaks, the Righteous Army, the Peddlers Guild, the Independence
> Club, the Ilchinwhoi, etc., are examples of how ready the Koreans are
> to form organizations for carrying out their objectives. At present the
> Ilchinwhoi is the only society that is permitted by the Japanese, for the
> simple reason that it is in sympathy with them. This being the case,
> scores of people in Seoul, finding no other outlet for their patriotic
> feelings, have been organizing themselves in YMCAs, and begun hold-
> ing meetings to discuss political questions. Many Christians, especially
> Methodist, were mixed up in this. The news quickly spread over the
> country that the YMCA, under the leadership of Americans, was work-
> ing in opposition to the Japanese. Consequently in different parts of the
> country, even where there were no Christians, movements to organize
> YMCAs were started.[30]

Nationalist leaders like Yun Chi-ho, Lee Sang-jai, and Syngman Rhee were all leaders of the YMCA. It was in this organization that the issue of self-determination came out for the first time in later years. The Koreans were not satisfied with the missionary leadership which attempted to depoliticize the YMCA; and they sought self-determination.

After the Annexation (1910) the patriotic feelings of the Korean Christians became more intensive. Already the Korean Church, if allowed to take on political matters, was ready to generate certain revolutionary dynamics in Korea. Miller wrote in 1908, "The church if forced to take sides would probably mean revolution in more than three or four provinces." Gale reports the political feelings of the Korean Christians in his letter dated November 11, 1910.

> Since you were here I seem to realize more and more that the young men in our schools are the most radically anti-government natives that one sees. They are ungovernable to a very large degree; want to dictate to directors, principals, superiors, king, cabinet and everybody. To govern the church is difficult enough, but to govern a lot of young men whose creed is . . . "down with the Japs" is quite impossible. . . . One marked feature of the present time is the fall in the value of the foreign missionary. In this intense political atmosphere, Koreans are so sensitive and fearful of being governed that even in church matters missionaries have to walk very carefully not to give offense.

Under the extreme conditions of political oppression by an alien regime and internal control by the missionaries, the Korean Christian koinonia had no positive outlet to express their feelings and aspirations other than in their dreams in the Christian language. But these dreams were not empty dreams; they were powerful for their historical self-understanding. As we shall next see, there was a remarkable imagination and creativity in their use of the biblical stories and symbols to do "creative political and historical hermeneutics."

The Emergent Language of the Christian Koinonia

Now we will examine some of the language of the Korean Christian koinonia, which was used not merely as a language of religious faith but as a historical language. This task is not easy because there was no Korean Christian theological leadership which thought through historical issues in their language. We will try to give an outline of the emerging language which was not identical with the official orthodox language or meaning dictated by missionary Christianity.

As we have already observed, the process of internalization of the Christian message was closely related to the social and political experiences of the Korean people. The Christian messianic language was related to the historical experiences of the people, though missionaries were not fully self-conscious of the process due to their own limitations and orientation. But there were several positive factors that facilitated the internalization process.

The first was the medium of communication. The fact that the Christian literature, especially the Bible, was translated and written in the Korean vernacular script had a significant implication in the shaping of the language of the Korean Christian koinonia. The first implication was social, then it became political. The vernacular language was the language of the lower class; and under the Japanese rule the vernacular language was the language of the ruled, not that of the ruler. One cannot separate the message from the medium—the language.

The second important factor was the nature of the message itself. The pure Korean language was undeveloped in conceptual, theoretical, and abstract expressions. If one wanted to express complex conceptual and theoretical ideas, he had to resort to Chinese character vocabulary, which the common people found hard to understand. The vernacular language was concrete, metaphorical, and symbolic rather than conceptual or theoretical. This meant that the Bible itself was the best form of presentation of the Christian message.

Another significant factor in the presentation of the Christian message was the mass education process. The Bible was presented in story form both in mass meetings and in carefully organized mass Bible classes throughout the land. We have indicated earlier that the process of Bible teaching was a mass process. Naturally, the response and internalization too were a mass process.

The true internalization of the message required not simply memory and intellectual grasp. It went beyond that. The whole process of the Great Revival around 1907 was not a revival as it is usually understood in the West. It was a collective social process in which alien stories, symbols, and parables were being integrated and internalized experientially in the life of the people. This occurred both on the individual level and on the collective social level.

The first meeting of the language of the Korean Christian koinonia with the historical experiences of the Korean people, however, was in the context of political persecution, that is, the Conspiracy Case.

For example, the theological reference to God—Hananim—underwent a transformation in its meaning as it was used as the name of the biblical God; and as it was related to the historical experience of the people, it underwent another transformation.

The term "Hananim" has a Shamanistic background. When it was adopted as a Christian term it was influenced by the biblical language. Moore describes the place of Hananim in the village life of Korea and its relation to Christianity.

> The chief of all the spirits is Hananim, who is the creator of all things and sends the sunshine and the rain. It is this spirit that comes nearest to the Christian's idea of God; so this is the term used by the Protestant

denominations for indicating God. Strange to say, this, the greatest of all the spirits, receives the least attention in the worship of the people. This is probably from the fact that he is considered good, and the religion of Korea is one of fear and not of love. It is not worthwhile to bother the good spirits, since they will do no harm; but the bad ones must be placated. In times of severe drought, by special command of the king, sheep are sacrificed to Hananim. There are no temples or shrines dedicated to Hananim except the altars on which the above-stated sacrifices are offered. So it can hardly be said that the village religion has much to do with the great spirit Hananim.[31]

But in the language of the Christian Independents or Christian koinonia the same Hananim was neither simply the Chief of the Spirits nor the God of historical aloofness, but the God who was the Lord of history, who would judge the oppressive Japanese power, and vindicate the innocent suffering Korean people. It was this God to whom Korean Christians prayed, "O, God (Hananim), save my country and save my soul," as their first and most important petition.

When missionaries used the term "Hananim," it was radically transformed by its use in biblical language. In addition, missionaries taught Korean Christians various philosophical descriptions of omnipotence, omnipresence, etc. However, until God, or Hananim, was related to the language of the historical experiences of Korean people, the term was less than fully serious.

Here, Korean Christians found the God of the Exodus most meaningful for their historical condition. For example a preface to a Sunday school lesson states:

> This Book of Exodus is written about the God who, with his power, saved the people of Israel from suffering and enslavement, and made them the people who enjoyed glorious freedom; He appeared as Jehovah before Israel, and as a whole and just God. He exists by himself and of himself, He has sympathy, and He is the Savior. Exodus is the book of the miracle of God's liberation of the people of Israel from the power of Pharaoh with His power. God has saved Israel first and established her holy. This book is a foreshadowing of the redemptive love of Jesus in the Gospels and of his power that cleanses, that is, the miracle of the grace shown forth.[32]

The Korean Christians had a special practice of prayer early morning every day, and every moment whenever they were able to do it. In these moments of prayer, one of their major themes was, "God, send us a leader like Moses, who can lead us from the present bondage to 'liberation'. God, have pity on this people." In this kind of spiritual situation the symbolic and parabolic use of the Book of Exodus was unusually powerful in determining the historical consciousness of the Korean Christian people.

Just as the drama of Israel and Egypt was governed by the God who is just, for the Korean Christians their destiny under Japanese rule was to be governed by the same just God.

> Egypt is the shadow of the power of sin just as Japan represented a symbol of evil in their situation. Just as the people of Israel got acquainted with the power of evil and sin, the Korean people are learning about the nature of evil; just as the people of Israel became aware of God, Korean people are getting to know God; and this is one of the strong reasons they preach the Gospel to the people of Korea, because as they know about the God who is just and powerful, there will be salvation for the Korean people. Thus Christian belief, for Korean Christians, is the power with which the people can be saved. Just as the people of Israel prospered due to God's help, Korean people can prosper even under the Japanese rule, if God helps. This was the subject of ardent prayer of the Korean people.
>
> The Book of Exodus teaches that the enemy of justice persecutes the people of God and oppresses them, but it cannot ruin the witness to the truth, nor can it prevent it. God's enemy harms and destroys us, but Jesus gives us life. Therefore, if we establish righteousness and rely upon God, then God will help us.[33]

One of the characteristics of the Sunday school lesson was a certain parabolization in the telling of biblical stories. The parabolization meant three things.

The Old Testament was read in terms of the New Testament analogy, especially the analogy or foreshadowing of Jesus the Messiah. The relationship between Moses and other prominent prophets and Jesus was the cardinal point that was emphasized.

Another way of parabolization was drawing spiritual and moral lessons for the life of the believer from the Bible.

The third way of parabolization was to symbolize the Old Testament in terms of the life of the people of Korea as well as in terms of the Christian life, particularly in the political context. It was this symbolization of the biblical stories, particularly the stories in the Book of Exodus, that gave the Christians and non-Christians a special power to fight the existing evil force, the Japanese colonial power. The story of Moses and the Exodus was so vividly related to the destiny of the people of Korea that it retained much of its historical character. The symbols of these stories gave the people of Korea the resources with which they could understand their present predicament, and direct their energies to overcome it. For Christians, everything depended on God, who liberated the people of Israel from the bondage of Egypt. Therefore, their primary task was to make the people of Korea the people of God so that they may get God's blessings of liberation and happiness. This was the most powerful incentive for the evangelical work of Korean Christian leaders.

The Book of Exodus was translated and published in 1909. It is reported that the Old Testament often became a political issue between the church and the Japanese government, and later the government banned it from the church. The power of the Book of Exodus was self-evident for the people, who came to the Christian church due to their poverty, oppression, and distress. The analogical and parabolic thinking of the Christian Koreans linked the destiny of the Korean people and not just the Korean church with that of Israel. They read the plight of Israel in Egypt as theirs, and they identified the Japanese with Egypt and other oppressors of Israel such as Assyria and Babylonia; and they yearned for liberation from oppression. They believed that their historical suffering was not merely because of their political weakness, but that it had a biblical significance, namely, that of God's judgment and deliverance of his people. Often, even the language of missionaries was affected by such analogical thinking.

> Among the mission fields of the world Korea is unique in several respects. It is unique geographically. As the Holy Land was a highway for larger and stronger nations than she, which used her to pass through to reach one another, or as a sort of neutral ground upon which to battle, so Korea lies between three of the great nations of the earth, Russia and China to the north and west and Japan to the south. Israel, when she failed to do the will of Jehovah of Hosts was delivered over to Syria or Babylonia; so Korea has been the checker board for these greater nations to play their game on. From time immemorial she has been under the influence and control of first one and then the other. She has been like Israel too—a means of communication influencing and in turn being influenced by the surrounding nations. Whether she will play a part among the mighty nations of the East commensurate with the part played by Israel among the nations that lay alongside her, only the future can show.[34]

Korean Christians took one step further in this line of thinking to link the historical experience of the people of Korea and the history of the people of Israel. The analogy was not between church and Israel; but between Korea and Israel, between the people of Korea and the people of Israel. The destiny of the people of Korea was the primary concern for the Korean Christians; whereas for the missionaries the destiny of the church, often more narrowly, the future of the mission, was the primary concern. The language of the Bible was directly applied to the history of the Korean people. It was becoming a historical language and not just a "churchy" language. For example, even in a very non-political letter written to Brown by a Korean Christian, he says,

We are thankful that the numerous souls of *our nation* who had fallen into sin are saved. . . . Because God has bestowed abundant grace on *the whole nation*, there are twelve churches and six schools in the county of Chairyong. . . . The reason why the church of our nation is prospering is due to God's abundant grace.[35]

This was based on "symbolic analogy" or creative symbolization as a means of interpreting the history of the Korean people. Korean Christians applied the analogy of Israel to the Korean situation extensively. Korea was to Korean Christians the Oriental Israel with a similar geography and with a similar political fate; Israel's relationship with God and its people's suffering and humiliation under foreign rule was like the destiny of the Korean people. The most striking analogy was the comparison of Exodus under Moses to Korea's struggle for national liberation from the Japanese colonial power and Jesus' struggle under the Roman domination of Israel.

This type of symbolization was not limited to a few people; in fact, it was the only way Koreans could make sense out of the biblical language, both on the level of common sense reading of the Bible and in more sophisticated reading of it. One of the most creative writings in this line is the *Tusurobon Hangugyoksa* (Korean History, Seen for Meaning), by Ham Sok-hon, one of the best known Christian writers in Korea today.

Besides the Book of Exodus, the other well-read books of the Bible were Revelation and other apocalyptic writings in the Old Testament. The commentaries or symbolic writings on these biblical materials, written especially by Koreans, are particularly important for us, for they show the way in which biblical language functioned in the thinking of Korean Christians.

One such important interpreter was Pastor Kil Son-ju (1869–1935), who was a famous preacher, evangelist, and revivalist, and one of the prominent signers of the March First Independence movement.

Kil Son-ju was born in Anju in North Korea. He was a leader of the early Korean Church and also was one of the leaders of the Korean people. He spent his life fighting for his people through religion. From time to time he stood in the front line of the people's national movement and Independence movement. In 1897 he together with Ahn Chang-ho organized a branch of the Independence Society at Pyongyang; he was the department of justice of that organization. He spoke before the people about official corruption; he was an advocate for human rights, for the sanctity of manual labor, and for respect for freedom and independence. He was one of the signers of the Independence Declaration of 1919. The latter part of his life was spent as an evangelist. He conducted many meetings; and through these he spoke to five million people.

He strongly emphasized eschatology to give hope to the Korean people who were suffering under oppression and poverty. He was by and large fundamentalist in his understanding of the Bible, but was more free in interpreting apocalyptic and eschatological writings. He believed that in 1974 the Mes-

siah would come again, and in A.D. 2002 the Heavenly Kingdom would be
established on earth. When socialist tendencies emerged in 1920, he organized
an evangelistic meeting for workers.

In his book *On the Second Coming of the Messiah*,[36] he took the position
that the Messiah is coming to earth to build a kingdom of a thousand years'
rule. But the time is unknown, except that the kingdom is near. "The eternal
hope of men is in the coming again of the Messiah to build a paradise of
peace. Be prepared to await the coming of the Messiah!"

Kil's message of the second coming of the Messiah is set in a context unmistakably similar to that of the Book of Revelation—the context of rule by a
colonial government and persecution of believers by the colonial power. The
language of the Book of Revelation is language about political persecution,
and the symbolism and language that describe Roman colonial power are the
same as the symbolisms that describe the political oppression by Japanese.

For example, Kil's interpretation of the third chapter of Revelation shows
a very interesting use of the book to understand the situation in which the
author was living:

> As evidenced by the wars (vs. 12, the Second Coming of the Messiah), a
> people shall rise to conquer other people; and nation will rise against
> nation. All the people hate war and demand peace. They call for peace
> between the nations and between peoples. They declare that war is evil
> and that peace is the only way to build paradise. But in the present
> world there is no peace. They say "peace" with their mouths, but they
> have guns and swords in their hands. They assert peace, but they have
> cannons behind them. They make treaties of peace on the one hand;
> and they prepare arms on the other hand. All mankind wants peace.
> They seek the peace. Two hundred million people shout peace with their
> mouths. But they are busy preparing arms at the same time.
>
> There is no need to mention again the war of 1914. If we look into the
> situation since the world war, they are preparing another world war.
> Wilson's 14 points, the Peace Conference in Paris, the Agreement of the
> Hague, Washington Conference, London agreement—all these are less
> important than one cannon ball for them. The League of Nations is
> only in name and not in reality. These are indeed dangerous times. The
> world is about to have war. There will be a great war. If we look into the
> world situation, the relations between Italy and Ethiopia, the relations
> between Italy and England, are getting into a very dangerous situation.
> How complex it is! The relations between China and Japan, the rela-
> tions between Russia and Japan! Everyone says there will be a war!
> There will be a war! The people cannot sleep in any nation because of
> the noise that is created by the war exercises of aeroplanes. People's
> minds are getting dizzy because of the gun noises made by armies and
> navies as they practice to kill people.[37]

There is a certain liberalization of the biblical writings, in that he took these words of the Book of Revelation as words that spoke to his time directly. The language and symbols of the Book of Revelation had an immediate relevance for Christians of his time.

Although he interpreted the Book of Revelation on the basis of an extremely other-worldly kingdom, yet he emphasizes the imminent coming of the Messianic Kingdom on earth. The kingdom of one thousand years would be realized at the coming of the Messiah who would judge the world at that time.

For the author and his followers there was no doubt that the earth would be turned into a paradise by the coming of the Messiah. Their yearning and aspiration is best expressed in a well-known hymn:

> When the paradise comes,
> Its joy my joy becomes,
> The cold weather of this world turns
> Into days of bright Spring.
> Glorious is the paradise,
> The House I behold over the sea from the mountain;
> It is the palace that our Messiah has prepared;
> It is built gloriously as my eternal house;
> It is not far from here to there;
> My Messiah will come and lead me with his hands;
> And that is my lifelong aspiration.[38]

Pastor Kil's language is the language of apocalyptic eschatology, which is a poetic, symbolic, and metaphysical drama of world history. History is characterized by the contradiction between the Messiah and the Anti-Messiah. The symbolic and imaginative language and description of the "powers that be" in the mouth of the eloquent preacher impressed the simple minds of the people, especially in mass meetings.

The descriptions of the Anti-Christ or Anti-Messiah in symbolic and metaphorical language served to stir the imagination of the people and remind them of their own predicament under Japanese power. The symbolic description of the Roman Empire was also a powerful symbol to describe Japan's oppression. The contradiction between the people of the Messiah and the Roman Empire, as it is described in Revelation, was symbolically applied to the contradiction between the people of Korea and the Japanese colonial domination.

The language of "the Coming Messiah," "the New Heaven," "the New Earth," and "the New Jerusalem" was an integral part of the symbolic language that stirred the hope and imagination of the people. It seems a fantastic and unreal language; but for those who were experiencing the persecutions under the oppressive rule of Japan, these symbols were real and functioned as perceptual tools to make sense of their history. The description of the resurrection of the believers was the radical language of change and transformation which was used as a tool to interpret the national destiny of Korea. This symbolic language in and of itself had no reality, but when it had a historical reference in the experiences of the people, it was just as real as the historical experience itself.

There was a super-abundance of literature on eschatology and the Book of Revelation.[39] One of the most interesting books in this category is entitled, *Sidae Taehan Hananim ui Kyongyun* (God's Providence in History), published in 1914.[40] In Chapter 13, there is an elaborate description of the nations of the world, which provides a political ethics of that time, or a sort of "politics" of God. It is a remarkable book which uses extensively a language of negative analysis to lay bare the power of this world in a way that was directly applicable to the Japanese power in Korea. The following are some excerpts:

Crucifixion as the Beginning of Messianic Politics

The crucifixion of the Lord is not only to redeem mankind, but also to restore man's original power to rule all things. But the Lord has redeemed it and, therefore, the power to rule belongs to Him. When man is restored to the original state, man will participate in the politics of the Messiah. Messianic politics continues with the powerful politics (like steel) of the Lord (Messiah) to bring to obedience those who are betrayers and disloyal, to restore humankind from the fallen state to the perfect state, to show forth divine providence for them, and to provide them with power to rule all things. . . . On the day when all people and all things are restored to their perfect state, politics on earth will be done according to the command of God; and man will be His representative who will rule with his politics to establish the Kingdom of God on earth [pp. 577–78].

Messianic Politics Versus the Conqueror of World Politics

There is a saying by philosophers of ancient times: The hope for the golden age never ceases. . . . Before too long, they (all created things, mankind) will be sons of God and witnesses to his redemptive work through the power of his Kingdom (Rom. 8:22, 19). Once God permitted to his descendants an evil politics. This was to teach that He provides us with a more beautiful politics when he realizes his good plan, that is, when he rules the world himself. He taught through prophets that (the kingdoms of this world) will undergo a great transformation. . . . The situation is that the political systems of the kingdoms of this world will be ruined on the day when his just and eternal politics is provided under the sovereignty of the Messiah, the King of Peace [pp. 586–87].

This book seems to be either a translation of a Western book, or was written by Western authors. It is in the vernacular Korean language. There is not sufficient evidence to determine the popularity of this book. However, it employs apocalyptic and eschatological language; and it clearly delineates the drama of conflict between the two kingdoms with concrete historical references. The language is political, not merely spiritual. It is very difficult to determine the level of articulateness and clarity of the Christian koinonia during the Japanese rule, for there are no writings on politics in a theological language by Koreans. It was probably impossible to publish such writings under the colonial rule, even if any existed.

To summarize the thrust of this book: God has created the world and humans, including the rule of man over the world. From the beginning, politics has a theological foundation and status, and is not a product of man after the fall. However, the fall was the moment in which the politics of man was demonized and satanized due to man's rebellion against God's rule. Man's rule was to be a representative rule of God. Thus, history is the struggle between the politics of God and the politics of Satan. The world is dominated by godless pagan politics, which are the manifestations of Satanic politics. But the politics of God is manifested in the politics of Israel and the politics of Jesus who was crucified. The politics of Jesus the Messiah is to conquer and overcome the politics of this world, of the pagan nations, and of Satan.

What is particularly remarkable about this book is that it advocates a republican form of government as the best government, and that today dictatorship is outdated, because there is a high degree of political consciousness among the people.

Taking into account the writings of this period, there is no doubt that the apocalyptic eschatological language of the Bible was the political language of the Korean Christian koinonia. This symbolic language was a powerful imaginative tool for the Korean Christians to interpret their historical experiences under the Japanese rule.

The biblical language, especially the language of the Book of Exodus, the Book of Revelation, the Gospels—the Stories of Jesus—became the historical language of the Korean Christian koinonia. It was not ideology, it was not a political program for revolution. But, it was the parable, the metaphor, and the symbol system to interpret history, to perceive historical suffering, and to transform history toward the Messianic Kingdom.

Another part of the language of the Korean Christian koinonia has to do with the notion of the Holy Spirit. Koreans were believers in spirits which were omnipresent for them. The language of spirits referred to nature spirits, which were the objects of manipulation through magical means. The context of the language of spirits was the interaction with natural forces, such as diseases and natural calamities, large or small. It has nothing to do with history and society.

However, the internationalization of the Christian language in the Christian koinonia had the effect of transforming the language concerning spirits. Much of it was similar to the indigenous language concerning spirits. However, the doctrine of the Spirit of the Christian Koinonia was posited over against the world of spirits of the Korean people. This had the effect of purging the content of spirit worship and substituting for it the content of the doctrine of the Holy Spirit in a biblical language.

The Christian language of the Holy Spirit was primarily related not to nature or natural forces but to the person. We will enumerate some of the categories of the work of the Holy Spirit in relation to persons.

The Holy Spirit was a power that worked both in the believer and within the Christian koinonia to complete the messianic mission of Jesus, the Messiah. The main work was the transformation of the person:

> The Holy Spirit effects a special transformation *(kaehwa)* in the spirit of man, and promotes new heart, new nature, and new life so that a Christian is created as a new man by realizing holiness and goodness.[41]

The language of the Holy Spirit was the chief correlate of the notions of regeneration and repentance. In the language of the Korean Christian koinonia these notions primarily applied to the person; and the contradictions and transformation were stated in terms of Christian and non-Christian, moral and immoral. Therefore, the process of transformation was from pagan to Christian, as it was understood in terms of missionary Christianity, and from the immoral and superstitious life to the moral and puritanical life. This form of transformation on the level of the personal self tended to alienate arbitrarily Korean Christians from their cultural environment, since the clarification and development of the new self was prescribed by moral codes and disciplines which were brought by their missionary teachers. Moreover, the contradiction in the personal self of Korean Christians was prescribed from the outside. It was not really a clarification of the contradictions inherent in a Korean person. The process of transformation was intended, therefore, to be a transition from a person who accepted the Confucian moral and personal disciplines to a person who generally accepted the moral and religious codes of the Western missionary.

However, the introduction of the notion of the Holy Spirit and its correlates as transformative categories was very significant for the Korean people. In contrast to the meta-psychology of Confucianism and the Confucian form of self-cultivation, a form of transformation which dealt with the basic structure of the human person was potentially revolutionary. The Confucian notion of self does not allow for a process of radical transformation, because the self is a metaphysical microcosm, which has permanent dispositions (four *tan* and seven *chong*). These dispositions are to be cultivated for a person to be a refined self, not a transformed self. However, there is a curious similarity between the discipline of Confucian self-cultivation and the discipline of missionary Christian self in their rigidity and puritanical spirit. Both were legalistic and formalistic; no emergence of creative self was necessary for Confucians and missionaries.

In spite of this, the notion of the Spirit, as it was understood by Korean Christians, was a dynamic notion, not necessarily controlled by the straitjacket of moral and religious regulations. They became new persons, open to the future, open to the West, and open to the historical process. Regrettably, this process was not clearly articulated in a definite and creative language. However, there is sufficient evidence that transformative categories became important notions for the Korean people, both collectively and individually.

Hyon Sang-yun, one of the forty-eight who participated in the March First Independence movement, wrote an article, "Let Us Regenerate Ourselves."

> The present Self (Korean people): There is still a defect in our Self. . . . But if the defect is partial, there is nothing to worry about. . . . Also if the defect and corruption is found only in one individual or in one community, there is very little to worry about. The reform of the individual and that community will be sufficient for the welfare of the whole people and the whole society. But the problem is that there is a defect, a lack and a corruption in the entire people and the entire society. What shall we do in this situation? . . . If we construct anything (in this situation), we must be regenerated and reborn, and thus, we must become new fundamentally and basically. . . . First of all, in our dispositions . . . we must build a new basis and a new foundation, and become a new man—new parents, new children, new youths, new adults, new students, new workers, new thinkers, and new businessmen. At the same time, . . . a village should become a new village; the city and citizenry should become new; and the entire society and the whole people should become a new society and a new people, just as the dark sky is turned and transformed into a clear sky. . . .[42]

Hyon goes on to describe a program to build a new society in terms of a new civilization. This article was written as a personal reflection on his life of three years' imprisonment and on his participation in the March First Independence movement. The Christian category of regeneration is used as a category for radical transformation in the history of the Korean people. Categories such as creation and resurrection are also used as historical categories in terms of creation of history and resurrection of the Korean people for a new nation and new civilization.

Another example is found in the editorial of the first issue of the magazine *Sinsaengmyong* (New Life) (Vol. 1, 1920), edited by Chang Tok-su:

> Time gives death, and also resurrection. History is a permanent process of death and resurrection. . . . The past five thousand years of history has robbed the great life of mankind, and thousands of lives were lost in bloodshed in a period of five years; now time is about to give resurrec-

tion and new life. Our history of four thousand years in the past let the life of our Korean people be lost. They lost God-given conscience, freedom and reason, and therefore, courage for progressive development, and desire for a happy life. Up to today our life has been that of a dead skull, and that of animals enslaved in a dead place. The great way of Christian reverence for God and love of man, great principle of freedom and justice of mankind, gave the power of new life. . . . The time that gave death will give resurrection and new life. . . .

The Korean Christian koinonia was hungry for historical categories with which they could meaningfully perceive their historical experiences and historical destiny. Transformative categories, which were intended to describe a narrow religious and moral transformation on the personal level, were turned into categories for historical transformation.

Furthermore, the symbolic world of the Korean people—or their spiritual world—was never wholly other-worldly. In fact, the spirits and symbols of the Korean people were radically oriented to this world. This is the power of apocalyptic books like *Chong Kam-nok*, the imagination of the popular novel like *The Tale of Hong Kil-dong*, and the language of the Donghaks. This language was not about the reality beyond the present world; rather it was a countervailing language, subversive of the established order, and was popular among the people of lower class origin.

Besides, the Confucian orientation, from which the Korean people were not completely free even after their conversion to Christianity, was radically this-worldly. This may be one of the reasons why Korean Confucians either committed suicide or rose up in arms in desperate attempts to save their nation from Japanese power. This also meant that Korean Christians could never become completely other-worldly just as they could never become politically neutral. For them, therefore, the language of apocalyptic eschatology and the Messianic Kingdom was a vehicle for social and historical imagination. There was always the possibility that their imagination could be translated into ideological and intellectual languages and to actions.

The next most prevalent language of Korean Christianity was the story of Jesus and his Kingdom of Heaven. The Gospel stories formed an important part of all Bible classes; and millions of copies of the Gospels were published. The pages of Sunday school lesson books, tracts, and other writings were filled with stories of the Bible.

The most significant portion of the story of Jesus for the history of the people of Korea had to do with his crucifixion under Pontius Pilate and his utopian teaching of the Kingdom of God. The suffering of the people of Korea and the Korean Christians under Japanese persecution was often seen in the light of the stories of the Last Supper, the stories of torture under the Roman military, the trial court of Pontius Pilate, the innocence of Jesus, and the suffering of Jesus on the Cross. These stories were too close to the life of

Korean people to permit complete spiritualization. King Herod and Pilate (Chongtok-Governor General) were symbols of oppression for the Koreans. The people identified with the suffering of Jesus on the Cross. Whatever the suffering of the people might be, it was the Cross for them.

Thus the language of Jesus' Cross was the language of the suffering of the Korean people. In traditional Korean culture there was no idea of innocent suffering being meaningful. The martyrdom of Catholic Christians may have been the beginning of a tradition that innocent suffering under political oppression is meaningful. Moreover, the suffering of the Protestant Christians, such as in the experience of the Conspiracy Case of 1911–12, gained a symbolic significance for the people of Korea. The suffering of the Christians was not different from the suffering of the oppressed people under the tyranny of Japanese power.

Thus, the Cross of Jesus was a historical reality for the people of Korea as well as for the Korean Christians. This is a sort of contrast to the messianic picture of Jesus who is coming with his Kingdom. Yet the story of Jesus was more than a symbolic reality for the suffering Christian koinonia; without this historical identification, the messianic Jesus and his Kingdom would not have had a powerful historical reference. For Korean Christians, Jesus on the Cross was the same Jesus the Messiah who was coming with his Messianic Kingdom.

> God has created this world and has established a good nation (Kingdom) like this; and later he will restore this good nation again. When we think about the evil world in which we live, we expect that there will be established a kingdom of grace. . . . The Kingdom of God is not going to be established in the otherworld; but it will be established in this world by overcoming the forces of evil.[43]

The emphasis on the Messianic Kingdom which was to come was increasingly made during Japan's rule. The symbolic power of the Kingdom of Heaven was never lost in the Christian koinonia.

The language of the Korean Christian koinonia was a new language for the Korean people. The complete and full system of the messianic language in Korean society, in the midst of intensifying historical contradictions, brought about a revolutionary change in the culture and language of the people.

This messianic language as the language of the oppressed people was a counter-language, subversive of the established and ruling ideology, be it Confucian orthodoxy or the Japanese "national polity." The language was utopian and at the same time transformative. But most important, the messianic language in Korea was concerned with historical transformation. The application of the messianic language to the historical experiences of the Korean people was bound to historicalize and secularize the Christian language and thus move it beyond the boundaries of the Christian church. Thus, such language could find expression in actions as it did in the March First Independence movement and other subsequent events.

NOTES

1. For a more detailed treatment see my dissertation "Historical Transformation, People's Movement and Messianic Koinonia," Princeton Theological Seminary 1976, especially chapter 4.

2. L. George Paik, *History of Protestant Missions in Korea, 1832–1910* (Pyongyang, Korea: Union Christian College Press, 1927; New York: Paragon, 1971), p. 261.

3. J. S. Gale, "A Few Words on Literature," *The Korean Repository* (September 1895), p. 424.

4. Harry A. Rhodes, *History of the Korean Mission* (Seoul: The Chosun Mission Presbyterian Church), p. 85.

5. Samuel D. Moffett, "Evangelistic Work," p. 17. The Quarterly Centennial Papers read before the Korean Mission of the Presbyterian Church in the USA, 1909.

6. Paik, *History*, p. 204.

7. Arthur Brown, *Mastery of the Far East* (New York: Charles Scribner, 1919), p. 517.

8. Robert Speer, *Missions and Politics in Asia* (New York: Revell & Co., 1898), p. 287.

9. Chang Chi-yon, editor of *Hwangsong Sinmun,* wrote this editorial on November 20, 1905.

10. *Taeil Minjok Sonon* (National Declaration against Japan), originally issued in 1907, p. 18.

11. Paik, *History*, p. 369. Italics mine.

12. George S. McCune's letter to Arthur Brown, Pyongyang, January 15, 1907.

13. Kim Yang-son, *Hanguk Kiodokysa Yongu* (A Study on Korean Christian History), (Seoul: General Assembly of Presbyterian Churches, 1956), p. 85f.

14. Paik, *History*, p. 374.

15. Brown, *Mastery of the Far East*, p. 545f.

16. Ibid.

17. Ibid., p. 540.

18. *Hanguk Tongrip Undongsa* (History of Korean Independence Movement) (Seoul: Kyoyuktoso Publishing Co., 1971), vol. 1, pp. 57–72.

19. Paik Nak-chun, "Hanguk Kyohoeui Pippak" (The Persecution of the Korean Church), *Sinhak Nondan* (Theological Forum) 6 (October 1962): p. 19.

20. Ibid., p. 7.

21. Federal Council of Boards of Foreign Mission, USA, *Korean Situation: Conspiracy Case* (New York, 1912), p. 25.

22. Ibid., pp. 25–26.

23. Sonu Hun, *Minjogui Sunan* (Seoul: Aeguktongji Wonhoe, 1959), pp. 11–12, 18–19. Min Young-whan and Chong Mong-ju were national patriotic martyrs.

24. Brown, *Mastery of the Far East*, pp. 7–8.

25. Paik, *History*, p. 261.

26. *The Independent*, June 10 and 17, 1886.

27. Speer, *Missions and Politics*, pp. 254f.

28. F. A. McKenzie, *Korea Struggles for Freedom* (New York: Revell & Co., 1920; New York: AMS Press, 1970), p. 71.

29. C. A. Clark's letter to Arthur Brown, February 9, 1909.

30. A. A. Pieter's letter to Arthur Brown, December 10, 1905.

31. J. Robert Moore, *Village Life in Korea* (Nashville, Tennessee, 1911), p. 191.

32. W. L. Swallen, *Sunday School Lessons on the Book of Exodus* (Seoul, Korea: Religious Tract Society, 1907), Preface.

33. Ibid., p. 4.

34. Ibid., Preface.

35. Hwang Tok-yong, et al., in a thank-you letter to Arthur Brown, 1907.

36. Kil Chin-Kyong, ed., *Kil Son-ju Moksa Chojakchip* (Works of Rev. Kil Son-ju), (Seoul: Korean Literature Society, 1968).

37. Ibid., pp. 48–49.

38. Ibid., p. 141.

39. To mention a few, there are James H. Brooks, *Till He Comes* (translated by W.M. Baird, 1922); Kim Chong-hyon, *Eschatology* (compilation of Pastor Kil's sermons and Bible classes, published 1935); Norman B. Harrison's *His Sure Return* (Chicago: The Bible Institute Colportage Assoc., 1926), translated by Paik Nam-suk and J. G. Haldcraft, 1932.

40. Published by Korean Religious Tract Society.

41. *Songyongnon* (On the Holy Spirit). This book is probably a translation published either before or around 1919.

42. *Kaepyok* (Creation) 19: 20f.

43. *Kuristo Simmun* (Christ Newspaper), vol. 5, no. 42, October 17, 1901.

SECTION FOUR:
MINJUNG PERSPECTIVES
IN THE BIBLE

Chapter VII

An Old Testament Understanding of Minjung

MOON HEE-SUK CYRIS

Since 1970, theologians in Korea have been confronted with a different theological agenda. In the streets and university campuses ordinary people, intellectuals, laborers, and even poets have begun to proclaim the message of the Bible in ways that are relevant to the current politico-socio-economic context of Korea. In this situation, scholars have been challenged to provide a biblical perspective for understanding the reality of the minjung (people)— those who are politically oppressed, impoverished, and subjected to insult and contempt.

In the latter part of the 1970s, clearly defined theologies of minjung, from many perspectives, began to appear in Korea. This led to the holding of a theological consultation on minjung in Seoul, Korea, from October 22 to 24, 1979, sponsored by the Christian Conference of Asia. At this consultation I presented a paper entitled ''An Old Testament Understanding of Minjung in the Narratives of the Exodus and the Creation Events.'' This paper (Part I of this essay) focused on Gen. 1:26f and its implications for understanding the rights of the people struggling for liberation in the Exodus.

History changes constantly and God's word is proclaimed in many different ways throughout history. But the fact which does not change is that God acts in history. He acts freely in history and his actions are not always repetitions of past actions. Often they are radically new. This is because he is sovereign over history.

While we cannot find a historical situation in the Bible which is identical to the one which exists in Korea today, a great similarity can be seen between the suffering and oppression experienced by minjung and that experienced by the oppressed class in Israel during the eighth century B.C., i.e., during the time of Amos and Micah. Although the Israelites were in a situation of oppression during the time of Moses, the liberation theology of the Exodus should be differentiated from that of minjung theology in Korea. Today Korea is no longer under foreign domination, as it was under imperial Japan a few decades ago. Today, the minjung in Korea are oppressed by their own rulers. Their cultural, social, and political rights have been infringed by the rulers of the country. A similar situation existed during the time of Amos and Micah in the eighth century B.C., as is shown in Part II of this essay. Although the historical context of Korea is somewhat different from that of the time of the prophets, it appears that God's intervention in history as perceived and proclaimed by these prophets can be proclaimed as relevant even to this day.

Part I: Minjung in the Narratives of the Exodus and Creation Events

In the Old Testament, there is no exact parallel for the term "minjung." Recently, however, the term "minjung" has appeared as an important word in the Korean situation. Scholars have sought to find an equivalent for "minjung" in the *'am-ha'aretz* of the Old Testament, or in the *laos* and in the *ochlos* of the New Testament. However, these attempts present some difficulties.

Suh Nam-dong has sought an understanding of the term "minjung" in the "relation of the ruler to the ruled," the ruled being the minjung. He speaks of the oppressed as being those who have their political, social, and cultural rights infringed. Furthermore, he regards the Exodus event as the biblical basis for the People's movement for liberation. In his opinion, it would be correct to say that minjung means those who are the "objects of liberation."

Kim Chi-ha has been looking for a different biblical basis for understanding the reality of minjung. He asserts that according to Gen. 1:28–30 the minjung are the real subjects of universal human history. Therefore, minjung means those who form human history by subduing and ruling the earth, and thus fulfilling God's purpose for Creation.

In essence, the Old Testament is the history of belief about the minjung's liberation movement (the Mosaic tradition) and is a creedal statement about their original status as the bearer of the image of God in the Creation narrative in Genesis chapter one. In contrast to that, when we discuss minjung generally we regard the minjung as economically under the dominion of the upper class and the powerful people or the ruling party. The Old Testament, however, describes the minjung subjectively, calling them the people of God, thus making them the subjects of history. Therefore, in a positive sense, we can find the meaning of minjung in their relation to God and their welfare becomes God's concern.

Minjung as the Objects of Liberation (Centering on the Exodus Event)

Some phrases appearing in the early part of the Book of Exodus are helpful in relating the story of the Exodus to the patriarchal age, but they also show the interruption between the two ages. There are no records on the period from the death of Jacob to the age of oppression in Egypt; and we have no accurate knowledge of how long the Hebrews lived in Egypt. The author/editor of the Book of Exodus seems to have had no intention of informing the reader of such details. The question then arises, "Why should the story of the Exodus be connected with the patriarchal age?" We can probably find the answer in the fact that the authors of the Bible had a deep interest in testifying to the identification of the Hebrews with "the sons of Israel" or the "sons of Jacob." Once the identification is made between the people who were oppressed under a totalitarian institution in Egypt and the descendants of Abraham, Isaac, and Jacob, the Hebrews become the objects who should be liberated from social and economic oppression (cf. Exod. 3:1–15).

The situation described in Exod. 1:8–14 coincides with historical information found outside the Bible, such as the accounts of the history of Egypt. The Semites, who would have included the descendants of Jacob, were given favorable treatment in the period of the Hyksos. Later, in 1550 B.C. the Semitic Hyksos rulers were expelled from Egypt by the 18th dynasty, as native Egyptians came to power. This development made it possible for Egypt to establish a powerful political leadership under the 19th dynasty, Seti I, and Ramses II. The only exception was the period of Ikhnaton (1387–1366 B.C.). As a part of their attempt to consolidate the internal power of Egypt, these powerful dynasties adopted a new policy toward the Semites. As a result, the Semites were forced into slavery and were cruelly treated.

The comment in Exod. 1:11 about the building of Pharaoh's store-cities, Pithom and Ramses, makes it possible to place the Exodus event in a chronicle of secular history. Furthermore, the mention of the policy of the Egyptian ruler in chapter 1 of Exodus indicates the fate awaiting the Hebrews. In this context, the minjung must be understood in contrast to the power. The minjung are the oppressed, who have their rights infringed.

Definitely, the Hebrews in Egypt were the socially outcast, politically enslaved, and religiously suppressed people who could be equated with the *'apiru*, as G. E. Mendenhall has recently stated. These had no national identity, were without legal protection, and were considered as outlaws. Thus, by worldly standards, it was acceptable for the Pharaoh to have the right to control and rule the Hebrews in Egypt. In human history, the weaker people almost always seem to have their rights infringed by the stronger. Today we see this fact in nations with dictatorships. In most civilizations of the world, the pattern of slavery, like that experienced by the Hebrews in Egypt, was not questioned and was considered reasonable. While the statesmen of Egypt regarded the Hebrews as a work force and thus an important factor in their economy, they never considered giving fair compensation for Hebrew work. This oppression by Egyptians may be regarded first as an oppression of a minority. However, the level of the life of the Hebrews in Egypt was probably about the same as that of Egyptian farmers in general. All land in Egypt belonged to Pharaoh (Gen. 47:13–26) and the people who cultivated it also belonged to Pharaoh. Therefore, the fact that the Egyptians oppressed the Hebrews merely reflected the fact that all foreign elements were subjugated in the Egyptian system. Long ago, the Egyptians had accepted a society with slaves as the natural and unchangeable order of things.

In my opinion, as indicated by the description of the diseased condition of Egyptian society, it was the intention of the writers of the Bible to record the oppression of Egypt in the simplest possible form. In their records we can see the following: a changeable political climate, distrust, avarice, excessive need for labor, insufficient wages, restrictions, lack of civil rights, and the treatment of humans as machines. Since the Hebrews were the objects of God's salvation history and the descendants of Abraham, Isaac, and Jacob, it is declared in the Bible that they should be liberated by God from Egyptian society.

Minjung as the Objects of Blessing in Creation

In Gen. 1:28–30 the minjung appear as the objects of God's blessing which was their original figure (prototype). God blessed them and said to them: "Be fruitful and multiply, and fill the earth and subdue it; and have dominion over all other living things." Nevertheless, as we see in the previous comments, there is the reverse figure (antitype) of the minjung in Egypt. Since the Hebrews were prolific and strong, Pharaoh tried to stifle their privilege to be fruitful and multiply by slaughtering the newborn males of Hebrews. Supervisors were placed over them and they suffered under exceptionally heavy burdens in all their work. These were the hardships of the Hebrews under slavery. For these reasons, the God-given call of the minjung to fill the earth and have dominion over it could not be realized. Moreover, they had fallen into the position of mere slaves ruled by Egypt, not even having enough food to eat. The distance between their situation in Egypt and the providence of God's Creation was great.

God's blessing was a bold and clear affirmation of the intention of his sovereignty. The intention was that his will could not be overcome, whatever the situation. His sovereignty would be asserted despite the captivity of the minjung. According to Genesis 1, God's assertion about his sovereignty is related to a reality filled with poverty, defeat, and despair. But the historical reality is changed to the reality of God's peace and joy. The five God-given privileges in the Genesis text affirm the gospel to the minjung. God completed the creation of human beings by entrusting them with the duty of maintaining the order of God's world, a world which he wishes to be fertile and plentiful.

If we compare the historical situation of the period of the exile in Babylon with that described in Gen. 1:28, since the Creation account was finally written during the exile, Genesis 1 becomes a refutation of helplessness and oppression. The call and blessing of Genesis promises an end to barrenness and a lack of heirs, as well as to being crowded out, subservient, and dominated.

This proclamation of Genesis is strikingly appropriate to a people in exile who are homeless, rootless, and alienated from their land and traditions. It is an affirmation that their God is still in charge and therefore their destiny still offers blessing and dominion. This word is an amazing challenge to a hopeless historical situation.

In today's complex world, the God-given rights of human beings will necessarily take on a new and broader meaning. The special relationship of human beings with the world and with other creatures needs to be emphasized. One of the purposes of Creation is that human beings dominate the earth and the animals, but it is not right for human beings to dominate their fellow human beings. It is not part of human destiny that any lord should dominate the people. This may be inevitable in certain situations, but that is not intrinsic to human life. The argument that some people were born to be slaves does not coincide with the biblical understanding of human beings as creatures of God.

Finally, all people have the right to bodily sustenance. This has special meaning if we remember that food is required to prolong life and that the body, as part of the human being, is the temple of God. Human beings have the responsibility to preserve that precious temple.

Dignity: Minjung Preserved as Human Beings

Some theologies emphasize only the salvation of the human soul. God's action is thus restricted to the work of forgiving sins and leading persons to heaven. But this emphasis misrepresents the totality of God's intention which is related to the concrete reality of human beings. As a result, many churches today are not interested in the dignity of humans which is an essential part of the biblical message. In Gen. 1:26-27 there is a comment on the dignity of human beings, and this theme is found throughout the Bible. The phrase about the creation of human beings, "Let us make man," indicates that man is more than spirit and thus does not accord with a purely spiritually oriented theology. The focus of this phrase is on what it means to be human. The emphasis is on the position of humans as God's creatures. This relation to God is decisive for an understanding of man. Thus, the dignity of human beings is emphasized. Here, the fact that God made the decision to create people in his own image indicates their special position as the head of Creation.

What is the meaning of the words, "God's image and likeness"? They are a proclamation about the creation of human beings. God decided to create people in his own image. That decision preceded the concrete act of creation. The content of creation is related to God himself. God's action of creating people in his image indicates the fact that there is a unique relationship of God to human beings. The Creator endowed his creature with the ability to communicate with him. The word "man" means "people" in the corporate sense. Creation in the image of God applies not to the individual but to the human race, the human species.

It is only in recent times that a consensus has come about as to the meaning of God's act to create man "in his own image." This phrase has attracted considerable attention but it has been difficult to understand its meaning.

The problem arises from the fact that the questions about it tend to suggest an individualistic view of man.

If the meaning of God's image is found not in the unique characteristics of human beings but rather in becoming human, then all differences between human beings, between religions, and between Christians and non-Christians would disappear. That human beings bear the image of God means, however, that the human has come from God. That is, one is "a part" of God. God is like a sculptor, as it were, who carves several stone statues out of a very large rock. In this aspect, every human has the image of God.

The fact that humans are created in the image of God explains the value of human beings. The basis of human dignity is the fact that the human being is God's creature. Human dignity is contained in all humans, in each individual member of the human race.

There is another very important problem in expressing human dignity correctly. Human dignity comes from outside the sphere of the human race. The Bible comments not only on human values but also on the meaning of being human. The human race is being created through certain events which occur between God and man. The meaning of being human originates in these events. Therefore, the term "minjung" preserves the full dignity of the human being.

The Struggle for the Restoration of the Rights of the Minjung

As noted in the preceding section, the Exodus event says that the Hebrews lost their rights and became slaves. Yet through their liberation by YHWH, their rights were restored. However, the question remains as to whether YHWH was the sole actor in the movement for their liberation. God asks the human, who is created in God's image, to act as his partner. People are to assist in the restoration of their rights. In the past, we entertained the notion that God fulfills all of human history under his sovereignty. That is, we were indifferent to the loss of our rights, evading our responsibility as the partners of God in affirming and upholding them. In contrast to such an attitude, the Bible says that Moses was ordered to meet Pharaoh and to help the Hebrews escape from slavery. Moreover, he had to persuade the Hebrews to struggle for their rights. According to Exod. 3:1-14, he had to make them realize that they had to escape from Egypt in order to obtain their freedom. One would think that since they led an oppressed life, the Hebrews would realize that the only way to freedom was to trust in God who acted to liberate them. However, we know that they did not have this kind of trust. They had developed the mentality of slaves. The Hebrews had lost their sense of humanity and were not disposed to struggle to change their situation.

In a system of domination, masters always separate the people from their leaders. Signs of rebellion are monitored. Thus the rulers can obstruct a people's rebellion before it takes place. Dominated people are concerned mainly about surviving and would find difficulty in escaping from a system that enslaves them but guarantees their survival. Participating in the struggle for human rights is dangerous. People must have an indefatigable spirit and courage. Today, there are many who would rather enjoy trivial human comforts than participate in acts aimed at the restoration of human rights. Moses had trouble persuading the Hebrews to act to achieve their liberty, even as God had difficulty persuading him. Although life in Egypt was filled with suffering, they could live in a situation which guaranteed their survival. And how were they to know whether those who would make the long journey away from the waters of the Nile would survive?

Anyone who participates in the struggle for human rights should be aware of God's guidance and protection. The writer of Exodus did not pretend to say that the Hebrews were valuable enough to receive God's protection or the restoration of their human rights. Instead, their freedom was the result of God's gracious action. Moreover, the writer describes how the Hebrews experienced God's presence symbolized by the pillar of cloud by day and the pillar of fire by night. In the struggle of the Hebrews, some people adhered to their faith while others grumbled and criticized Moses. They said that Moses had led them to their death in the desert.

Not a few Hebrews longed to return to Goshen; others, however, were penitent and realized their stupidity in not trusting God and Moses. Many of them could not discern God's liberating act for and with them. They had a faint notion, if at all, of the value of the struggle for their rights.

The Purpose of the Restoration of Human Rights

In the Old Testament, the purpose of the restoration of the rights of the minjung is seen not only from a political, social, and economic point of view but also in the light of the relationship between YHWH and his people. God was present among the Hebrews. He led them. Moses acknowledged this fact in Exod. 33:16: "For how shall it be known that I have found favor in thy sight, I and thy people? Is it not in thy going with us, so that we are distinct, I and thy people, from all other people that are upon the face of the earth?" God disciplined the Hebrews for their ungrateful act (Exod. 32:35). He made a covenant with them (34:10), and bestowed upon them commandments concerning the worship of God (34:11–26). God continually maintained this covenant relationship with Israel. He did that by "speaking to Moses" (34:27).

However, that covenant renewal was not the final one. In Josh. 24:1–8, a renewal rite of a new form is dramatically described. Perhaps that became the pattern for the Israelite community. Thus, the writers of the Bible continually emphasized the renewal of the covenant, especially from the eighth century B.C. to the seventh century B.C. when the prophets reproached the Israelite community for failing to see the spiritual meaning of their covenant relationship with God. As a result, the Hebrews became insensitive to the rights of human beings. That contributed to the process that led to their loss of national freedom. As a person loses health because of a lack of proper food, so a human community can suffer spiritual malnutrition when they ignore their relationship with God. A poorly fed body is apt to be infected with disease. Similarly, the community of Israel lost its spiritual well-being.

The Book of Exodus contains guidance on the struggle for the restoration of human rights and on the proper education of people in it. These are expressed in terms of explanation and encouragement. The narrative of the Passover is filled not only with explanations of the ceremony, but also with encouragement for parents who try to satisfy the curiosity of their children. People today should plan and participate in religious services which nourish the spiritual life of adults and raise the curiosity of children. Therefore, our religious ceremonies and services should involve visual materials which would help nurture the children in the heritage of our faith. Apart from the concrete examples of encouragement in Exodus, there are many statements that affirm that community life should be upheld in the light of the covenant relationship. When we realize that worship is central to covenant life, we will acknowledge the value of God in the community. We can see the covenant as the symbol of human relationships which respects human rights. In this sense, service becomes a witness to the will of God to create communities based on mutual respect of human rights. Safeguarding human rights and praising the Lord God are inseparable. To hold them together is to be in harmony with God's creation. Only then will God admire what he has created, including the human person, and say that it is good. The phrase, "It is very good," indicates the whole structure of human rights and God's authority over it, because he is the Lord of Creation.

The phrase, "It is good," is not to be understood on the basis of objective standards of judgment or established rules. Instead, it should be seen as coinciding with the purpose which is being accomplished now. "It is good" means the process of attaining a goal. God created the world for humans. God looked at it and said, "It is good." God relates to human beings in a unique way; and God intends to establish communities in which the rights, privileges, and responsibilities of every individual person are safeguarded.

Part II: Minjung in the Prophetic Writings of Micah and Amos

In Part I, I have primarily dealt with the Exodus event through which the Hebrews (minjung) were the objects of God's liberation. In the second part of this chapter, I will deal with a few passages, especially in Micah, which deal with issues related to the oppression of "my people." They were supposed to be the image-bearers of God who should be the subjects of history. Yet they had become an oppressed people. Their oppression was brought upon them not by pharaoh, who was a king of a foreign nation, but by their own countrymen, especially "this people." He says:

> Do not my words do good
> to him who walks uprightly?
> But you rise against my people as an enemy;

you strip the robe from the peaceful,
from those who pass by trustingly
with no thought of war.
The women of my people you drive out
from their pleasant houses;
from their young children you take away their dignity forever.

[Mic. 2:7b–9]

Micah singles out two terms in particular, "my people" and "enemy." The concept of "my people" in Micah corresponds to the concept of minjung developed by Suh Nam-dong. Suh says, "The term 'minjung' should be interpreted not as a people, crowd, or folk, but as a political and social concept." Like Micah, Suh also makes a distinction between "my people" and minjung from among the people of the same nation. While Suh distinguishes minjung from the people or folk in general, Micah differentiates the "enemy" from the people. Whereas "my people" are always on the side of the prophet, the "enemy" is always on the opposite side. Probably the most striking example of a conflict between a suffering people and the ruling class in the Old Testament is found in Mic. 2:8. Since the formal features of minjung theology are based on this text it is important to undertake an exegesis of this verse and of other related passages.

"My People" and "This People"

In Mic. 1:9, 2:9, and 3: 3–5, the prophet uses the term "my people." What does Micah mean by "my people"? In 1:9 he says, "It has reached to the gate of my people, to Jerusalem." Why does he call Jerusalem "the gate of my people"? Jerusalem was the seat of the government of the Kingdom of Judah. Whether "the gate of my people" is understood as the government seat or as the place of entrance for the enemy, "my people" for Micah should be understood not as the rich ruling class who lived in Jerusalem but as the country people who lived in the vicinity of Moresheth. In 1:14 the prophet refers to Moresheth-Gath, his hometown. In it, he mentions "the people" and conveys the meaning referred to above. That Micah was a representative of the people is found in 2:9. He censures the ruling class for the following action: driving "the women of my people from their pleasant houses." The context of this accusation is found in 2:6–11. Through an analysis of 2:9 we can come to an understanding of the background of this prophecy.

In 2:4 Micah makes the following condemnation: "In that day a taunt-song shall be raised over you; a lament shall be sung, saying: 'We are utterly ruined. The property of my people is measured; there is none to return it again. Our fields are divided up.' " In this passage Micah censures the taking of houses, land, and property from his people. Their wicked actions are fully described in 2:9a. "The women of my people" were powerless widows who had lost all their property to the greed of the ruling class. Micah feels the plight of the poor country people. He enjoins strict morality, unbending devotion to justice both in law and in action, and sympathy for the poor.

Although the term "my people" is not found in Mic. 2:2, the people whose property has been taken away belong to the group "my people." Micah identifies the widows in 2:9 with the women mentioned in 2:2 who lost all their property and freedom of movement. Women with powerful husbands are not called "my people." In a word, "my people" stands for the have-nots, the victims of social injustice. Thus the term must be understood in the light of unjust structures giving rise to serious socio-economic problems. It is interesting to note that Micah proclaimed the message appearing in chapter 2 not in the city of Jerusalem, but in Moresheth. The ancient site of Moresheth has been identified as the modern Tell el-Judeideh, a site occupying a strategic location about two kilometers north of Beit Jibrin (Eleutheropolis). Five cities (2 Chron. 11:7–9) built by Rehoboam were located within ten kilometers of Moresheth. Their names were Azekah, Socoh, Adullam, Maresha, and Lachish. Control of these cities was essential for the security of Jerusalem. Government officials and soldiers moved in and out of these fortress cities in the vicinity of Moresheth (2 Chron. 19:5). Located about nine kilometers west of Gath and thirty-three kilometers southwest of Jerusalem, Moresheth came under their influence. Micah calls government officials and soldiers not "my people" but "this people" in 2:11. He obviously contrasts "my people" with "this people." For Micah "this people" is the enemy of "my people"; and he stands between the two. He reproaches the former; and his attitude makes it clear that he belongs to the latter. At the same time he sees himself as not subject to "my people." He regards himself as a judge who distinguishes between "my people" and "this people." In fact he discovers "my people" as a distinct group.

"This people" were not the foreign occupation forces or officials but were Micah's own people. Moreover, "this people" were not from Israel which lay to the north but were Judeans of the same nation as the people they oppressed. If this is so, it appears that Micah divides the people of his nation into two groups. Coming from the poorer class, Micah was acutely aware of the injustice and avarice of the rich. While he was interested in the political affairs of his nation it was only as they were connected with the social and moral situation that Micah spoke to them. It can be assumed that the most fertile land and best houses in the village of Moresheth had been expropriated. "This people" were those who had taken houses and land from the poor by physical force and coercion.

In Mic. 2:8 the prophet declares, "But you arise against my people as an enemy." "My people" should have constituted all the people of the nation; however, when the ruling class became the "enemy" the integration of the nation was broken down and a distinction between "my people" and "this people" was established.

Let us consider the concept of "my people" found in 3:3. Whereas in chapter 2 high government officials and officers robbed the country people of Moresheth of their property, in chapter 3 we find statesmen, judicial officers, and the religious men of Jerusalem exploiting the laborers. It is clear that chapter 2 speaks of robbery and that chapter 3 deals with oppression. In 3:3 he speaks of the statesmen, judicial officers, and the religious men of Jerusalem as follows: "They eat the flesh of my people, and strip their skin off them." Moreover, in 3:10 he proclaims that they had built "Zion at the cost of bloodshed, Jerusalem by means of violence." It can be supposed that the rich who lived in the city could easily exploit the laborers. We can identify "my people" in chapter 3 with the country people mentioned in chapter 2. As a native of the Shephelah he felt the plight of poor country people. Micah was a man of courage, conviction, and rare personal faith.

Micah was an elder in the country and judged with justice the oppressed people who were alienated from society. It is no wonder that for Micah the judicial officers who were appointed by the government in Jerusalem hated good and loved evil (Mic. 3:2). In 3:8 the prophet shows interest in the political affairs of his nation only insofar as they are related to the religious and social situations. In chapter 2 he points out the injustice and illegality occurring in the country. In chapter 3:8 he calls attention to the injustice and illegality in Jerusalem perpetrated by the ruling class. In chapter 3 "my people" is used to refer not only to the country people but also to those who were exploited in Jerusalem. Mic. 5:11 speaks of those who had their property and labor expropriated by the prophets and priests in Jerusalem. The religious leaders used forced labor and money gained through coercion to promote their religious affairs. This brought about social injustice which Micah denounced.

For Amos, the people who had been robbed of their property and human rights were "the poor," the "oppressed," and the "powerless." Like Amos, Micah prophesied against the people who disregarded inheritance rights, the nobility who seized the fields of the poor, and evictors of widows. Amos often mentions those who were sold into slavery because of their debt (Amos 2:6), those who had their clothes and wine taken by the bond holder (2:8), and those who became slaves out of their poverty (8:6). In addition, Micah mentions the powerless whose property was expropriated although technically they remained freemen (Mic. 2:2,5).

In terms of the social structure, those who lived in the time of Micah were freer than those who lived in the time of Amos. However, they were robbed of their houses and land and the fruits of their labor not by the hands of those from another nation, as Israel had experienced in Egypt, but by their own countrymen who shared a common heritage with them. The condition of the people in the time of Micah was due basically to unjust power structures. There are similarities between the living conditions of the farmer, laborer, and the unemployed who live like slaves in Korea and the living conditions of the oppressed in the time of Micah. The situation described in Mic. 3:10 bears a striking resemblance to the present situation of Korean laborers who are exploited and have little control over their own destinies.

The Prophet as an Advocate of the Minjung

Micah called the inhabitants of his hometown "my people." He would go to Jerusalem in order to settle their grievances brought about by the oppression by the ruling class. In him we see a prophet seeking out his suffering people and espousing their cause.We see the same concern in the action of a few pastors who were imprisoned for the sake of the oppressed people in Korea. Their example demonstrates the meaning of minjung.

In 2:9 Micah speaks of women and children who were robbed of their houses. These old widows, children, and other powerless people led a nomadic life. Since they could not support themselves they became a burden to society. Micah, however, calls them "my people." He points out that God rules over things and people. He is concerned not only with those who have lost their property but also with those who have lost their freedom. In 2:7 Micah says that the ruling class presume on God's mercy for their evil purposes. However, God is merciful not to the plunderer but to the powerless who have been exploited.

Even though we are people of the same nation we bite and devour one another. The result will be that both the haves and the have-nots will perish. When the rich get richer and the poor get poorer the integrity and quality of the nation break down.

In 3:8 Micah says, "But as for me, I am filled with power, with the spirit of YHWH, and with justice and might." Here the prophet speaks of God's judgment in terms of justice and righteousness. For Micah, justice is a law which is binding upon the ruler and the ruled alike. In 3:1 he insists that everyone should live by the demands of justice and righteousness. "Here, you heads of Jacob and the rulers of the house of Israel! Is it not for you to know justice?" Micah bewails the fact that the ruling class, who were supposed to know the law, turned out to be "haters of good and lovers of evil" (3:2). They did not practice justice and righteousness. In 3:9 he says that they "detest justice and pervert the right (way)." For Micah, the law serves not to promote national development or social order but to ensure freedom from oppression and extortion. He also points out that the legitimate interests of minority groups should not be ignored. In 3:12 he makes it clear that even if Zion and Jerusalem were made of fine materials, "Zion shall become a plowed field, Jerusalem a heap of rubble, and the mount of the house a wooded height."

The remarkable feature of "my people" is silence. We see in 3:1–3 that in spite of their sufferings, they remain silent. They do not appeal even to God as the thieves do. In 2:6f the ruling class argues theologically against the prophet. "Do not preach"—thus they preach—"one should not preach of such things; disgrace will not overtake us." They devise a false faith and theology to justify their prosperity, security, and happiness. Thus, they reject the word of God. Their minds are closed not only to God but also to the prophet. They always think of ways to maintain and increase their wealth. The oracles of false prophets and the faith of the ruling class serve only to maintain their prosperity and happiness. For this reason they attempt to silence a prophet who speaks the truth. For instance, Amaziah tells Amos never again to prophesy in Bethel. Amaziah represents the ruling class which seeks to suppress dissent in order to safeguard their interests. They enlist the service of false prophets to legitimize their position theologically. The false religious leaders conspire with unjust politicians in exploiting the poor and the powerless. They are therefore not on the side of God. In contrast, the true prophet reminds the rulers that God demands that they rule in justice and righteousness.

Prophet Confronts Kings

In Micah's time, false prophets supported the ruling class uncritically and promised peace to those who lavish them with gifts. They denounced those who did not bribe them. False prophets lived in Jerusalem, and in close proximity to the rich who lived ostentatiously. Micah was not like these false prophets. He did not stand on the side of the rich but championed the cause of the poor, exploited, and oppressed. Like the good shepherd (John 10:11f.), he identifies with a suffering people. He prefigured the Christ who came to proclaim release to the captives and liberation to victims of systemic injustice.

In 1:6 and 3:12 Micah proclaimed judgment on Samaria. Micah saw the defeat of the northern kingdom and the fall of Samaria to Assyria in 722/721. Of Samaria he prophesied: "I will make Samaria into a ruin in the field, a place to plant vineyards. I will pour down her stones into the valley and uncover her foundations." After the fall of Samaria was proclaimed, Micah began to mourn. In 1:8f. he proclaims, "For this I will mourn and wail; I will go stripped and naked. I will raise a mourning like the jackals, and grieving like the ostrich. For her wound is incurable, and it has come to Judah. He has reached to the gate of my people, to Jerusalem."

It was very important for Micah himself to be involved with "my people" (minjung). In Mic. 1:8 he dramatizes his lament over his people. He stripped himself naked and wailed like the ostrich and the jackal. According to the ancient war custom, victorious soldiers humiliated men and women of a vanquished nation by stripping them naked. Micah says that he would also go into exile with his people. He identified with his people. He shared their suffering. He was on the side of the minjung. It could be said that Micah's suffering prefigured that of Christ's.

The central issue for Micah was not the king's diplomatic policy which was a main concern of Isaiah but the suffering of "my people" who were oppressed and robbed of their property. He strongly denounces nobles, civil rulers (3:1–4), and false prophets for using their position of power, authority, and influence to oppress their people.

In the time of Amos it was common for those who had money and power to commit crimes. Amos 2:6–8 describes how the more powerful sold the poor for silver and the needy for a pair of shoes. However, those who bought and sold the poor for silver and a pair of shoes were not the rich but the small merchants who were poor themselves. We learn in Amos 2:8 that they were poor to the extent that they laid themselves down upon garments taken in pledge. In Amos 2:7 the father and the son who visited the same prostitute were also poor.

According to Amos, the upper class stole the property of the middle class and the middle class took the possessions of the lower class. In Amos, we vividly see a nation that was biting and devouring itself. Amos severely denounced the rulers who lived in the city of Samaria and denounced low-class thieves (chapters 2 and 8). In Amos 6: 1, 3, 6 he says, "Woe to those who are at ease in Zion, and to those who feel secure on the moutain of Samaria, the notable men of the first of the nations, to whom the house of Israel come! O you who put far away the evil day, and bring near the seat of violence! Who drink wine in bowls, and anoint themselves with the finest oils, but are not grieved over the ruin of Joseph!" The fact that they did not grieve over the affliction of Joseph makes it clear that they were preoccupied with what they regarded as more important national affairs. They had high-ranking positions (4:1). The rich possessed houses made of ivory. In the time of Amos, religious, legal, military, and political leaders conspired to promote their interests. Instead of working for the well-being of society as a whole, they created unjust situations. Prophets like Micah and Amos denounced the corrupt and oppressive rulers of their day. Judgment will come upon the oppressors. In 6:6–7 Amos says that those "who drink wine in bowls, and anoint themselves with the finest oils, but are not grieved over the ruin of Joseph! . . . shall be the first of those to go into exile, and the revelry of those who stretch themselves shall pass away."

Where Hosea speaks of the possibility of repentance and forgiveness for oppressors, Amos and Micah pronounce judgment on them. For them, the sins of the rulers against the minjung were unpardonable.

In the Pentateuch, the minjung are understood primarily as the subjects destined to subdue the earth and to live with God under his blessing. However, they became slaves of the oppressive pharaoh of Egypt. They were endowed with the right to be fruitful, to multiply, to fill the earth and to subdue it. However, as slaves they could not carry out that mandate. In the midst of their suffering God acted to liberate them from bondage.

In the messages of the prophets Amos and Micah, the theme of social justice and the message of liberation, embodied in the Exodus event, should be differentiated. The former speaks of God's judgment upon the ruling class who oppressed their own people; the latter of God's judgment upon a country conquering and dominating another. Whereas the Exodus pointed to God's act to liberate the Hebrews from their bondage and oppression in Egypt, the mission of Amos and Micah was to set the minjung free from robbery and oppression at the hands of their brethren. Minjung theology presupposes God's liberating concern and action. God is advocate of the minjung. He denounces oppression and seeks to liberate the oppressed.

Three characteristics marked the mission of Moses, Amos, and Micah. First, they always stood on the side of the oppressed people as their advocates. Second, they were commoners, not professional prophets. Third, they lived and identified with people. In this sense, God's liberating act is the same whether the minjung were oppressed by a foreign power such as pharaoh in Egypt or by their countrymen such as "this people" in Micah.

Like Moses, Amos, and Micah, we in Korea must resolve to follow the footsteps of the true prophet living among our oppressed people and standing against political, social, and economic oppression. To work for the transformation of our society is to participate in the task of ushering in the Kingdom of God.

Chapter VIII

Jesus and the Minjung in the Gospel of Mark

AHN BYUNG-MU

Although New Testament scholarship has focused a great deal of attention on the people who were the audience and the object of Jesus' teaching, not much attention has been paid to the social character of his audience. Consequently, the words and deeds of Jesus have been desocialized. Whom did Jesus address and what was the character of what he said? This question will clarify the historical character of Jesus' words. The social characteristics of the "whom" can be clarified by investigating the economic, political, and cultural make-up of the people. To understand this subject more comprehensively we need to see the total social structure and the place of the people surrounding Jesus. This is what this chapter will seek to do on the basis of the editorial phrases in the Gospel of Mark and the words of Jesus himself.

Ochlos in the Gospel according to Mark

From the beginning, the Gospel according to Mark mentions the crowds surrounding Jesus. Form critics view the editorial sections about the people surrounding Jesus as only the framework for the words of Jesus or for the kerygma that Jesus is the Christ. Therefore the people have been excluded and, as a result, a very important aspect has been lost.

In contrast to the approach of form critics, redaction critics consider the redactional framework important both for understanding the viewpoint of the author and the import of Jesus' sayings in context. However, surprisingly, these too have paid little attention to the audience of Jesus, preferring to concentrate on "the theology" of the author as found in his redactional statements and redactional arrangements. Redaction critics also seem to have missed the point that the authors of the Gospels put so much emphasis on "the people" because they considered the relationship between Jesus and the people to be crucial for understanding the identity and mission of Jesus. Therefore, while this paper will reflect essentially the approach of redaction criticism, it will pay greater attention to the reality of "the people" and their relationship to Jesus.

As early as Mark 1:22 the crowd is mentioned, and it continually appears on the scene. At the beginning, "the people," or the third person plural, "all," is used to refer to them. In this way attention is drawn to the people (Mark 1:22, 30, 32, 33, 37, 44, 45; 2:2). However, their identity does not become clear. This kind of descriptive method makes the readers pay attention to the social composition of the people. Eventually the concept which represents the many people *(polloi)* appears on the stage: this is *ochlos* (2:4). In the Gospel according to Mark, without counting the indicative pronouns, there are 36 occurrences of the word *ochlos*.[1] This indicates a definite intention in the use of the word.[2]

Besides the frequency in the use of the word, there is another reason why our attention is drawn to this word. For we would normally expect the term *laos* rather than *ochlos* to be used for the people, since the term *laos* occurs far more frequently in the language of the biblical writers. The term *laos* is used around 2,000 times in the Septuagint. This word consistently indicates the people of Israel as the people of God.[3] However, in the Gospel according to Mark, there is no use of the word *laos* except in a quotation from the Old Testament in 7:6 and in the words of the chief priests and lawyers (14:2).

Besides these two uses of *laos,* there is one occurrence of *plethos* as a noun, and "the many" as an adjective, which do not describe any characteristic group (3:8).

It is certain that in the New Testament, Mark is the first writer to introduce the term *ochlos*. It does not appear in any New Testament writing before Mark, but the documents written after Mark, such as the other Gospels and Acts, contain this word many times, proving the influence of Mark. *Ochlos* appears three times in Revelation, which we know to have been written during the persecution of Christians (7:9; 19:1, 6). It is noteworthy that in the Epistles of Paul, which were written before Mark, this word does not appear even once.

All these facts indicate that we must pay close attention to Mark's use of the word *ochlos*. A comparison of the contexts and intentions of Paul's writings and those of Mark will indicate in a preliminary way Mark's predilection for this term.

The Epistles of Paul were written ten years before Mark's Gospel, that is, about A.D. 50–60. Paul's writings were intended to explicate the mission to the Gentiles and were addressed to the Gentile churches to exhort and to teach them the faith. These concentrate on Christology and soteriology, and therefore have an apologetic and a didactic character. For his purpose, Paul does not think it important to mention anything about the historical Jesus. In fact, he declares that he does not really want to know about the historical Jesus (2 Cor. 5:16).

In contrast, the Gospel of Mark was written when the Jewish War had already started, or when Jerusalem was already occupied in 70 A.D. (I believe the latter) and the Jews were being expelled *en masse* from the land of Judea.[4] Unlike Paul, Mark concentrates on the traditions of the historical Jesus. Although Mark's basic position is similar to that of Paul, namely, that Jesus is the Christ (the kerygma), his concern is to present the historical Jesus prior to the Resurrection. Hence the kerygmatic materials that were already established as the basis for Christology were insufficient. He uses other materials of a historical nature. Therefore, we cannot agree with Bultmann that Mark is only an expanded kerygma. Thus Mark, unlike Paul, is not apologetic, and neither is he interested in developing a Christology or a soteriology, which are abstract and idealistic. His descriptive style is simple and folksy, containing historical facts.

In the above comparison we can see certain factors that are related to our subject matter. Mark was in a different social situation from Paul's. Therefore, not only could Mark not accept the highly concentrated kerygmatic theology, but it seems he also consciously had to maintain a certain distance from Paul. Such a position made Mark move toward a historical rather than kerygmatic Jesus. Under such a premise, the term *"ochlos,"* which Mark introduces, has a very important function which was demanded by Mark's historical situation. During Mark's time, the Jewish people, including the Jewish Christians, were expelled from their land and were on the way to exile like lost sheep without a shepherd.

The Characteristics of *Ochlos* in the Gospel according to Mark

Normally, we would begin with a semantic and conceptual clarification of a term and then see how this is reflected in a writing. We are not going to follow this procedure. Rather, we will first determine the character of the *ochlos* by examining the occurrences of this term in Mark. By so doing we will reduce to a minimum the subjective interpretation of this term. We will later examine its semantic field and usage in other literature.

The Characteristics of Ochlos

1. Wherever Jesus went, there were always people who gathered around him. They are called the *ochlos* (2:4, 13; 3:9, 20, 32; 4:1; 5:21, 24, 31; 8:1; 10:1). In most instances, there is no clear reason as to why these people followed Jesus. They form the background of Jesus' activities.

2. These people were the so-called sinners, who stood condemned in their society. Especially at the beginning of his Gospel, Mark applies the term *ochlos* in a typical way to the tax collectors and sinners. As we shall show more fully later, Mark describes in this scene how the dogmatic legalists criti-

cize Jesus for meeting with these people, who are the outcasts of society (2:13–17).

3. There are cases where they (the *ochlos*) are differentiated from the disciples (8:34; 9:14; 10:46). In some instances Jesus teaches only the disciples (4:36; 6:46; 7:17, 33). Thus it seems that Jesus placed the disciples above the *ochlos*. However, we must note that Jesus often fiercely criticized the disciples.[5] On the contrary, there are no instances of Jesus rebuking the *ochlos*. Matthew and Luke either boldly suppress the criticism of the disciples or beautify Jesus' attitude toward the disciples. This fact should be remembered when we view the disciples as representatives of the church.[6]

4. The *ochlos* are contrasted with the ruling class from Jerusalem who attack and criticize Jesus as their enemy. The *ochlos* took an anti-Jerusalem position and were clearly on the side of Jesus (2:4–6; 3:2–21; 4:1; 11:18, 27, 32). In this connection, it is important to note that they were the minjung of Galilee.[7]

5. Because the *ochlos* were against the rulers, the rulers were afraid of them and tried not to arouse their anger (11:18, 32; 12:12; 15:8, 15). Accordingly, to get the *ochlos* on their side, the rulers had to bribe them. For instance, when Jesus was arrested the rulers are said to have given money to mobilize the *ochlos*—a fact which indicates the strength of the *ochlos*. However, the fact that they were mobilized in such a way does not mean that they were necessarily anti-Jesus but that they could be manipulated.[8]

The Attitude of Jesus toward the Ochlos

1. "Jesus had compassion on them, because they were like sheep without a shepherd" (6:34). The expression "sheep without a shepherd" comes from the Old Testament. Such an expression implies a tradition of criticism against the rulers, who had a responsibility to take care of the people (for example, Ezek. 34:5), as well as against the crowd, who were cursed with directionlessness because of their betrayal of Yahweh. The latter tradition, however, does not appear in the Gospels. In the prayer of Moses requesting a successor, he says, "Please do not abandon the congregation of Yahweh like lost sheep without a shepherd" (Num. 27:17). Moses regards the *ochlos,* who were hungry and following him, as a crowd without leaders. At the same time, he seems to suggest that they were also alienated from the rulers.

2. After the brief narration in Mark 3:34 ("And looking around on those who sat about him . . .") Jesus announces that they (the people) were his mother and his brothers. Previously in verse 32, it is written, "A crowd was sitting about him. . . ." This editorial phrase specifically refers to the *ochlos*. The announcement indicates, on the one hand, a deliberate extrication of Jesus from the ties and demands of kinship and, on the other, it announces that the *ochlos* are the members of a new community (family). This statement was not easily accepted in those days. Therefore, in Matthew we have *mathetai* (disciples) instead of *ochlos,* and in Luke it has been eliminated.

3. "As was his custom, Jesus taught the *ochlos*" (10:1; see also 2:13;

4:11–12; 7:4; 11:18). This means that the *ochlos* were fascinated with his teachings (13:18b). In Matthew and Luke the instances noted above of Jesus teaching the *ochlos* have either been partially eliminated or altered. Such alteration certainly weakens the position of the *ochlos* as the people whom Jesus taught and as the object of his teachings. Although the *ochlos* is not totally ignored in the other Gospels, there is evidence of the expanding authority of the apostles and the church.

Synthesis

Taking into consideration all these factors, we may state the following:

1. There is no evidence of a qualitative evaluation of the *ochlos*. In other words, there is no attempt to evaluate the *ochlos* either in terms of an established religious or ethical standard or in terms of a new ethic. (Mark 3:35 is patently a later addition.)

2. Those who were the *ochlos* gathered around Jesus and followed him: if Jesus was the *Wanderprediger,* they were the *Wanderochlos.* In 8:2 we see that they followed Jesus for three days without eating. This shows us that they had neither an established position in their society nor were they members of an identifiable economic class.

3. When we consider the fact that the *ochlos* are contrasted with the ruling class of that time and that Jesus was criticized for associating with the *ochlos,* it becomes evident that the *ochlos* were the condemned and alienated class.

4. Finally, there is a consistent attitude of Jesus toward the *ochlos*. He accepted and supported them without making any conditions. He received them as they were. He also promised them the future (the Kingdom of God). Such action was unacceptable to the leaders—the Pharisees and the Sadducees—and even to the religious groups who were anti-Jerusalem, i.e., the Essenes and the followers of John the Baptist.

The Composition of the *Ochlos*—Those Who Followed Jesus

There are a variety of people who followed Jesus and about whom Jesus spoke. However, socially all these are seen as belonging to one social class, namely, the *ochlos*. In Mark 2:13–17, the *ochlos* is presented in a paradigmatic way, as we shall see in the following analysis.

Mark 2:13–17 can be divided into two parts: (1) verses 13–14 and (2) verses 15–17. The first part is concerned with the invitation "Follow me!" addressed to Levi (14b); and the second focuses on the joy of sharing a meal in which Levi does not have a major role. These two parts were transmitted independently, as is particularly evident in Luke 5:29 where Luke clarifies the link Mark makes in 2:15a by saying that Levi invited Jesus and his disciples for a meal.

It is important to make a connection between these two passages without which it is not possible to see the significance of the two. If we keep the two separate, we do not really get the significance of Levi being a tax collector and the meaning of the meal also becomes vague. When we combine these two, the dinner becomes a joyful feast celebrating the fact that certain types of people were called to be the disciples of Jesus.

To make this connection, Mark does not rely simply on the connection he makes in 2:15a, which Luke amplifies. He perceives and states a more substantial connection in verses 13 and 15c, which scholars agree are Mark's own editorial compositions. In verse 13b Mark says that those who followed Jesus and listened to his teaching were "the whole crowd" *(pas ho ochlos);* and in verse 15a he says that many tax collectors and sinners sat at the meal with Jesus and his disciples. In so saying, he sees the tax collectors and sinners as part of those who followed him. In other words, the "many who followed him" are the very *ochlos* referred to in verse 13 (cf. 2:2-4).

The presence of the *ochlos* is what provides a substantial connection between these two parts, i.e., verses 13-14 and 15-17, and indeed provides the overall connection and background for Jesus' teaching and ministry. We will now turn to an examination of the composition of the *ochlos.*

The sinners and tax collectors already referred to are mentioned in the old so-called Q source (Matt. 11:19) and in Luke's special source. There is thus early and convincing agreement that "tax collectors and sinners" were a part of the *ochlos.* In Matthew the category of prostitutes is also mentioned in "tax collectors and prostitutes" (Matt. 21:31) so this category too formed a part of the designation "sinners." Although there are many references to the sick (fifteen times), to the hungry (16:34-35; 8:1ff.), and to widows (12:41f.) who appear more often in Luke as part of the *ochlos,* the category "tax-collectors and sinners" seems to be a more pervasive group in the *ochlos.* Hence, a clarification, in particular, of the concept of sinners and the social composition of tax collectors, identified in terms of their occupation, would provide us with a good idea of the contours of this amorphous group of people called the *ochlos.*

Sinners (Hamartolos)

There is no argument about the fact that Jesus associated with sinners. The question is who are the types of people called sinners, or what is the meaning of sinner?

A sinner in the Judaic tradition primarily signified one who is a criminal before God. Concretely, it is an overall designation for people who cannot accomplish the duty of the law. From the time the Pharisees appeared on the religious scene, the law of cleanliness, previously limited to the priests, was applied to the Israelites as a whole.[9] This raised a new problem vis-à-vis the classification of sinners.

In discussing this problem, Jeremias points out that the sinner in Jewish society was defined in two ways.[10] One was a publicly recognized criminal (offender against the law), and the other was a person in a lowly, i.e. a socially unacceptable, occupation as defined in those days. He differentiates these two and says that the latter was despised because of "immoral conduct of life" or "dishonorable occupation." But the reason why the occupation made a person a sinner was because the occupation violated the law, either directly or indirectly, and not because of the occupation itself. These were persons who could not rest on the Sabbath day because of the character of their occupations (boatmen, shepherds, and prostitutes). Or, persons who were ill-smelling or those who had to handle things defined as impure (leather-makers, coppersmiths, and butchers). They were alienated and could not participate in worship. While drawing attention to these categories of sinners, Jeremias overlooked another important group. Even persons who could not fulfill the requirements of the law because of sickness or poverty were also designated sinners.

The notion that sickness was the result of crime was pervasive in Judaism. Such a notion appears continually not only among the orthodox in the Old Testament (for example, Psalm 73, Job, etc.), but also in the New Testament (John 9:1f.). In particular, lepers, hemophiliacs, and the mentally ill were regarded either as unclean according to the law or as those upon whom the wrath of God had come. These are not really criminals, but were forced into these situations because of outside pressures and religious-social thinking. Poverty also brought about this condition for it prevented people from keeping the Sabbath or the law of cleanliness.

These persons were different from those who violated the law on purpose. But in effect they were also branded as sinners by the law which upheld a particular system.

The tradition of the three Gospels views the scholars of religious and civil law and the Pharisees as Jesus' antagonists. These understood sinners in terms of the categories given above. As we have already noted, in Pharisaic thinking the label "sinner" was applied widely, especially to those who infringed the law of cleanliness, so that the realm of the law was expanded. This brought about the social alienation of those in humble occupations, the poor, and the sick. Therefore, both persons defined according to their occupations and those who were criminals were forcibly marginalized and alienated by the system. They were sinners because they violated the law or could not adapt themselves to the system of the law. From this standpoint, religious sin and social alienation were really two sides of the same coin.

Tax Collectors

Tax collectors are not included in the comprehensive category of sinners, but are another conspicuous parallel category. As already noted, the usage "tax collectors and sinners" can be seen in the Q source (Matt. 11:19), in the special source of Luke (15:1), and in the Gospel of Mark.

If the tax collectors were regarded as Jesus' people (minjung), the minjung cannot be limited just to politically and economically alienated people. For the tax collectors were agents of the Roman Empire and cannot be characterized as the poor class. Mark dares to describe the tax collector Levi as a person who could afford to give a dinner. But there is a difficulty in characterizing tax collectors as a group because among them too there were the rich and the poor. There was a class which received contracts from the Roman Empire to collect taxes and these exploited the people. There were also a number of others who worked under these people as their employees. Among the employee category, there were many people who worked part-time. All of them were treated as tax collectors in that society and were alienated. This can be seen in the fact that they were often referred to like Gentiles (Matt. 5:46–48; cf. 6:7, 32; 10:5).

When the anti-Roman movement eventually became a guerrilla movement, an attempt was made to get a general nationalist response. In order to do this the people rose in revolt at the time of a census for the purpose of tax-collection. They made Galilee their stronghold and made the refusal to pay taxes the beginning of their struggle. This fact indicates the general animosity towards tax collectors. Even in the Rabbinic tradition, they convicted the tax collectors and arrayed them with murderers and burglars.[11]

Why did Mark include them in the category of *ochlos?* First of all, it is precisely because of the tradition that Jesus associated with them (Matt. 11:9). The distinguishing character of this tradition about Jesus is that, no matter what, he unconditionally embraced the alienated and despised class in the community. It is clear that tax collectors were excluded not only by the nationalists, but also by the religious ruling class, landowners, and merchants. The tax collectors were denied the right to make offerings for the poor (Baba Qamma 10:1, 2), and they were not permitted as witnesses in the Judaic court *(Babylonian Talmud).*

Jesus' attitude to the tax collectors is implied in the saying "those who are well have no need of a physician, but those who are sick; I came not to call the righteous, but sinners" (16b–17), which was given in answer to the question "Why does he eat with tax collectors and sinners?" As already indicated, Jesus includes tax collectors with sinners and says that he has come to call the sinners.

Here it is necessary to note the meaning of *kalesai* (to call) in order to understand Jesus' attitude to tax collectors. Unlike Mark, Luke speaks of making one repent or the sinner who repents (Luke 15:7–10, 18). This idea is not present in Mark; and he uses the word *"kalesai,"* which is used to call one as a disciple.

Jesus shows this basic attitude also to other groups, that is, the ill, fishermen, women, and children. Though tax collectors were different in some respects from these people, they have something in common. They too were alienated from the system and were therefore despised. Taking into account the fact that Zealots were also included with tax collectors among Jesus' disciples (Mark 3:18), we know that Jesus' attitude toward the minjung was never limited to people who were politically oppressed.

The Sick

In Judaism, sickness like other forms of ill fortune was considered to be punishment for sin. There are evidences of this notion also in the Gospels (cf. John 9:1; Luke 13:2; Mark 2:5, etc.). This idea became even more dominant when the Pharisees applied the law of cleanliness to the common people. Consequently, in particular, lepers, the mentally ill and hemophiliacs were also alienated. The sick appear many times in the Gospels, and in many cases it seems that they have already been deserted by their family and neighbors. The reason why the sick were socially alienated was because they were poor and their condition contrary to the law of cleanliness. They were thus also alienated on religious grounds. The belief that their unfortunate lot was punishment for crime made it possible to exclude them from the community.

Some people feel that, according to Mark 2:5b, Jesus also had such an idea, but this is wrong. Mark speaks of belief here, but he does not speak about the belief of the patient himself, but of the people who carried the sick person on their shoulders. There are two more cases like this (5:36; 9:23) where belief is seen as a precondition for healing. We must recognize the fact that here belief means pure trust, regardless of belief about redemption. If this text gives weight to the idea of absolution from sin, the advent of the Kingdom of God must be regarded as bringing liberation not just from sins but rather from the whole dominating system and from the ideas upon which it is founded.[12]

In this connection, we must take note of two things regarding the character of the healing story. One is that most of the sick had already left their dwelling houses and were in the alienated situation of wanderers. The other is that, in most cases, Jesus sent them to their homes after curing them.[13]

A good illustration of this character of the healing story, namely, the restoration of lost rights, occurs in those stories concerning lepers, who were typical of persons alienated by the law of cleanliness (cf. Bill. I.474). Furthermore, lepers were isolated from places where others lived. Hence, an important aspect of the restoration is for the cured leper to show himself to the priest to prove that he is cured and to offer the sacrifice that Moses ordered. Except for cases where the sick were children (5:35ff.; 7:24ff.) and where healing stories have another purpose (3:1ff.), Jesus says, "Go back home!" or "Go!" (2:11; 5:19; 5:34; 8:26; 10:52). The phrase in 5:19 that "the cured man wanted to follow Jesus" emphasizes the fact that Jesus sent him home in spite of the fact that he wanted to remain with Jesus. The restoration here is different from "to call him" *(kalesai),* which was a different process for the restoration of rights of people in the society.

Sayings in Mark about Jesus' Attitude to the *Ochlos*

1. "I came not to call the righteous, but sinners" (2:17b). In this logion we have an indication of Jesus' basic attitude of love. We must not overlook in this logion the terms "not" and "but." It cannot be interpreted as saying "not only . . . but also. . . ." Jesus never showed what may be called universal love. He loved people with partiality. He always stood on the side of the oppressed, the aggrieved, and the weak. This fact is clarified in the Q source, as for example in the parable in Luke 15:2ff. (Q). It says, "He leaves the other

ninety-nine sheep in the pasture and goes looking for the one that got lost until he finds it.''

As we have already said, Mark views sinners as the *ochlos* and says definitely that Jesus came to the world for the *ochlos*.

Then it is necessary to clarify whether the sinners were defined from Jesus' standpoint or defined by the society. Luke, in using Mark, adds at the end ''who repent,'' so that they are sinners from the point of view of Jesus. The King James version adds this phrase to the text of Mark and understands it from Luke's standpoint. But ''who repent'' is Luke's, not Mark's. However, Luke's understanding of ''sinners who repent'' is clarified in Luke 15 in the parables of the lost sheep, lost coin, and lost son. The sinner who repents is the one who is lost and is returned to the place to which he or she belongs. Therefore Luke 15 also reflects in some measure Jesus' attitude to the *ochlos* as found in Mark. Hence, ''sinner'' must be given the added prefix ''so-called.'' For Jesus, those labelled sinners by the current ideology of the rulers were the victims who were robbed and oppressed.

2. ''There is nothing outside a man which by going into him can defile him; but the things which come out of a man are what defile him'' (7:15). This is Jesus' saying about the law of cleanliness. This logion reflects situational language related to verses 1, 2, 5, 14b, 15. The original meaning became unclear because of the insertion of verses 6-14, which are unrelated to the original content. When this section is bracketed out, the original speech shows a stand opposing the law of cleanliness as generalized in the Pharisaic system which, as noted above, alienated many people. Incidentally, the speech of Jesus opposes the absolute rule of cult over life. Most people have discussed this revolutionary declaration in terms of Judaism and anti-Judaism, but have not asked the question as to why he made it.

The situation which provided the background for this speech was that of the Pharisees and the scholars of law from Jerusalem criticizing Jesus' disciples for eating with unwashed hands. Eating with unwashed hands contravened the law of cleanliness. In Jewish society of that time, people who violated the law of cleanliness were branded as *'am ha'aretz*.[14] In his editorial phrases (7:14a), Mark confirms the important fact that the hearers are the *ochlos*. They demonstrate their liberation from the system by disregarding the law of cleanliness which is a heavy burden on the *ochlos*—a fact which is confirmed in the saying in 7:15. Like this saying, the statement ''The sabbath was made for man, not man for the sabbath'' (2:27) also is a declaration which liberates the people oppressed by the Sabbath law. In the Gospel of Matthew, it is for ''all who labor and are heavy-laden'' (11:28).

3. The saying, in 9:37 and 10:13-15 require respect for children. In 9:37 children are identified with Jesus and through him with God. In 10:13-15 he says that the Kingdom of God belongs to children. It is said that Judaism is the religion of adults because there is the responsibility to know the law and to keep it. In this situation women and children were treated contemptuously. There are many arguments about what the words ''with children'' mean. In

the context of the quarrel over who is higher or who is the first, Mark makes children the symbol of low persons (9:37). Mark 10:13-15 is the same because Jesus reacts to the bad attitude of the disciples toward the children. Luke (9:48) adds to the text of Mark the words "for he who is least among you all is the one who is great" and indicates that a child is the symbol of a person who is treated coldly by society. In fact, the children stand in common with the minority *(mikroi).*[15]

Bultmann considers Luke 17:1-2 to be the basic source reflecting this attitude of Jesus which was later Christianized by identifying "little ones" with *"ton pisteuonton"* (believers) (Matt. 18:6-7). Kummel identifies the little ones with "the poor in spirit" (Matt. 5:3). However, "little ones" does not designate a modest attitude, but a social position. It is proper that they are understood in relation to the poor, the crying, and the hungry and as participants in the Kingdom of God. The attitude of Jesus to the children is similar to his attitude toward the crowd, *ochlos.*

The Linguistic Meaning of *Ochlos*

We have noted that Mark introduced the term *ochlos* into the New Testament and that he identified the followers of Jesus and the persons whom Jesus loved with partiality as the *ochlos.* We must now inquire into the linguistic tradition of this word. By so doing, we will be able to discover Mark's understanding of the meaning of "minjung." We will focus on the characteristics of the minjung (people) mainly through an analysis of materials in Kittel's New Testament dictionary.[16]

Laos *and* Ochlos

a. Before the New Testament. The Septuagint introduces the term *laos* into Jewish usage. It translates the Hebrew term *'am* as many as 2,000 times. In Greek sources it is mostly used to denote a national group and often means belonging to some ruling community. For example, the expression "Pharaoh's *laos*" is found in Homer, Pindar, and Herodotus. The Septuagint reflects the meaning of "national group," and this word especially indicates the Israelites who are referred to as *'am* in Hebrew. For non-Israelites the term *ethnos* is used in most cases. Of course, *laos* is used especially for "God's people" *('am).* Another characteristic usage of the Septuagint is that *laoi,* plural of *laos,* is used only 140 times, and it has the meaning of "crowd" or *ochlos.* In this case, there is not the substantial meaning of *laos.* This is a significant characteristic, since ordinary common people hardly make an appearance in the use of *laos* in the Septuagint.

This tradition is also followed in Rabbinic documents. Usually, these documents employ *laos* also to designate non-Israelites, but the added description "offended the law" differentiates them from the Israelites. Also epigraphic material from the Jewish diaspora often designates Israel as *laos.*

Compared with the use of *laos, ochlos* is used only about sixty times in the

Septuagint. However, it does not occur in the ancient Old Testament documents but in the documents of the later period. It is used to translate several
Hebrew words, except *hamon,* which mean minjung. The common meaning
of all these usages is "the crowd." But, it does not mean a particular social
group or a member of a social group. Typical uses of the term are *"ochlos
laou"*—a crowd of Israelites—or *"ochloi ethnou"*—a crowd of Gentiles.

After Pindar, the term *ochlos* appears in Greek documents referring to a
confused majority or to the ordinary soldiers in a combat unit but not to
officers. It also refers to non-combat people who follow the army and perform menial duties. We must note that the anonymous people referred to as
the *ochlos* are differentiated from the ruling class. The term *ochlos* refers to
an ignorant crowd under a burden.

The Septuagint uses this Greek word with this general meaning of "the
mass." As a descriptive term its precise meaning varies from context to context. It could mean "insurgents," "tactical troops," or just refer to the majority. It sometimes designates a crowd of children or women. Its usage in
Rabbinic literature is not very different.

b. Usage in the New Testament. In the New Testament, unlike in the Septuagint, the term *ochlos* is used more often than *laos.* It occurs 174 times
while the term *laos* occurs 141 times.

Looking at the use of the term *laos* in the New Testament, it occurs some 84
times in Luke, so that the majority of its uses are here. Luke seems to use it
consciously since there are several aspects peculiar to his use of this term.
First, quite often *laos* and *ochlos* are used interchangeably and carry the same
meaning as *ochlos* in Mark. Second, Luke, however, seems to prefer the term
laos for Israelites, though understood on the same lines as *ochlos* in Mark, to
distinguish them from other national groups who are the *ethnoi* (Luke 19:47;
22:66; Acts 4:8; 23:5; etc.). This usage of *laos* betrays the influence of the
Septuagint. It is worth noting in this connection that non-Christian Jews who
oppress Christians are also called *ochlos* or *ochloi.* Third, the *laos* is in a
situation of confrontation with those in power. This is similar to the use of
ochlos in Mark. However, sometimes, Luke takes the *laos* and the ruling class
together: *presbuteroi tou laou,* the elders of the *laos* (Luke 22:66). Mark
never uses the term *ochlos* in relation to the Jews of the ruling class.

By and large, it is Mark's use of the term *ochlos* for people that is distinctive in the New Testament and has even influenced Luke's use of *laos.* Besides
this use of *laos* in Luke, other uses of this word in the New Testament are by
and large in quotations from or allusions to the Old Testament and in the
language of the rulers. References to Israel as the people of God also have
laos, following the Septuagint.

Ochlos *and the* 'Am Ha'aretz

In order to understand the meaning of *'am ha'aretz,* we should look not at
its usage in the whole Old Testament but rather at its everyday use at the
beginning of the first century B.C.

Before the Israelites were taken into exile, this term designated land-owners, aristocrats, etc. who were the upper class of Israelite society. However, the meaning of this word changed during the exilic and post-exilic periods. Once the leading members of the society were taken into exile, the ownership of the land passed to the common people, including the Samaritans, who were left behind. Thus, these became the *'am ha'aretz.*

However, this term became a pejorative and was used both in a religious sense and in a "national sense for a low class of people as the people of the land," while the cream of the society was considered to be that which was taken into exile. From the time of Ezra onwards, it became a sociological term designating a class of people that was uneducated and ignorant of the law.

We must remember that it was during this time that Rabbinic Judaism was established; and it was Rabbinic Judaism that systematized the law and set up the social and religious system of its time. Defining the term *'am ha'aretz* in the way it did, Rabbinic Judaism made it refer to the poor and the powerless class which was despised and marginalized. According to Rabbinic Judaism, Jews were forbidden to marry the daughters of the *'am ha'aretz* or sit together with them at meals. This attitude was clearly evident during the time of Jesus.

In the *Babylonian Pesachim,* there are the following prohibitions concerning the *'am ha'aretz.* These are worth noting in relation to the *ochlos.* (1) They cannot be witnesses. (2) Their witness cannot be believed. (3) No secret is to be revealed to them. (4) They are not permitted to be the guardians of orphans. (5) They are not permitted to take charge of contributions for the poor. (6) No Jew is to travel with them.

As we have already mentioned, at least during the time of Mark, if not before, the *'am ha'aretz* designates a social status and indicates an object of contempt. It is close in meaning to *ochlos.* Geographically, Galilee symbolizes the *'am ha'aretz.* Mark selected the word *ochlos,* which was used in a negative sense at that time, to refer to the *'am ha'aretz* and took Galilee as the background to show the victims of the society of that time.

Summary

1. Mark deliberately avoided the term *laos* and used the term *ochlos* to indicate the minjung. This is different from the people of God, who are those within the national and religious framework as defined by the Pharisees. It is also different from the *laos* in Luke, which refers to those who repent and become the new people of God. The minjung do not belong to either group, nor are they the baptized crowd. They belong to a class of society which has been marginalized and abandoned.

2. However, the term *ochlos* is not consolidated into a concept but is defined in a relational way, and is therefore a fluid notion. For example, the poor are *ochlos* in relation to the rich or the ruler. The tax collector is minjung

only in relation to the Jewish nationalist establishment. Accordingly, a certain value or beautification cannot be attributed to the term.

3. The *ochlos* are feared by the unjust and powerful, but they are not organized into a power group. Therefore, we cannot regard them as a political power bloc; rather, they should be regarded existentially as a crowd. They are minjung not because they have a common destiny, but simply because they are alienated, dispossessed, and powerless. They are never represented as a class which has a power base. They yearn for something. In this sense, they are different from the people in the Gospel of John who sought to crown Jesus as a king. The *ochlos* in the Gospel of Mark follow Jesus, but they do not force Jesus to conform to a course of action set up by them. In this sense they are different from the Zealots in Galilee. The Zealots, in their social character and position, have some things in common with the *ochlos,* but the Zealots have a clear purpose which the *ochlos* do not have.

4. Jesus sides with the *ochlos* and accepts them as they are without making any conditions. Jesus never rebukes these persons who are called sinners; rather he rebukes only those who criticize and attack the *ochlos*. (This reconfirms the statement in 2 above.)

5. Jesus does not give the impression that he intends to organize the *ochlos* into a force. He does not provide a program for their movement, nor does he make them an object of his movement. He does not forcibly demand anything from them. He does not ask to be their ruler or head. He "passively" stands with them. A relationship between Jesus and the minjung takes place and then is broken. They follow him without condition. They welcome him. They also betray him.

6. In a word, Jesus informed the minjung of the advent of God's Kingdom. Significantly, Mark summarizes Jesus' preaching thus: "The time is fulfilled, and the kingdom of God is at hand" (1:15). This eschatological declaration announces that there is the creation of a new world as the old world ends. And this declaration gave the *ochlos* a new way and a new hope. Jesus struggled together with the suffering minjung on the frontline of this advent. In this sense, he is the Messiah—a viewpoint Mark reflects.

7. Jesus proclaims the coming of God's Kingdom. He stands with the minjung, and promises them the future of God. The God whom Jesus presented is not like Yahweh of the Old Testament who manifests a tension between love and justice. God's will is to side with the minjung completely and unconditionally. This notion was not comprehensible within the framework of established ethics, cult, and laws. God's will is revealed in the event of Jesus being with them in which he loves the minjung.

NOTES

1. B. Citron, *The Multitude in the Synoptic Gospels* (1954), p. 410, points out that the term *ochlos* is used forty-one times, but the Nestle-Aland text has it only thirty-six times.

2. J. Gnilka, *Das Evangelium nach Markus, EKK*, I (1978) p. 28, says it is wrong to regard the *ochlos* as a choir like the ones in Greek plays. Although he makes this remark, he does not show any interest in Mark's use of this form.

3. Herman Strathmann, *Theologische Worterbuch zum Neuem Testament* IV, pp. 29, 34.

4. Often Chapter 13 of the Gospel of Mark is taken as the criterion for determining the date of the authorship of the Gospel, depending on whether one takes the account as a prophecy of the Fall of Jerusalem or as an expression of the reality after the Fall of Jerusalem. However, considering the situation of the *ochlos* as they appear in Mark—the four thousand people who followed Jesus for three days without food (Mark 8:1ff.)—I conclude that Mark 13 reflects the situation of the people of Israel, including Christians, who had been expelled from their homeland after the Jewish war. Even the expression in Mark 6:34 regarding Jesus' attitude to the five thousand, "Jesus was moved with compassion as they were as sheep without a shepherd," is a reflection of the historical reality of the people.

5. Jesus mainly rebukes their ignorance, for example, their misunderstanding of the parables (4:13; 7:18), their unbelief during the storm (4:35–41; 6:51f.), and their lack of understanding of Jesus' suffering (8:32ff.; 9:32; 10:32, etc.).

6. See especially J. Gnilka, *Das Evangelium,* p. 279.

7. The first to contrast Galilee with Jerusalem were Ernst Lohmeyer, *Galiläa und Jerusalem* (Gottingen: Vandenhoek & Ruprecht, 1936) and W. Marxen, *Der Evangelist Markus*, (1969[2]). But both simply note the contrasting characteristics of the two words in the light of the history of the church, but do not investigate the use of these words in terms of the socio-economic context.

8. The attempt to distinguish between the minjung of Galilee who stood by Jesus and the minjung of Jerusalem who turned against him—for example, Lohmeyer, *Galilee*—is not tenable. The real intention of this attempt seems to be to beautify the minjung.

9. There is still much confusion about the identity of the Pharisees. This is because there is an opinion which puts Pharisees on the side of the minjung. The Pharisees originally came from the pietistic Chassidim, who fought in the Maccabean War. The Pharisees are known from the time of Simon of the house of Hasmon, who appointed himself as arch-priest and ethnarch in 140 B.C. (A. Gunneweg, *Geschichte Israels bis Bar Kochba,* 1972, p. 270). They popularized the law; therefore they conscientized the minjung. First they were in conflict with the royal family of Hasmon. But after the death of Jannai, their policies were accepted by the next ruler, who was Jannai's wife, Alexandra (76–67 B.C.). From then on their position changed, so that they became the defenders of the system. During the time of Herod the Great, they were in conflict with the regime, and ten Pharisees were even executed. However, after the death of Herod, they became part of the establishment. They were allowed to participate in the decision-making assemblies of the ruling regime centered around Jerusalem, i.e., the arch-priest Hannas (A.D. 6–15), who was appointed by the Roman governor-general, Quirinus, A.D. 6–11. (Bo Reike, *N.T. Zeitgeschichte,* 1968 [2], p. 106). Therefore their role changed. From working for the minjung they now became inspectors enforcing submission to the establishment. At least, this is the way the Gospel of Mark presents the Pharisees. For example, they attacked Jesus and his disciples for their violation of rules concerning fasting (2:18), and their eating without washing their hands (7:15). These rules were made by the Pharisees, and therefore express the Pharisees' attitude about the minjung. Also they called themselves Pharisees in order to distinguish themselves, as elites, from the minjung.

10. J. Jeremias (*ZNW* 30, 1931, p. 293ff.) *Jerusalem zur Zeit Jesu,* 1962 (3) expanded this. Eng. ed., Philadelphia: Fortress Press, 1969.

11. *Nedarim* III 4: Bill I, 379.

12. J. Schniewind and others understand this in a similar fashion, and John 9:2–3 also clearly indicates such an attitude.

13. G. Theissen, *Urchristliche Wundergeschichten* (1974), p. 71, points out that sending home the sick after their cure is a special characteristic of the miracle, but he does not clarify the reasons. However, Arai Ken, *Jesus and His Times* (1974), p. 84ff, points out that sending them home was an act restoring their rights.

14. J. Jeremias, *ZNW* 30 (1931), p. 294. See also discussion of *'am ha'aretz* in this paper.

15. Mark 9:42; Matt. 10:42; 17:2 (Q). Cf. R. Bultmann, *History of the Synoptic Tradition* (Oxford: Blackwell, 1963), p. 84.

16. *Theol. Begriffslexikon,* edited by L. Coenen, 1970.

SECTION FIVE:
MINJUNG THEOLOGY—
HISTORICAL VOCATION
AND HOPE

Chapter IX

Historical References for a Theology of Minjung

SUH NAM-DONG

The well-known Korean minjung poet, Kim Chi-ha, clarifies the concept of minjung in a statement he made when on trial at the Seoul District Court:

In Genesis God says to them, "Be fruitful, multiply and fill the earth." The minjung are those who have increased and occupied the ends of the earth, revolutionized the world, built societies, and advanced the course of human history. They physically make up the substance of, what we call, humanity. In other words, the minjung are those who eat the food produced by their own labor, who till and cultivate the soil, and protect their country and its culture not just with words but with their very lives. I think of the minjung in these concrete terms.

The concept of the minjung should be contrasted with the concept of the regime or the ruling authority and differentiated from the intellectuals who take a middle position between the minjung and the rulers. Authority or power originally comes from the minjung. But when it is institutionalized it becomes a tool to suppress the minjung in whom its roots lie. Therefore, in the course of history, the minjung have risen up in revolts to reappropriate the power which they lost and in so doing restore social justice. In my opinion, when the ruling power or authority perverts justice and takes an anti-minjung stand, then justice is on the side of the minjung and injustice on the side of the ruling authority. Throughout the course of human history we witness the constant change from the rule of power to the rule of the minjung, from the history of dictatorship and oppression to that of liberation and democracy.

In answer to the question, "Why are the urban humble (lower) people the protagonists in your works?" Kim Chi-ha replied:

> The reason is that the Christian Gospel (Jesus) came to earth first of all to save the sinners and the humble people. At the present time, the church should be filled with the exploding force of the life and toil of the humble people. The most miserable of the lower people should become the subjects and the vanguard of the work of salvation. In my works my purpose is to point to a certain mystery in the glory of God which reveals itself in the salvation effected through those in extreme misery. Through my experience I have the strange conviction that the Messiah, whom we Christians are longing for and calling upon in our daily prayers, does not come from those who are sophisticated like ourselves, but from these people (wicked prisoners) who are suppressed by us and live in the bitterness of starvation. So, I have tried to formulate and express in my works this conviction concerning the Messiah who comes from the bottom.[1]

In these words, Kim Chi-ha expresses clearly what is the substance of the minjung, their historical destiny and their way of salvation. From the beginning the minjung are the partners of the covenant with God and the true subjects of human history—subduing the earth, producing the values of life, revolutionizing the world, and pushing human history ahead. These have been alienated, suppressed, and have fallen into the category of lower people and sinners. Now, in order to advance the course of history, the minjung have to strive for their own salvation. They themselves must bring about the upheavals which will retake the power which has been taken from them and used against them and thus restore God's justice. For Kim Chi-ha, salvation from the biblical point of view is the salvation of the minjung for which God works through human history, especially through the event of Jesus Christ. Here it is clear that even though he looks at the beginning of Genesis as the place which speaks about the proper place of the minjung in human history, he does not indulge in a kind of retrospective romanticism. Rather, he seeks the reactualization of these ideas in a new future in history. In other words, the significance of what is said about the minjung in Genesis is not to be sought in the past alone (remembrance-idea), but in the future (prophecy-action).

In my opinion, the literature of Kim Chi-ha indicates that the Korean church in the Korean historical and political situation should unify God (spiritual renewal) and revolution (structural renewal) concretely, and that it should refine the historical tradition of the Korean minjung movement with the chisel of a liberation-oriented theology so that it may suggest the direction along which the people's rights movement should go. In so doing, theology will take upon itself the task of interpreting the Mission of God in the present.

In order to interpret the people's rights movement, which is the essence of the Mission of God in Korea today, we need some *references;* and these should be ones which most Korean Christians can recognize. I think that the three most clear *references* are, first, the events of the Exodus and the Cruci-fixion-Resurrection; second, the history of the church, which has received the traditions of the Exodus and the Crucifixion-Resurrection; and third, the tradition of the minjung movement in Korean history. The word "reference" is used here in preference to and in contrast with the word "revelation," which is a term from and a tenet of traditional theology. While the word "revelation" belongs to the category of, shall we say, pure religion, the word "reference" belongs to that of history. The most powerful references from historical theology may be called "paradigms" or "archetypes." We may say that the present people's rights movement, which we will attempt to interpret in this chapter, may be viewed as the reactualization or the re-incarnation of these paradigms or archetypes.

In order to interpret these references we will view them in terms of socio-economic history and in terms of the sociology of literature. It seems to me that a new theological era will begin when we use these two approaches or perspectives for understanding historical references. We may then see the history and thinking of the church going beyond a mere confrontation with communism to a new understanding of historical theology.

The limitations in the situation of the minjung, who are to be contrasted with the ruling regime, may be clarified when we use the approach of socio-economic history.[2] Once we clarify the history of the minjung through this approach, we can then see through the *social biography of the minjung* their corporate spirit, that is, their consciousness and aspirations, by using the method of the sociology of literature.[3] These new hermeneutics follow the proposal of Bonhoeffer, who attempted a "wordly interpretation of the Bible." This theological method or hermeneutical framework provides a new perspective for theologians. Previously, Augustine's theology had as its framework Plato's philosophy of ideas. Thomas Aquinas' theology made Aristotelian philosophy its framework. The liberal theology of the nineteenth century made Kantian philosophy its frame of reference. The recent existentialist theology made the philosophy of existentialism its framework. Today, we are convinced that the perspectives or framework of socio-economic history and the sociology of literature will reveal the identity of the minjung, who will become the subjects of their own history and destiny.

The approach we propose goes a step beyond that of Paul Tillich. He criti-cized existentialist theology for dissolving the kerygma in the realm of per-sonal existence and, on the other, traditional dogmatic theology for repeating the traditional dogma without concerning itself with the situation or the con-text of the present time. Instead, he proposed that theology should relate the kerygma to the situation through the method of question-and-answer.[4] Now, political theology, to which category the themes of revolution, liberation, and minjung belong, uses as its framework for interpretation not just the personal existence of the human being but the social conditions of human existence which both dogmatic and existentialist theology neglect. These two theologies assume that one's being determines one's situation rather than that one's environmental condition determines one's being.

Actually, there is a reciprocal relationship between the two. But in order to overthrow the view-point or prejudice of dogmatic theology, political theology takes the stand that social conditions determine humanity. In making this assertion, the humanity we have in mind is not just that of individual personal existence but rather the social existence of groups like race groups, classes, sex groups, historical groups, the ruled vis-à-vis the rulers, etc., that is, social units which are the essential elements in the make-up of a society which advances the course of human history. To use an illustration: the question is whether one should concentrate on the innumerable cells which compose the human body or focus attention on the organs of the body. In contrast to traditional theology, which tends to concentrate on individual cells, minjung theology and theologies of liberation focus on the organs.

The Biblical Paradigms

The event of the Exodus recorded in the Old Testament is one paradigm for the theology of minjung. This historical event is one of the nuclear events for the salvation of God's people together with the event of Jesus's Crucifixion-Resurrection in the New Testament. The total witness of the Bible may be clarified and understood in terms of these two nuclear historical events. According to the witness of the Bible, God's self-revelation (God's salvation for human beings) is a historical event rather than a mysterious religious experience. The historical event is, so to speak, the language of God. On the basis of the event of the Exodus in the Old Testament, which it considers a paradigm, the Korean church understands the historical experience of the March First Independence movement of 1919 and the liberation on August 15, 1945, as events of God's salvation of the nation.[5] However, if the historical church interprets the event of the Exodus as simply in the area of religion, it cannot perform the role of a revolutionary power to transform reality, but it can only accept and play a role dictated to it by the ideology of the ruler to maintain the status quo.

The event of the Exodus is a political event which occurred in the area of socio-economic history. It is an event in the socio-economic history of the people of Israel who were used as slaves for the vast public works and as serfs working the farms of Egypt. These rebelled against the oppressive ruling system of Egypt, and under the leadership of Moses escaped from Egypt. This political event is the nucleus of the story. Nevertheless, for two thousand years, the Christian church has viewed the event of the Exodus as in the realm of religious ideas, thus ridding the event of its historical nucleus. If the dominant reference, the paradigm, the archetype of God's intervention in history, was the political event occurring in the dimension of socio-economic history, now, at the present time too, God's intervention in history has to occur in the dimension of socio-economic history.[6]

Both the event of the Exodus in the Old Testament and the event of the Crucifixion-Resurrection in the New Testament are equally paradigms for the theology of the minjung. And yet there are some differences and points of contrast between the two. In terms of the minjung, Moses was a heroic leader. But Jesus was a resister who kept company with the minjung. In the case of Moses, the revolution was a success. But in the case of Jesus it seems to have failed, if we evaluate it in the same terms as that of Moses. Actually, if we use the term "revolution" for Jesus, we must recognize the fact that the style of his revolution is different from that of Moses. In the case of the Exodus, the revolution occurred only once at a historical point, while the event of the Crucifixion-Resurrection was aimed at permanent revolution. In the case of a one-time revolution, the minjung are the objects of salvation (salvation from outside). In the case of permanent revolution, the minjung become the subjects of salvation (self-reliant salvation). Moses answered the cry (aspiration) of the people; but Jesus was the very cry (aspiration) of the people themselves. In this sense, Jesus was truly *a part of* the minjung, not just *for* the minjung. Therefore, Jesus was the personification of the minjung and their symbol.

As scholars have shown, there are two traditions concerning this companion-in-resistance whose life gradually reaches its peak at the point of the crucifixion. The first tradition is that of the Q source (a book of the sayings of Jesus). The second is the Gospel of Mark. According to the Q source, the characteristic impression given by Jesus when he was teaching is that he was not like the lawyers, but was one who had authority. In the Gospel of Mark, the statement which characterizes Jesus' style of action is that he was the friend of tax collectors and sinners. These two sources present a montage of the "criminal" Jesus.

Wherever Jesus went many nameless crowds followed him. The crowds surrounding Jesus were the shadow which demonstrated that Jesus was not an abstract figure but a historical being with a particular existence. It is said that John the Baptist also attracted crowds, but these were drawn by his preaching. In other words, they were seekers after truth. But the crowds of Galilee who sought Jesus, though they contained some seekers after truth, were essentially the poor, the sick, the crippled (especially those sick and crippled who had been driven out of their villages), widows, tax collectors, and prostitutes, that is, those who were the forsaken people at the bottom of society. These were the *'am ha'aretz* who were called "sinners" by the ruling religious people of the time. According to biblical scholars, the group of disciples, which was composed of people from the crowds surrounding Jesus, did not appear at the beginning of Jesus' mission. At the beginning, they were hardly distinguishable from the ordinary people.[7] That is to say, the mission of Jesus was a mission directed to these nameless crowds.

The Japanese scholar Tagawa says in interpreting Mark 3:31–35 that the crowds in this text are to be differentiated from the group of disciples, the lawyers from Jerusalem, and Jesus' relative James who was later the head of the Jerusalem Church. For a clear comprehension of the *ochlos* he proposes: "In view of the contrast evident between the *ochlos* and others in this context, we find that the crowd in Mark 3:32, 34 means more than just a crowd. It has the same meaning as the word 'minjung.' According to Mark, minjung is a concept in contrast to the ruling group. Jesus appears as one whose existence is embodied concretely in the minjung. Therefore, the minjung in Mark is never an independent object, but is always described as the shape of the situation in which Jesus lived. The minjung themselves, in fact, do not exist in any place. The minjung can come to take the name of Jesus when they appear as a self-aware existence."[8]

As far as I understand Tagawa, first, he perceives the subject matter of Mark's theology to be the minjung rather than Jesus himself. Second, more than the generalized meaning of "crowd," *ochlos* has the meaning of minjung, the groups which were oppressed and alienated by the ruling regime. In the light of the assertion of Tagawa, I would like to clarify the main points of today's minjung theology. First, the subject matter of minjung theology is not Jesus but the minjung. In the case of minjung theology, Jesus is the means for understanding the minjung correctly, rather than the concept of "minjung" being the instrument for understanding Jesus. Second, the term "minjung" in Korean and also in Japanese has its place and technical meaning in the area of political theology. It should be differentiated from the term *"ochlos."* Minjung is also quite different from *"laos"* (found in the Old Testament and the Gospel of Luke). *"Laos"* has a biblical tradition and is used quite often for the national people of Israel. The minjung is rather close to the meaning of "the poor" in the Covenant Code (Exod. 20:22–23, 39), in the Prophets, and in the Epistle of James. The (common) people, crowd, and *volk* must be differentiated from the minjung, which is none of these. It must not and in fact cannot be translated into English, but must be written "minjung" as a special word for a political theological concept. In other words, Mark needed the concept of the minjung for his theology, but there was no word to express it. Hence he used the term *"ochlos"* for it. Jesus was a friend of tax collectors and sinners, that is, the minjung. He was the educator and the liberator of the minjung. He was not in the same way a friend of the leaders. Therefore, the main focus of our theological concern should be the tax collectors and sinners, that is, the minjung.

In the Gospel accounts, especially as presented in Mark, Jesus always asked the minjung to decide for themselves and to be responsible for their own lives. In other words, the minjung had to become their own subjects. In making this demand, Jesus stood on the side of the minjung. He walked with them and became their friend. This stance is related to the fact that he did not act like the lawyers. Instead, he impressed the people as a man with authority. The authority of the lawyers was based upon the fact that they spoke according to the law; and the authority of the prophets was based upon the fact that they spoke the word of God. But Jesus did not draw the basis for his authority either from the law or from God. He spoke his own word. In this sense, he was the true God and the true man. Jesus did not attempt to empower his word with God's word. This reticence may be due to the fact that the language of God had already become or was in the process of becoming the language of the rulers and of their ideology to oppress the minjung. The stance of Jesus is the reference for minjung theology in which the oppressed and alienated minjung become the protagonists of history and in control of their destiny.

Living a life of companion-in-resistance, Jesus was forced to the cross. As he had already been labelled a friend of tax collectors and sinners, it was natural that his stance as a friend of the minjung should be seen as in opposition to the system of the rulers. Besides, he criticized the laws of Judaism, especially the Sabbath law—"The Sabbath exists for human beings and not human beings for the Sabbath." Jesus also publicly challenged the regulations imposed by the priestly rulers of the Jerusalem Temple, which was the central organization exploiting the minjung. This challenge became the immediate basis for accusing him; and he was crucified as a political offender. Even though all the historical facts about Jesus are not clear because of the limited documentary evidence that is available, one fact is clear, namely, that he was executed as a political offender. The crucifixion of Jesus was not an incidental occurrence, but the inevitable conclusion and climax of the life of the companion-in-resistance. The crucifixion is the peak in the process of struggle in which the minjung become the protagonists of their own history and destiny.

The salvation of the minjung starts in the political realm, in the realm of their socio-political history. Thereafter, the church seems to have stepped aside from the political realm in which this salvation occurred. Therefore, the crucifixion of Jesus was changed into a religious symbol, the Cross, and the image of the Messiah, which had political implications, was changed into the Christ and carried a religious connotation. Consequently, the event of salvation lost its historical nucleus of meaning; and the purely religious symbol of the Cross could not have the power to change the course of human history. The basis of minjung theology is the crucifixion of Jesus which occurred in the political realm as a historical event. I think the way to recapture this historical nucleus of meaning is through a correct interpretation of the socio-economic history of the minjung. Jesus was resurrected after three days and promised to meet with his disciples in Galilee. This is one of the earliest testimonies about the resurrection of Jesus. In Mark, Galilee is the birthplace of the minjung; and Jerusalem is the seat of authority of the rulers. It is our conviction that the Risen Jesus lives among the minjung, who have been continually oppressed and alienated in the course of socio-economic history.

The Paradigm from Church History

After the writing of the documents which are now included in the Old Testament, Judaism appeared and edited the Old Testament. Similarly, after the writing of the documents of the New Testament, Christianity appeared and edited the New Testament. It seems to me that in the historical processes which took place between the situation of the church which edited the Scriptures and the historical nucleus of the Scriptures itself, the content and real import of the Bible were de-politicized. We can point to two cultural and historical reasons for this process of de-politicization.

First, there was the change in thinking and worldview: a change from the historical and eschatological thinking of Hebrew culture to the cosmological and metaphysical worldview of Hellenism. In terms of Hebrew eschatology, we wait for the Day of Yahweh as a future event. But, in Hellenistic metaphysical thinking, we find the idea that this world, which we perceive through our senses, is unreal and transitory. The image of the original Messiah, who is to come and save the afflicted minjung, became non-political; and it changed into the image of the heavenly Christ. Accordingly, as the Messiah became a non-political figure, the Crucifixion, which was to be understood in the dimension of politics, became the non-political symbol of the Cross in the dimension of religion.

Second, from the time Constantine the Great accepted Christianity in A.D. 313, the Christianity which had been an underground religion of the oppressed became the state religion of the rulers and oppressors. The faith which contained the sigh and protest of the oppressed, as a religion revealing a revolutionary potential, was co-opted by the Roman political power. Hence, this religion degenerated into the ideology of the ruler; and its original essence, that is, the themes of liberation of the oppressed and the minjung's aspiration for the realization of justice, was projected onto a transcendental dimension of the heavenly world which has nothing to do with an eschatological understanding of history. Thus it became essentially a faith focusing on a supra-temporal eternal heaven beyond human history. In this way it began to function as an opiate. However, even though religion may tend to function or be used as an opiate, it is yet for all that the sigh and protest of the oppressed. Therefore, the way forward is not to become irreligious but to recover the political and historical essence of religion.

The Gospel writers summarize the message of Jesus in these words: "God's kingdom has come near." These words deepen the meaning of the Day of Yahweh, which the prophets proclaimed. But it must be remembered that the motif of the Kingdom of God became a non-political category after the time of the Constantinian era. Therefore, the aspiration of the oppressed took the form of a longing for a Millennium which is in a historical future rather than the form of the Kingdom of God which is beyond human history.

In this connection, let me say in summary form what I have argued elsewhere concerning the symbols of the Millennium and the Kingdom of God.[9] While the Kingdom of God is a heavenly and ultimate symbol, the Millennium is a historical, earthly, and semi-ultimate symbol. Accordingly, the Kingdom of God is understood as the place the believer enters when he dies, but the Millennium is understood as the point at which history and society are renewed. Therefore, in the Kingdom of God the salvation of the individual person is secured, but in the Millennium is secured the salvation of the whole social reality of humankind. Consequently, while the Kingdom of God is used in the ideology of the ruler, the Millennium is the symbol of the aspiration of the minjung.

In fact, the religion of the Millennium was the orthodox doctrine of the church of the first century. However, the Christianity of Constantine's church repelled the belief in the Millennium, the aspiration for the future, and other such beliefs as heterodoxies. Thus the church suppressed the aspiration of the minjung. As a matter of fact, Augustine identified the era of the church with that of the Millennium, and established the theology of an absolute church,[10] so that the idea of a new historical dispensation could no longer be entertained in history.

Because the religion of the Millennium was removed and forgotten, Western social thought adopted in its place the symbol of the Utopia, which originated in Greece. But, without exception, Utopia signifies an ideal land which certain elites, who leave their irrational society, establish on an isolated island. It is, so to speak, the dream of the bourgeoisie. In contrast, the Millennium is the minjung's aspiration, in which the whole society is renewed in history. Therefore, as a rule, I have insisted on restoring the symbol of the Millennium over against that of the Utopia and as a counterbalance to that of the Kingdom of God. The symbol of the Millennium, which secures social justice, must be restored and must run parallel to the symbol of the Kingdom of God, which secures the salvation of the individual. Otherwise, the symbol of the Kingdom of God is apt to promote an otherworldly faith, and the Millennium is apt to bring about a form of fanaticism.

In the twelfth century, Joachim of Floris reintroduced the belief in the Millennium, removed from the church in the Constantinian era, as a variation of the "third Age of the Holy Spirit."[11] He did not accept the traditional understanding of the Trinity of the Holy Father, the Holy Son, and the Holy Spirit as three persons in one divine unity. Rather, he viewed the Trinity in a historical perspective as revealed in three successive historical periods: the period of the Holy Father, the period of the Holy Son and the period of the Holy Spirit. He developed a clear historical theology. He said that man was a *slave* in the period of the Holy Father, and was a *son* in the period of the Holy Son, and then became a *friend* who had spiritual freedom in the period of the Holy Spirit. Thus, in the third spiritual period, all the people surpass the institutional church and the literal word of the Bible, and their souls and bodies become filled with wisdom and happiness in the historical reality of this world. There, a democratic community of the poor and the minjung will be realized. In it there will be no fear, class, monopoly of wealth, or domination by the strong. His statement that "the poor must suffer from hunger again whenever the altar is adorned" reveals his deep insight into the irrational entanglement between the ruler and the oppressed minjung.

According to Augustine, the absolute and permanent truth is the monopoly of the church, and only the church spreads the absolute truth. But, according to Joachim of Floris, the truth grows and spreads itself from a bud to a stem and then to flowers and fruits as history develops. Augustine's outlook on truth takes the form of a fence which protects the concessions granted to the rulers and persons who have vested interests. However, that of Joachim of Floris responds to the aspirations of the oppressed minjung. In accepting the viewpoint of Augustine, the church turned away from the Holy Spirit and the minjung.

By contemplating on both the Old and the New Testaments, Joachim of Floris believed that God is the inner power of the process of humanization in history and that he incarnates himself by progressively increasing his presence in history.

More recently, historical theology has been presented in terms of the activity rather than just the presence of the three persons of the Trinity by the English theologian R. P. C. Hanson. In his "The Divinity of the Holy Spirit," he argues that the protagonist of the Old Testament is the Holy Father, and the Holy Son is not yet clearly present.[12] Though the activity of the Spirit is mentioned quite often, the Spirit in the Old Testament is merely God's supernatural power. In the New Testament the protagonist is the Holy Son. The Holy Father withdraws and the Holy Spirit as yet has no real recognition. Then, when the doctrine of the Trinity was established in the church, the activity of the Holy Spirit was recognized; and the Holy Spirit was given the same status as that of the Holy Father and the Holy Son. The divine status of the Holy Spirit is recognized in the writings of persons like Basil of Caesarea in the fourth century. Thus, God develops his own presence and activity in this way: the Holy Son surpasses the Holy Father, and in turn the Holy Spirit surpasses the Holy Son, and moves in an eschatological direction. Finally, he says that the Holy Spirit will be poured out over all the people at the end. This is the paradigm of minjung theology.

A similar process may be discerned in the history of Christian art. According to André Malraux, a French art critic, God's figure as the subject of Western art changes as the periods go by.[13] First, God was depicted in the Byzantine period as a mysterious glimmering symbol hovering over the universe as a transcendent and an almighty judge. Second, in Western art, the figure of God changes to take on an anthropomorphic form. Third, in Romanesque cathedrals, God is usually portrayed as the Christ who takes the human form. Fourth, in the Gothic art of the thirteenth century, although the Christ figure is increasingly depicted as that of an earthly human being, it still retains the theme of king and victor. Fifth, in the fourteenth century, the Christ figure changes into one in which distress and agony are accentuated. Sixth, in the fifteenth century, Jesus is portrayed as a man in actual historical situations of the time of the artist. Seventh, in the sixteenth and seventeenth centuries, the figure of Christ gradually disappears from the canvas and a general human figure appears. Eighth, in the next stage, the inner thoughts of the artist find expression in abstract forms rather than in a human form.

In this history of art, which reflects the various periods, the Christ figure withdraws and vanishes in the process of the transformation of the Holy

Father to the Holy Son and to the Holy Spirit who is God as he exists in human beings. The Holy Spirit is Christ's successor (cf. John 16). He is the transformation of Christ and is intrinsic God dwelling in humanity. As such, he becomes the basis for the conviction regarding the equal rights and dignity of all human beings. Therefore, the period of the Holy Spirit is that of the minjung.

These historical processes are also evident in Korean history as set out by Lee Gi-baik.[14] While in the Christian cultural and historical context, this historical process is seen as that of humanization and incarnation, in the Korean historical context, as we shall see below, the same historical process may be seen as demonstrating that humanity is heaven itself.

Muentzer's appearance in Germany in the sixteenth century helped to clarify minjung theology and revolutionary theology.[15] While Luther received his inspiration regarding the reformation in a cloistered room, Muentzer perceived the need for revolution by participating in the social movements of his time. Consequently, while Luther's reformation, by disregarding the dimension of social reformation, brought into being a church for citizens of the middle class, Muentzer pushed simultaneously for a religious reformation and for a social reformation which would secure the rights of the urban poor and the peasants. In this way, he called for a much more radical reformation. In Muentzer's theology we find the impact of the suffering of the minjung evident in the irrational society of his time. He believed that "the chosen people" for the revolution would come from among the urban poor and the peasants. He said: "All the members of society must have the power of the sword. Then the minjung become free and only God remains the Lord of the minjung." He pushed for a social reformation with the power of the sword; and he thought this was the inevitable program for the salvation of the individual as well as society.

According to Muentzer, "individual purification" (inward reformation) and "social reformation" (outward reformation) were not properly related. The struggle for social reformation needs the inner purification of the person, and personal religious salvation itself cannot be realized without revolutionary action. If the existing ruling power as an outward organization of sin is to be overcome, the salvation of individuals must itself move and be subsumed in a social reformation. Muentzer believed that under an oppressive system the image of God in man would be distorted, so that man cannot speak correctly of God in a situation of oppression. In this perception he was different from many other founders of Christian sects in the sixteenth century; and he moved toward an understanding of the universal church of the Holy Spirit. In this respect, he is a pioneer of the theology of secularization and of the contemporary theology of the minjung.

Following this tradition, we believe that the Holy Spirit is the principle and the power through which we interpret the Bible correctly and at depth. Such interpretation becomes a new possibility for revelation. In order to preserve its vested interests, the institutional church will deny this new possibility for revelation. According to Muentzer, Luther's "literal religion" depending "only upon the Bible" makes the minjung wait passively for the infusion of God's grace. Thus the minjung continue to be the objects of history and do not function as actual subjects.

Muentzer's movement for radical reformation failed in the peasant wars; and he was executed by the combined forces of the princes and the governors. In his failure he felt that the appropriate time had not yet come, because the self-consciousness of the minjung had not matured. He felt that when the minjung awake, there will be an authentic revolution of the minjung themselves. In actual fact, if he had succeeded in his revolution, he may have betrayed the revolution of the minjung which he himself advocated. His most important contribution to minjung theology is the assertion that the minjung themselves must achieve their own salvation. All the revolutionaries who lead the liberation and the salvation of the minjung may push forward their revolution, but, unlike Jesus, will not achieve the goal. This is the reason why the deserted people at the bottom of society appear as the protagonists of self-liberation in Kim Chi-ha's works, and the reason why the Bodhisattva Jijang resolves to enter Nirvana only after saving the last one who remains in hell.

The theology arising out of today's secular world, which is based on hope, revolution, liberation, politics, the minjung, and the Holy Spirit, is the theology of the post-Christian era. It stands over against the tradition which divorced the Gospel from its original historical situation and then politicized it to play an ideological role for the rulers. This is why theological movements that claim to stand for revolution, the future, and the Holy Spirit are usually branded as heterodoxy and banned from the church. In turn, the church itself advocates the internal and spiritual purification of persons and projects onto an otherworldly heaven, existing outside history, the vision of an ideal society. As a consequence, revolutionary movements which have attempted to reform the social system have broken away from the church, since the church has shown nothing but hostility toward these movements and the Holy Spirit.

It is not impossible that Christianity might once again appropriate the Gospel of the liberation of the minjung who are already engaged in a revolutionary struggle for the future. Already, Christendom has collapsed, and Christianity has entered the Oikoumene; and the post-Christian era has begun especially in the third world. When did the post-Christian era begin? The French Revolution would be its first epoch-making manifestation. When did revolutionary political theology become the main subject of church theology? Clearly, the starting points would be the sharp confrontations and debates which happened during the Church and Society Conference of the World Council of Churches in 1966 and the Second Vatican Council of 1965.

In the post-Christian era, the minjung church and minjung theology attempt to deal simultaneously with the purification of the person, which is the realm of freedom, and the humanization of the social structure, which is the realm of necessity. It is, as Kim Chi-ha perceives, "the unification of God and revolution." The unification will be achieved in the form of the Minjung

Church. It will come into being neither as an accident nor as a supernatural event. It will not be brought about by heroes or the elite through their ideology. Rather, this unification will be achieved by the minjung themselves through their wisdom, conviction, and courage.

The Paradigm of the Minjung Movement in Korean History

The uncovering of minjung history, which has been hidden in the usual research into Korean history, has been accomplished largely through the method of socio-economic history. In saying this, I do not intend to imply that the approach of socio-economic history is indispensable for grasping the reality of the minjung. The Priestly author/redactor of the Pentateuch in the Old Testament, the Prophets, the author of Mark's Gospel, and the author of the Epistle of James all understand the substance and the aspiration of the minjung without resorting to a study or analysis of the socio-economic history of the people. Neither does the Korean revolutionary Chon Bong-jun[16] resort to the method of socio-economic analysis to understand the reality of the minjung. But here too, it seems to me, these persons may have had some perception or intuitive understanding of socio-economic history which enabled them to grasp the situation of the minjung.

Korean historians, whether they hold the historical view of state-nationalism or the historical view of minjung-nationalism, are agreed on the significance of a study of the socio-economic history of Korea and consider the minjung to be the subject of the nation's history. For instance, Ahn Byung-jik's research into the March First Independence movement has surfaced the reality of the minjung.[17] Also, Lee Gi-baik uses the method of socio-economic history for his schematic presentation of Korean history. In recent research, the historical view of the minjung has taken the place of the earlier tradition of the history of dynasties.[18] Thus, a study of the socio-economic history of Korea is enabling us to grasp the reality of the minjung objectively; and the research into the sociology of literature will help to bring into relief the reality of the minjung and their corporate spirit.

Let us begin our inquiry into the tradition of the minjung in the course of Korean history, which is one of the paradigms of Korean minjung theology, by looking at Lee Gi-baik's presentation of Korean history in his *Korean History: A New Study*. In this work, he divides Korean history into sixteen eras and deals with it in sixteen chapters. He points out that after an initial narrowing, there is a progressive expansion of the social base of the ruling power.

1. *The Primitive Community* (Neolitic fourth century B.C.): All the members of the community participate in the process of government.

2. *The Castle States and Allied Kingdom:* The chief's families built up the Castle States and formed the Allied Kingdom (ancient Chosen of Dangun Wangkom)[19] by federating the states. The power to rule was restricted to the upper echelon of society.

3. *The Rule of the Royal Family and the Aristocracy:* The era of the Three Kingdoms during which the king, the king's family, and the queen's family monopolized the power to rule.

4. *Establishing of Autocracy:* The era of Unified Silla.[20] The autocrat was the single ruler; and only the king's family was responsible for the administration of the state. The queen's family was excluded.

5. *The Era of Provincial Lords:* From the end of Silla to the beginning of Koryo. Yukdupum,[21] a system which ranked next to the royal Jingol,[22] was at the center. The Provincial Lords were the ruling power in the country. These established the dynasty of Koryo.[23]

6. *The Rule of the Literati Aristocrats:* The first term of Koryo. Because there was an increase in number of the aristocrats and rulers composed of the royal family, Yukdupum, and the Provincial Lords, a public civil service examination was instituted to select the administrators. The literati aristocrats vied for the posts that were available.

7. *The Rule of the Warrior Aristocrats:* The Musin (the military faction of the aristocracy), who were based in the countryside, increased in numbers. Although they were lower in social status than the Munsin (literati aristocrats), they became part of the ruling power.

8. *Appearance of the Sadaibu:*[24] From the end of Koryo to the beginning of Chosen,[25] the Sadaibu emerged from among the local landlords whose social status was lower than that of the Munsin nobility.

9. *Establishment of the Yangban*[26] *Society:* The beginning of Chosen. The Sadaibu held official posts, both civil and military, and in this period became part of the ruling class.

10. *The Increasing Power of Confucian Scholars:* From the era of King Songjong,[27] the classical scholars who were in the country emerged as a new force, and the number of the ruling class increased.

11. *The Rise of Big Farmers and Wholesale Dealers:* From the era of Kwanghaegun's reign[28] independent middle-class farmers and wholesale dealers became part of the ruling class.

12. *Crisis in the Yangban Social System and the Minjung Rebellion:* Beginning from the era of King Sunjo's[29] reign the Chungin,[30] who were just below the yangban class, the Sori[31] (technicians), merchants, industrialists, and peasants became the ruling power. Lowly persons, such as slaves, were liberated.

13. *The Period of the Enlightenment:* Opening the ports to the outside world, the Chungin, Sori, merchants, industrialists, and peasants, became active participants in their society. In the Donghak[32] movement, the minjung played an active role in politics for a short period.

14. *The Beginning of the Nation-State and the Imperial Invasion of Japan*—from the Independence Association to the March First movement (1919): Through the movement of the Independence Association,[33] whose members were mostly intellectuals, merchants, and industrialists, and through the Donghak movement, the minjung emerged as an integral part of

the ruling. These two movements joined together to form the society. These two movements joined together to form the March First movement,[34] which was the broadest in scope of the minjung movements.

15. *Development of the Nationalist Movement*—from the March First movement to National Liberation: the minjung was the main power of the National movement which resisted the colonial Japanese government.

16. *The Growth of Democracy*—from National Liberation to the April 1960 Student Revolution:[35] Because of the liberation, it was now possible for the minjung and not just the ruling class to participate directly in politics. The nation thereby became a democratic country.

To summarize this historical development: First, for a long time, the minjung were the objects of the ruling power. Second, the minjung did not attempt to become the ruling power through a revolutionary process, but prepared the way to bring about a historical transformation. Third, step by step, the minjung prepared the ground to become the ruling power.

This is a meaningful paradigm for minjung theology which shows that the minjung gradually liberate themselves from the position of being a historical object and become a historical subject. Minjung history and theology testify to the fact that the minjung overcome with their own power the external conditions which determine and confine them and become the subjects who determine their own social situation and destiny.

Having indicated the development of Korean history from a minjung perspective, we will now trace the genealogy of the minjung movement in which the minjung define themselves and struggle for their own liberation. The minjung movement originated in Korean history only with the establishment of Ancient Chosen.

1. In the Chronicle of the Three Kingdoms,[36] there is an account of a minjung revolution. When King Bongsang[37] exploited the people, they achieved a peaceful turnover of political power in A.D. 300 under the leadership of Prime Minister Changjori.[38] It was the voice of the minjung which helped bring about this revolution.

2. Again, the minjung were the social base for the political power of Kungye of Taebong[39] and Kyonhwon[40] of Hubaikje, who challenged the ruling system of Unified Silla. The evidence for this is found in the government document of Silla which was compiled for government revenue and administrative purposes. This document was recently discovered in Japan in Chung Chang Won.[41] It is stated here that the minjung in resisting the exploiting ruling class proclaimed the coming down of the Maitreya, which is the aspiration of the minjung. Both Kungye and Kyonhwon claimed to be incarnations of the Maitreya.

3. Next, I think it is very important in tracing the history of the minjung movement to compare the historical view of the *Samguk Sagi* by Kim Bu-sik[42] with that of the *Samguk Yusa* by Il Yon[43] in the Koryo Dynasty. Because Kim Bu-sik was in the position of the ruling power, he was not able to see the history of Ancient Korea (Ko-Chosen) and wrote Korean history from the

perspective of the Chinese, who were claiming suzerainty over Korea. In Kim Bu-sik's *Samguk Sagi*, there is no record of the story of Dangun Wangkom, the first ancestor of the Korean nation. In Kim Bu-sik's view of history, the origin of Ancient Korea was, so to speak, replaced by that of Ancient China. He describes the invasion of Korea by China as subjugation of the bandits and conversely the invasion of China by Korea as an illicit invasion by bandits. Thus the place of the subject and the object is reversed. Moreover, this is conspicuously clear in the confrontation of Kim Bu-sik with Myo Chung,[44] who was regarded as the advocate of the national culture of the lower stratum of society, on the matter of transferring the capital city.

On the other hand, Il Yon's way of recording history *(Samguk Yusa)* was to collect the legends and folk stories which were popular among the people. The story of Dangun Wangkom, the first ancestor, was recorded for the first time here along with other Korean historical records. Here Dangun is the symbol of the soul of the Korean nation. Il Yon's position and social status enabled him to write of the minjung's joys and sorrows.

4. The matter of which class or group in fact takes responsibility for protecting the nation, that is, whether it is the ruling class or the minjung, can be seen in the following example. When Koryo submitted to the Won[45] dynasty in China, the Sambyolcho,[46] refused to submit. They represented the very will of the minjung. They were driven out from Kangwhado to Jindo and again to Chejudo,[47] but they refused to submit and steadfastly stood up to the invaders.

5. The insurrection of the slave Manjuk,[48] which happened before the rebellion of Sambyolcho, is another case in point. In this insurrection there was a general shake-up of the social order of Koryo at the end of the twelfth century. It was an obvious minjung movement in which the minjung tried to liberate the Nobee (slaves) and improve their social status.

6. During the Japanese (Imjin)[49] and the Mongol (Byongja)[50] invasion, the ruling class did not display the needed courage to protect the nation. But the minjung resisted the invaders and protected the nation through its Righteous Army.[51]

7. The Insurrection of Hong Kyung-rae:[52] Hong Kyung-rae mobilized the inhabitants of the northwestern provinces and stood against the central government, because the government discriminated against the people from this district. In this insurrection, the political consciousness of ordinary people of the district was awakened and mobilized, exerting great influence upon the central regime.

8. The Imsul[53] uprising, which took place in the year of Imsul, was made up of more than forty separate peasant rebellions all over the country. These were occasioned by the tremendous corruption and disorder in the administration of taxes—farm tax, military tax, and the tax on the loaning of grain. In this uprising the political consciousness of the minjung found nationwide expression.

9. The Donghak Revolution in many ways represents the peak of the Kor-

rean minjung movement in history. With the ideology "humanity is heaven,"[54] it fought, on the one hand, the feudal social system in Korea and, on the other, the invasion of Korea by foreign capital. In this revolution the oppressed minjung defined themselves as the subject of their own history and destiny. It must also be stressed that the aspiration of the minjung went beyond a mere longing for political liberation. There was a deep-seated hope for a Messianic Kingdom, since Chon Bong-jun, the leader of the Donghak revolution, was accepted as the Messiah of the minjung. As defined by Ho Kyun,[55] Chon Bong-jun was a "homin."[56]

10. The Righteous Army movement, which spread all over the country when the Eulsa Agreement[57] was signed, was another important minjung movement. Although the leaders of the Righteous Army during the early stages were upper class Confucianists, during the latter stages the leadership moved into the hands of the common people, such as Shin Dol-suk.[58]

11. In the early twentieth century in every part of the country, bands of armed peasants called Hwalbindang[59] rose up. These robbed the rich in order to help the poor. The Hwalbindang had a social ideal which came from the Hong Kil-dong story of Ho Kyun, which was written during the sixteenth century. This social ideal was concerned with the national rights and equality of all and the desire to eliminate the gap between the poor and the rich.

12. The Independence Association movement and the All People's Assembly.[60]

13. The March First movement, in which there was the clearly minjung-led nationalism of the revolutionaries Han Yong-un[61] and Shin Chae-ho.[62]

14. The April 19 (1960) Student Revolution was also an enlightened minjung movement, which was inspired by the ideology of democracy.

In Korean history the minjung movement changes and develops to play an increasingly prominent role. It is this movement that acts as a paradigm for the human rights struggle in Korea today. It is not too much to say that today's struggle for human rights hears the outcry and the protest of persons who participated in the March First movement and the April 1960 Revolution. For it is evident that those who participate in the human rights struggle see their genealogy beginning with the Donghak movement and coming down through the Independence Association movement, the March First movement, and the April 1960 movement. The historical consciousness which has this genealogy of the minjung movement needs to be manifested and realized as an appropriate political hermeneutic for today.

I have given an outline of the Korean minjung reality in terms of some of the significant historical events in which the minjung asserted their identity and claimed their right to be the subjects of history. The events in the history of the minjung movement, however, must be seen only as stepping stones to the onward movement of Korean minjung history. In some ways, therefore, the interim period between events deserves more attention, for it is in these periods that there was the progressive formation of the historical consciousness of the minjung which burst to the surface of history in the kinds of events we have outlined above. This fact is important. Otherwise, we would tend to read minjung history in terms of the biography of minjung heroes, who are no more than the visible peaks of the minjung historical consciousness thrown up during particular historical engagements, rather than in terms of the social biography of the minjung themselves.

We will next look at the corporate spirit of the minjung by looking at the style of literature and art forms that developed during the course of Korean history. It will not be possible in a brief paper like this to go into detailed discussions. All that will be possible is to indicate certain significant moments in this process.

There seems to be a clear correlation between the change and transformations in art styles and the process of humanization and liberation. The transformation in art seems to be concerned with the enlargement of its base moving from the nobility to the minjung; and it concerns all aspects—author, spectator, reader, and content—whether it be in subject matter, orientation or styles of expression. In a way the thesis of André Malraux concerning the transformation of gods in the history of fine arts is also perceivable in the history of Korean art. Its change can be diagrammed as follows: Hyangga[63] → Kyonggichega → Byolgok → Koryo Kayo[64] Jangga → Sokyo → Sijo (a particular kind of verse) → Gasa[65] (another kind of verse more free than Sijo) → Pungyo (novels in Korean ancient times) → Pansori (Korean opera) → Talchum (Mask Dance) → Kaehwagasa[66] (poetic prose) → modern poetry. This process of popularization culminates in the minjung art styles evident particularly in Talchum and Pansori.

A fair amount of research has gone into the history of art in Korea. According to Park Song-ui,[67] Sijo literature, which was aristocratic, emerged earlier than the more popular (minjung) Gasa literature. When we examine further the Sijo and Gasa literature which is extant today, we discover that the names of authors which are known are all noblemen. The names of the authors of later creations, who would be common people, are not known. Also, the Gasa of a known writer is in 3.4 jo rhythm, while that of an anonymous writer or that of a woman would be in 4.4 jo, which is more popular. Judging from these facts, the direction of change in literature was toward the popularization and democratization of what was originally aristocratic in character.

A new trend emerged in the fine arts with the development of Korean novels, such as *Chunhyangjon* and *Shimchungjon*[68] in the seventeenth century. Also, in painting, as for instance in that of Heum Chong,[69] real landscapes, mountains, and streams are depicted. There are also depictions of the actual manners and customs of people as by the painters Kim Hong-do and Shin Yun-bok.[70] These are in contrast to the ethereal and highly imaginative paintings which imitated Chinese fine arts and were acceptable to the nobility.

When the consciousness of minjung painters and artists is awakened, they depict life and reality as it is. Then these art forms become a way of looking at us Koreans as we really are. The consciousness of the ruling class, their learning and their ideologies, are not the window through which we can find our peculiarity. Rather, these have always been obstacles to finding ourselves. In minjung literature there is, or course, much that a refined person would find objectionable, particularly the rudeness, bawdiness, and vulgarities. But these reflect our dirty lives and moreover are a protest against the ruling class. Such protest is particularly evident in the Pansori (Korean opera) and Talchum (mask dance). It is said that these art forms are the artistic sublimation of the repressed *han* of the minjung. When a Pansori is sung in its Kyemyunjo mode,[71] Koreans intuitively feel the *han* of the minjung. Pansori and Talchum are not only expressions of the *han* of the minjung, but also criticize the morality, power, and the pretensions of the ruling class.

In Pansori there is an internal theme and an external theme. The external theme is carried largely in a well-embroidered dialogue/narrative. The internal theme is implicit in the development of the events in the scenes and in the conversations which employ many vulgar words and sayings. If we only perceive the external theme of Pansori, we will see a portrayal of traditional morality. The internal theme is not easily recognized, but for one who understands Pansori it is not too difficult. For instance, in the Pansori *Chunhyangjon*, the internal theme is in the conflict within Chunhyang. Although by birth Chunhyang is a kisaeng,[72] one of a low social class, by virtue she is not a kisaeng. In the conflict between Chunhyang-a-kisaeng and Chunhyang-not-a-kisaeng the latter wins, overcoming the limitation of social status, and achieves her liberation. The internal theme is also found in the conflicts portrayed in other Pansori. For instance in *Sugungga*[73] and *Jugbyukga*[74] the minjung grope for a way to survive under the oppression of tyrants like Jojo (a powerful and crafty Chinese politician of the Tri-States Era)[75] and Yongwang (Dragon King). Seeing Jojo and Yongwang defeated by their own tricks, the low-class people can take courage.

The mask dance also reflects the awakening of the consciousness of the minjung. For instance, Maltugi, a servant in a yangban family, through his satire expresses the resistance of the minjung. In the conflict between Maltugi and the ruling class (yangban), there is the struggle to be free of the restrictions of social status. The conflict is expressed in terms of the interplay between two different ways of thinking and behavior. On the one hand, there is the way of the ruling class which lives in a world that is removed from the reality of people. Living in this world the ruling class are largely nonactive and indulge themselves in a world of fantasy. They are therefore no match for the way of Maltugi, who not only understands reality but also possesses the ability to change and improve it. Through the antics of Maltugi and the behavior of the yangban, there is expressed the idea that all feudal privileges, which oppress the minjung and sap their vitality, must be gotten rid of. Only then would the energy of the minjung, represented in the character of Maltugi, be released. Maltugi boldly ridicules the ruling class, which is defeated because it sticks to its dignity and authority. The mask dance shows that feudal privileges cannot be maintained anymore and that the liberation of the minjung is near.

In the Maltugi scene there is a criticism of feudal privileges. In the Nojang (the Buddhist monk) scene there is a criticism of pretentious ideology; and in the Miyal (old woman) scene there is a criticism of man's oppression of woman. These are the three basic targets of criticism in the mask dance. Through these the minjung express their thirst for liberation.[76]

Pansori and Talchum may be called vehicles for expressing the potential liberation of the oppressed minjung and for finding their own identity, that is, their corporate spirit. While this is true, the ruling class has also used Talchum and Pansori for its own purposes. These have become means of entertainment for the ruling class and have been incorporated into their culture and then used as a means for manipulating and domesticating the minjung. Many scholars have been drawn into the task of making the Pansori and Talchum part of the culture of the ruling class, so that there is the creation of an aesthetics of Talchum. In this process, minjung heroes are introduced in Korean textbooks as the loyal subjects of the ruling class; and the resistance of the minjung is reworked into the aesthetics and culture of the nobility. When this happens, Talchum and Pansori are converted into an opiate for the minjung. Thus, rulers exploit not only the physical blood and sweat of the minjung, but also their spiritual blood and sweat. This kind of exploitation is the most insidious. Harvey Cox calls this the seduction of the spirit, which means that the minjung's religion, their ceremony of resistance and yearning for liberation, is seduced. But the wisdom of the minjung will not always yield to such manipulation. As Kim Chi-ha's hero Maltugi[77] shows, at first Maltugi (the minjung) is swallowed up by the ruling class. The ruling class then gets sick in the stomach and vomits out Maltugi. As the ruler vomits, he is defeated, and Maltugi wins and revives. The same idea is present in a popular novel of Cho Se-hee, *Little Ball Which Is Tossed Up by a Dwarf*.[78] Here, fish are caught in the net of the ruler. But then the thorns of the fish pierce the ruler.

The history of literature and art reflects the process of awakening of the minjung. In this process the minjung's resistance gets stronger and stronger. This is their way of surviving under the oppression of the ruler and finally defeating the ruler.

Another way of looking at the formation of the minjung historical tradition is through their belief in Maitreya. The historical aspiration of the minjung seems to be focused more intensely and meaningfully in this belief than in any other. The poet Ko Eun has recently made this point very forcefully. Let me present his analysis and observations as found in his article "Belief in Maitreya and Minjung,"[79] together with those of other researchers.

Historically, the belief in the Maitreya arose among the oppressed minjung who were against the existing social system. The rulers regarded this belief as heretical and attempted to suppress it.

Maitreya was one of Siddhartha's disciples who died before Siddhartha. He is a popular minjung Buddha whose character and practice are future-oriented. The same is true of his other disciple whom we call Jijang. The stone statue of Maitreya, carved with an axe, which stands on the levee of a rice field, represents the minjung's will for revolution, while the goldplated statue of Buddha in a temple represents salvation from the point of view of nobility.

According to Buddhist cosmology, from the beginning of the cosmos to its end there are several kalpas (aeons). During each kalpa there will appear a Buddha. The first is Kuryuson Buddha, the second is Kunahammuni Buddha, the third is Kapasa Buddha, the fourth is Siddhartha, and the fifth is Maitreya. Siddhartha Buddha is of the present Sava world, while Maitreya is the Buddha of the future Yongwha world, which follows the Sava world. If we make supplication to the Siddhartha Buddha (Amita Buddha), we will enter the Buddhist paradise in the West after our death. If, however, we make supplication to Maitreya, we will realize the future Yongwha world which follows the Sava world. Here we find a contrast between belief in Amita, that is reaching paradise, and belief in Maitreya, that is realization of the Yongwha world. Also, the belief in Maitreya is divided into the belief of Maitreya going up to the heaven of Dosol, and the belief of Maitreya coming down to establish the Yongwha world. In other words, he will come to this dirty world to make it pure; and the Saint King Jun-ryun[80] will appear to realize the just and ideal society of the Yongwha world.

The belief in Amita is the promise of paradise after death. It cannot be the hope of people who are living the lives of slaves, experiencing poverty, violence, and oppression. These are alientated from the movement of history, which is controlled by the ruling class. The Buddhism of the ruling class (Amita) was used to teach people the doctrines of renunciation and the transitoriness of all forms of material existence. This was done in order that the people might give up resisting. It also glossed over what was happening in society by saying that wealth is the result of one's former good life. In the period of the Silla dynasty, Amita Buddhism was used to placate the minjung by saying that even a slave could enter the Buddhist paradise.

However, belief in the Maitreya became a countervailing view of the people. They believed that the Maitreya would come soon even though he was supposed to come some billion years later. Belief in Maitreya and the thirst for coming ignited many resistance movements. This was so in the case of the resistance of the Latter Baikje,[81] to the Silla dynasty.[82] Here, in this resistance, Kyonhwon, the founder of Latter Baikje, was suppressed by the Buddhism of Kaesong (capital of Koryo dynasty), and the belief in the Amita was encouraged. Later, Kungye, who came from the royal Silla dynasty, claimed that he was the prince of the Maitreya. He proclaimed, "Now is the time of the Maitreya!" He called his two sons Bodhisattva. He began a revolution to overthrow the Silla dynasty.

Wangkon (A.D. 918), the founder of the Koryo dynasty, also participated in the people's belief in the Maitreya and revolution. His Maitreya revolution with the people brought the history of the Old Age to an end and began the history of the Middle Age.

Maitreya Buddhism has contributed to the revolutionary practice and belief of the minjung. It is a self-helping belief which is different from Amita Buddhism in that it is concerned with the realization of the new Yongwha world.

Under the Confucianist society of the Yi dynasty,[83] the belief in Maitreya atrophied into a superstitious belief which was mixed up with shamanism. This superstitious belief was that of the lowest classes. However, we can still see the belief in Maitreya coming up on the historical stage at certain times, for instance, when the suffering of the people becomes extremely intense, when there is the purge of the literati, or when there is a foreign invasion.

During the period of King Sukjong (1674–1720), Chang Kil-san, who was called the "bandit of Maitreya," began a guerrilla movement as a Maitreya revolution to overthrow the Confucianist system. The revolutionary thought of Chang Kil-san has informed and inspired many revolts and revolutions. It is significant that the Donghak revolution also claims this ancestry.

After the Japanese invasion, revolutionary movements were not possible, and the people fell into deep despair. During this period the belief in Maitreya was transformed into various distorted pseudo-religions, such as Baikbaikkyo, Yongwhakyo,[84] and others, which are still found in the valley of Mount Keryong.[85]

In the sketch given above we can see clearly that the historical aspiration of the minjung is constantly focused on the belief in the Maitreya. Up to the present, the belief in the Maitreya is widely prevalent among the Korean minjung. It is associated with the dragon (Miruk), and in many places the Maitreya is carved on stone. Eujin Miruk, the largest stone statue of Buddha in Korea, is called Maitreya, even though it is actually of Kwaneum, the goddess of mercy. Also, large stones are usually called Maitreya. We see here how deeply embedded the belief in Maitreya is in the corporate spirit of the minjung.

Belief in Amita and belief in Maitreya conflict with each other, both in dogma and in their historical appearances. In China and Japan, Amita Buddhism flourished while Maitreya Buddhism disappeared. One rarely finds traces of Maitreya Buddhism in these two countries. However, in Korea it is still alive together with Amita Buddhism.[86] This fact is important, for it eloquently bears testimony to the survival of the oppressed minjung throughout history—their resistance and their yearning for the coming new world and their refusal to accept the promise of an otherworldly paradise. Hatata,[87] a Japanese historian, admits that Korean people in spite of their powerlessness have been able to resist powerful foreign invasions because of the belief in the Maitreya.

We have seen Korean minjung history from four perspectives, all of which bear witness to the inner power which made the minjung survive throughout history.

Memo for a Scheme of Minjung Theology

Now, the task for Korean minjung theology is to testify that in the Mission of God in Korea there is a confluence of the minjung tradition in Christianity and the Korean minjung tradition. It is to participate and interpret theologically the events which we consider to be God's intervention in history and the work of the Holy Spirit. To participate in and to interpret these events we need to maintain both traditions. I call this the pneumatological historical interpretation, which I would contrast with the traditional Christological interpretation.

However, I would maintain that the traditional Christological interpretation is also necessary, for it affirms that Jesus of Nazareth has redeemed me from sin. The pneumatological interpretation goes further and asserts that I imitate the life of Jesus and repeat in my life the events of the life of Jesus. Although these two viewpoints are not antagonistic but supplementary, in minjung theology we must give greater emphasis to the work of the Holy Spirit.

On this basis, let me introduce an example of Korean minjung theology, namely, Kim Chi-ha's theological thoughts in a memo for the plot of *Chang Il-dam*.[88] Let me summarize some of the points he makes in this unique minjung theology.

1. Chang Il-dam is a preacher of liberation, who is an heir to both the Korean minjung tradition and the Christian minjung tradition. The starting point of his mission is "coincidence with the bottom" which is his spiritual awakening. He calls this experience "complete conformity with the *han* of hell." It is the experience of being "in one mind with" those who have been cursed by society and expelled from it. These are the robbers, murderers, etc. Kim Chi-ha views such trangressions as the internally reversed expression of *han*, which is formed by oppression. However, Chang Il-dam also meets here the true mind that is God in the mind of the dehumanized persons. Therefore, when the bottom is reversed outward and upward, it becomes heaven and the Messiah of the minjung can appear there. In this context, he believes that humanity is heaven.

Chang Il-dam goes to a brothel and sees a prostitute delivering a child. Her body is ravaged with venereal disease and tuberculosis and she is mentally deranged. She is the living dead. Chang Il-dam receives a deep realization of truth seeing a new life (God) in this filthy cesspool of humanity. He decides to preach human liberation. It is not the workers or peasants, the leading class of the communist revolution, but the most dehumanized and immoral persons in the bottommost place that will be the heirs of the Kingdom of the Messiah.

2. The most important thesis of Kim Chi-ha's minjung theology is "the unification of God and revolution." For him, minjung theology is the unification of Donghak and Christianity, the unification of the renewal of the human spirit and the revolutionary change for justice in the social structure, the unification of idea and practice, the unification of personal prayer and the corporate Mass, the coincidence of heaven and earth, and the coincidence of worldly food (bread) and heavenly food (freedom).

Kim Chi-ha repeatedly emphasizes the fact that this unification is not a compromise or a mixture of two polarities, but that both must be accomplished simultaneously. Kim Chi-ha says that he was able to find this insight and experience not in Marxian thought but in Catholic belief.

3. The unification of God and revolution is of course also a revolution. But Kim Chi-ha calls it a "great revolution" which is of a higher order than a social revolution. He expresses this in poetic words and calls it "eternal revolution" or "the road travelled by a wayfarer." A passage from his memo states it as follows:

> My paradise is not in this land. It is a single white road which is like a wind moved by time, passing Seoul towards the world, universe and sky. This road is the paradise; and I am a wayfarer who follows the road.

In these words we can see Chang Il-dam's dimension of revolution. In another passage Kim Chi-ha writes, "his task is to travel against the flow of the stream of the unfortunate minjung's degradation." This flowing stream of degradation may be diagrammed as follows: farmer→ urban immigrant→ worker→ unemployed→ slum dweller→ losing of humanity and morality→ theft→ crime→ prison.

4. Kim Chi-ha's theology is the theology of *han*. He decides to act as "the messenger of *han*, the medium of murmuring grievances, because this peninsula is full of the *han* of aggrieved and weeping ghosts." Kim Chi-ha writes that as the priest of *han* he goes beyond socialism:

> When I compare my literature with that of Solzhenitsyn, there is one thing in common. Both of us reveal the *han* of the oppressed and the facts which are buried without being known to the world. My task and theme is to show the facts which are filled with the *han* of the miserable ghosts of people who have been sacrificed. We existed before Solzhenitsyn did. The world has experienced the historical limit of socialism. I am younger than Solzhenitsyn. I am a humorous optimist. But I think we are both the same in that we are priests of *han*.

The accumulation of the *han* of the oppressed minjung will be changed and activated into revolutionary energy through the act of "cutting":

Fundamentally it means to cut all adherence to the secular world in order that one may be for the revolution of the secular world. It is to sever the link which permits circulation. There is a terrible accumulation of *han* which will burn in endless hate, massacre, revenge and destruction. Therefore we need the repeated cutting which stops the vicious circular explosion and sublimates it to a higher spiritual power.

This priest of *han* sees the vocation of the minjung church as consoling and resolving the *han* of the minjung. The church must break the vicious circle of violence caused by *han*. The church must convert circulation into movement. The church must accept limited violence to do so. The church must be a sanctuary for radicals. It must be a repository for all progressive thought.

Kim Chi-ha's theology of *han* is different from both socialism and the traditional theology of redemption. The dialectics of *han* and of cutting are different from the socialist understanding of dialectical materialism and revolution. In Western theology, the church is responsible for redeeming the people and preaches the need for repentance from sin and penitence. This is the ideology of the ruling class. In Kim Chi-ha's theology the church resolves the *han* of the minjung and consoles them. But the minjung themselves seek their own liberation and salvation in the process of establishing their identity as the subjects of history.

5. Chang Il-dam is, in fact, the Jesus of Korea, born in Korea in the 1970s. His birth, itinerating, preaching of liberation, trial, and execution are the reproduction of the life of Jesus. Chang Il-dam is executed when he is thirty-three—the same age as Kim Chi-ha when he wrote the notes for *Chang Il-dam*. Here the poet transposes his own image upon that of Chang Il-dam, who is himself a duplicate figure of Jesus. The biography of Chang Il-dam is the social biography of the Korean minjung and means far more than the Hong Kil-dong story of Ho Kyun. While the story of Hong Kil-dong and his kingdom of Yuldo savor of a Utopia, Chang Il-dam's idea of an Eastern Paradise has the character of the Millennium. This is why Chang Il-dam is more popular.

6. Chang Il-dam is beheaded as a vicious criminal, but he revives three days later and cuts off the head of the betrayer and places his own head upon the betrayer's body. This peculiar combination of the body of the evil man and the head of truth indicates that Kim Chi-ha thought that even the most wicked villain will be saved at the end. Through the carrier that is the body of the evil man, Chang Il-dam's good news of liberation, like a wild and stormy wind, goes everywhere.

7. What is the meaning of the metaphor of the body of evil which carries on it the good news of liberation? According to Kim Chi-ha, the good news of liberation is the substance or content of theology becoming indigenous in Korea. He wants to combine the Gospel (the story of Jesus) with the depictions of the *han* of the minjung to establish Korean minjung theology. Chang

Il-dam's story is similar to the story of Jesus and is written in the form of the Pansori, which is one of the traditional forms for expressing the *han* of the minjung.

8. Finally, Kim Chi-ha vehemently protests against his minjung theology being branded as communism. His theology, and in fact all minjung theology, move beyond communism to speak in terms of the *han* of the wretched of the earth. This effort has to be carried on and developed further, not only theoretically but also practically. This should be the continuing task of all minjung theologians.

NOTES

(In the notes there are citations of publications from Seoul and Tokyo. Many of these are either in Korean or Japanese. Some of these are now being translated into English.)

1. From the transcript of Kim Chi-ha's court statements during his trial, May-September 1976; in English see Kim Chi Ha, *The Gold Crowned Jesus and Other Writings*, ed. Chong Sun Kim and Shelly Killen (Maryknoll, N.Y.: Orbis Books, 1978).
2. Here "methodology of socio-economic history" comprises a broad spectrum of social scientific methods, and it should be distinguished from the method of historical materialism. Cf. Lee Gi-baik, *Korean History: A New Study,* revised edition (Seoul, 1976); Ahn Byung-jik, *March First Movement* (Seoul, 1975). After this paper was published in 1979, I became aware of some theological works on this line. Cf. Suh In-suk, *The Cry of God: The Liberation of the Poor* (Seoul, 1979); Norman Gottwald, *The Tribes of Yahweh* (Maryknoll, N.Y.: Orbis Books, 1979).
3. Cf. Gerd Theissen, *Sociologie der Jesusbewegung,* 1979; Sasagu Arai, *Jesus and His Age* (Tokyo, 1974).
4. Paul Tillich, *Systematic Theology* (Chicago: University of Chicago Press, 1951), vol. 1.
5. Cf. Choo Jae-yong, "100 Years' History of Korean Protestant Church," in *Theological Studies,* 21 (1979); Suh Nam-dong, "Our Resurrection and the April Revolution" in *The Voice of the People,* April 1979.
6. A more thorough discussion of this point is found in Norman Gottwald's *Tribes of Yahweh,* which was published after this paper.
7. Sasagu Arai, *Jesus and His Age,* pp. 145–146, cf. 102f. It is interesting to note how even the bearers of the Q source (probably collected by the so-called "wandering charismatics") saw the tax-collectors and sinners, that is, the *'am ha'aretz,* as a negative existence to be converted, in contrast to the viewpoint of Mark's Gospel which probably can be traced back to the historical Jesus. Cf. Arai, *Jesus and His Age;* Tagawa, *The Gospel of Mark* (Tokyo, 1972), p. 218f and *A Cross-Section of Primitive Christianity* (Tokyo, 1968).
8. Tagawa, *Gospel of Mark,* p. 251f.
9. See my article, "Our Resurrection and the April Revolution."
10. Rosemary Reuther, *The Radical Kingdom* (New York: Harper & Row, 1970), p. 15. Cf. Ernst Benz, *Evolution and Christian Hope: Man's Concept of the Future from the Early Fathers to Teilhard de Chardin* (Garden City, N.Y.: Doubleday, 1965), p. 15; Karl Loewith, *Meaning in History* (Chicago: University of Chicago Press, 1949), p. 160f.
11. Karl Loewith, *Meaning in History,* pp. 145–159; Ernst Benz, *Evolution and Christian Hope,* pp. 35–48. Also see my article, "The Third Age of the Holy Spirit," *Christian Thought,* October 1975, which is included in my collection of theological essays, *Theology in an Age of Transition* (Seoul, 1976).
12. R.P.C. Hanson, "The Divinity of the Holy Spirit," 1969, in *New Theology No. 7,* ed. Martin Marty and Dean Peerman (New York: Macmillan, 1970).
13. André Malraux, *The Voices of Silence* (Garden City, N.Y.: Doubleday, 1953); *The Metamorphosis of the Gods* (Garden City, N.Y.: Doubleday, 1960). Cf. J. Cobb, *Christ in a Pluralistic Age* (Philadelphia: Westminster, 1975), p. 31ff.
14. Lee Gi-baik, *Korean History*.

15. Eric Gritsch, *Reformer Without a Church* (Philadelphia: Fortress, 1967); M. Bensing, *Thomas Muentzer* (Leipzig, 1965); Kurazuka et al., tr. and ed., *Documents from the Radical Reformers;* Ernst Benz, *Evolution and Christian Hope.*

16. Chun Bong-joon (1854–1895): the chief leader of the Donghak Peasant Revolution (1894–1895).

17. Ahn Byung-jik, *March First Movement.*

18. See in particular Lee Wu-song and Kang Man-gil, *Understanding of Korean History,* 2 vols. (Seoul, 1976).

19. Ancient Chosen: the first kingdom of Korean history. Dangun Wangkom: the legendary ancestor of the Korean nation around 4 B.C.

20. Unified Silla Kingdom, A.D. 668-918.

21. Yukdupum: The second rank in the bureaucratic system of Silla Kingdom.

22. Jingol: The first rank in the bureaucratic system of Silla Kingdom.

23. Dynasty of Koryo, A.D. 918–1388.

24. Sadaibu: Scholar-bureaucrat.

25. Chosen: The Yi Dynasty (1388–1910).

26. Yangban: Bureaucratic nobility of Yi Dynasty.

27. King Sungjong, 1469–1494.

28. King Kwanghae Gun, 1608–1623.

29. King Soonjo, 1800–1834.

30. Chungin: The class ranking just below the bureaucratic nobility in Yi Dynasty.

31. Sori: A lower class government official in Yi Dynasty.

32. Donghak movement: Donghak Peasant Revolution (1894–1895).

33. Independence Association, 1896–1898.

34. March First Movement, 1919: The great nationwide demonstration for independence from Japan.

35. The April Student Revolution of 1960 which toppled the Syngman Rhee dictatorship.

36. *Chronicle of the Three Kingdoms* (Koguryo, Silla, Baekje), ed. Kim Bu-sik, the Prime Minister during Koryo Dynasty, 1145. Koguryo Kingdom, 37 B.C.–A.D. 668.

37. King Bongsang, Koguryo Kingdom, A.D. 292–300.

38. Prime Minister Changjori, A.D. 300.

39. Kungye: Founder of Taebong Kingdom, A.D. 918.

40. Kyonhwon: Founder of Hubaikje Kingdom, A.D. 892–918.

41. Chung Chang Won: A Buddhist temple in Nara City, Japan.

42. *Samguk Sagi: The Chronicle of the Three Kingdoms.* (See note 36 above.)

43. *Samguk Yusa:* A collection of historical stories edited by a Buddhist monk Il-yon (A.D. 1281).

44. Myo Chung: Buddhist monk, advisor to the King, and leader of the Myo Chung Insurrection, 1135. Here Myo Chung is regarded as the advocate of the traditional culture of the low, fundamental stratum of society.

45. Won Dynasty, 1271–1368 (Mongolian rule).

46. Sambyolcho: The name of a battalion of Koryo Dynasty.

47. Kangwhado: A big island off the west coast from Seoul. Jindo: A big island at the southwest end of Korea. Chejudo: The biggest island, a province, off the south coast of Korea.

48. Manjuk: A slave who instigated an insurrection in 1198.

49. Imjin: The year 1592.

50. Byongja: The year 1636.

51. The volunteer army which was formed to resist a foreign invasion, in contrast to government mercenaries.

52. Hong Kyung-rae Insurrection, 1811.

53. Imsul Uprising, 1862.

54. The core doctrine of Donghak religion. Donghak means "Eastern learning" as contrasted to "Western learning" (Amita).

55. Ho Kyun, a well-known man of letters during the reign of King Kwanghaegun (1608–1623) and the author of *The Tale of Hong Kil-dong,* the first novel to be written in the Korean alphabet (Hangul). The hero, Hong Kil-dong, is a Korean Robin Hood.

56. Homin: Ho Kyun wrote *An Essay on Homin,* and he meant by Homin the mobilizer of the *han* of the minjung for revolution, who himself comes out of the minjung. Someone similar to the Judges in the Old Testament.

57. Eulsa Protectorate Agreement, 1905: The Korea-Japan agreement which deprived Korea of its diplomatic rights, which happened before the Japanese annexation of Korea, 1910.

58. Shin Dol-suk, a commander of the Righteous Army, 1907.

59. Hwalbindang, a gang of bandits for the cause of social justice, during the time of late Yi Korea.

60. All-People's Assembly: People's rally for civil rights and modernization, 1898.

61. Han Yong-un (1879–1944), a Buddhist monk, a well-known writer and one of the thirty-three persons who signed the "Independence Statement" of March 1, 1919.

62. Shin Chae-ho (1880–1936), a Korean historian, theorist, and fighter in the Independence movement.

63. Hyangga: A specific style of poem in the era of the Silla dynasty.

64. Kyonggichega, Byolgok, Koryo Kayo: Specific types of poetry in the era of the Koryo dynasty.

65. Jangga, Sokyo, Sijo, Gasa: Particular types of poetry in the era of the Yi dynasty.

66. Kaehwagasa: The latest type of poetry of the era of the Yi dynasty.

67. Park Song-ui, *An Outline of the History of Korean Culture,* vol. IV (Seoul, 1972).

68. *Chunhyangjon* and *Shimchungjon:* Classical novels of the seventeenth century, written in Hangul.

69. Heum Chong: A painter who lived at the time of King Soohjong (1674–1720).

70. Kim Hong-do and Shin Yun-bok: Painters during the same time as Heum Chong.

71. Kyemyunjo mode: A melancholic melody in Pansori which expresses the sorrow and transitoriness of life.

72. Kisaeng: A girl who sings and dances at a special place of entertainment.

73. Sugungga: "The Song of the Undersea Royal Palace," from a script of a Pansori.

74. Jugbyukga, a script of a Pansori, a chapter from a Chinese classical novel, *Stories of the Tri-States.*

75. Tri-States Era: A.D. 3–4 in Chinese history.

76. See further Cho Dong-il and Kim Heung-kyu, *Understanding Pansori* (Seoul, 1978), pp. 26f. and Cho Dong-il, *Aesthetics of Korean Mask Dance* (Seoul, 1975), p. 226ff.

77. Kim Chi-ha's idea of Maltugi, quoted from his "Memo in Prison, 1974–75."

78. Cho Se-hee, *Little Ball Which Is Tossed Up by a Dwarf* (Seoul, 1978).

79. Ko Eun, "Belief in Maitreya and Minjung," in *Literature and Intelligence,* Spring 1979. Cf. Kim Chi-kyun and Che In-whan, eds., *Studies on Buddhism of Silla Era* (Tokyo, 1975); Han Jong-man, ed., *The Idea and Its Development: Minjung Buddhism in Recent Korea* (Seoul, 1980).

80. Junryun the Saint King is awaited as the ruler of the Yongwha World, which is equivalent to the millennium.

81. Latter Baikje, A.D. 892–936.

82. Silla Kingdom, 57 B.C.–A.D. 935.

83. Yi Dynasty, 1392–1910.

84. Both Baikbaikkyo and Yongwhakyo were conspicuous pseudo-religions which used sex and property as means to dazzle and exploit the people. Together with numerous other sects these flourished during the period of the harsh Japanese rule in Korea. Most of these sects preached the coming of Maitreya Buddha.

85. Mt. Keryong: A mountain in the middle of South Korea which was believed by the people to be the place of the advent of the Messiah Chong Doryong, who is mentioned in *Chongkamnok,* an apocalyptic and astrological work which is anonymous. It was widely read by Koreans in the eighteenth and nineteenth centuries. See Ryu Tong-shik, *The History and Structure of Korean Shamanism* (Seoul, 1975); *Folk Religions and Culture of Korea* (Seoul, 1978).

86. See Minamoto, "The Characteristics of the Silla Jongto Buddhism," in Kim Chi-kyun, *Studies on Buddhism,* p. 315.

87. Hatata Takasi, *The History of Korea* (Iwanami: Tokyo, 1951).

88. Based on Kim Chi-ha's own prison transcript "Memo in Prison, 1974–75," and on the transcript of his court statements during his trial, May–September 1976. Cf. *Asceticism,* by Kim Chi-ha, ed. by the Publication Committee for Kim Chi-ha's Writings, Tokyo, 1978.

CHAPTER X

Messiah and Minjung: Discerning Messianic Politics over against Political Messianism

KIM YONG-BOCK

In this essay we intend to use the category of messianism as a conceptual tool to determine the relation between minjung and power. We shall first define the term "minjung" as the subject of history and clarify an approach to historical reality. In the context of such an understanding of history, the relationship between the people and power will be clarified. To do this we will do three things. First, we will trace messianic traditions in Korea. Second, we will use messianic categories to analyze Japanese colonial power in Korea, the Korean Communist regime, and the present government of Korea. Finally, we will seek to shed light on the messianic politics of the minjung in terms of the liberation of the minjung.

The minjung are the permanent reality of history. Kingdoms, dynasties, and states rise and fall; but the minjung remain as a concrete reality in history, experiencing the comings and goings of political powers. Although the minjung understand themselves in relation to the power which is in command, they are not confined by that power. The minjung transcend the power structures which attempt to confine them through the unfolding of their stories. Power has its basis in the minjung. But power as it expresses itself in political powers does not belong to the minjung. These powers seek to maintain themselves; and they rule the minjung.

When we view minjung in relation to power, we define the minjung in political terms. The political definition of minjung also includes their socio-economic determination. The political and socio-economic conditions of the minjung are not just objective realities for socio-economic analysis. Rather, we have in mind the total subjective experiences of the minjung—their aspirations and sufferings, their struggles and defeats which form their social biography. Therefore, our reflection on the minjung involves not only objective socio-economic analysis, but also an empathy for their expressive language and culture.

The identity and reality of the minjung is known not by a philosophical or scientific definition of their essence or nature, but rather through their own stories—their social biographies which the minjung themselves create and therefore can tell best. This story of the minjung or their social biography is told vis-à-vis the power structure that rules the people; and therefore power is the antagonist in the story, while the people are the subjects. The minjung themselves are the protagonists. Thus the story of the minjung entails a historical understanding which regards them as subjects—not as objects—of their own story and destiny.

In discussions of the minjung as the subjects of history there have arisen several questions. The first is about the unclearness of the concept of the minjung. The second is about the social determination or definition of the minjung; the third is whether or not the minjung have been "glorified" into an ideal notion.

We have an obligation to clarify these questions, but before we do so we should indicate our basic position. "Minjung" is not a concept or object which can be easily explained or defined. "Minjung" signifies a living reality which is dynamic, changing, and complex. This living reality defines its own existence and generates new acts and dramas in history; and it refuses in principle to be defined conceptually.

One of the issues involved in the above questions is the difference between the minjung and the Marxist proletariat. The proletariat is defined socio-economically, while the minjung is known politically. Politics as power relations is understood comprehensively and thus includes socio-economic relations. Philosophically speaking, the proletariat is "confined" to socio-economic (materialistic) determination, so that it is bound to historical possibilities and the internal logic of history. The minjung suffers these limitations in reality; yet the minjung as historical subject transcends the socio-economic determination of history, and unfolds its stories beyond mere historical possibilities to historical novelty—a new drama beyond the present history to a new and transformed history.

This difference between the minjung and the proletariat entails different views of history. Minjung history has a strong transcendental or transcending dimension—a beyond history—which is often expressed in religious form. There is a close relationship between religion and the minjung's perception of history. Even if minjung history does not involve religious elements in an explicit manner, its folklore or cultural elements play a transcending function similar to religion in the perception of history.

In scope too there is a difference between the minjung and the proletariat. The former is a dynamic, changing concept. Woman belongs to minjung when she is politically dominated by man. An ethnic group is a minjung group when it is politically dominated by another group. A race is minjung when it is dominated by another powerful ruling race. When intellectuals are suppressed by the military power elite, they belong to minjung. Of course, the same applies to the workers and farmers. However, the proletariat is rigidly defined in socio-economic terms in all political circumstances. It is even a name through which a totalitarian political dictatorship is justified.

Historically, the minjung is always in the condition of being ruled, a situation which they seek to overcome. Therefore, minjung history will never permit the glorification of the minjung so that its name may be used to justify any kind of political dictatorship, especially the totalitarian kind. In many ways, the minjung view of history has an affinity with the cultural values of Western democracy; but the constituency of the minjung is the poor and the suppressed who are alienated in their political and socio-economic condition.

Often we are asked about the difference between the idea of minjung and the Maoist notion of "inmin" (人民). Here, we should recognize the fact that the Maoist notion upholds the supremacy of the proletariat, and that total dictatorship—which is antagonistic to the minjung and therefore contrary to minjung politics—is an integral part of Maoism.

The minjung is not a self-contained or completely defined concept, but a living entity, which has an ever-unfolding drama and story. The minjung has a social and political biography. The minjung reality is known only through its biography, its story, its hope, and sufferings. The socio-political biography of the minjung is the key historical point of reference for minjung theology in addition to references of biblical stories. The problem with philosophical and ideological views of history is that they reduce the total socio-political biography (the record of socio-political experiences) of the minjung to an appendix to their systems or concepts. Rather than co-opt the story of the minjung into their systems, philosophy and ideology should serve to clarify the story of the minjung, in which the pain and suffering of the people as well as their hopes and aspirations are expressed.

The next question we need to clarify concerns the historical subjecthood or subjectivity of the minjung. The minjung is the protagonist in the historical drama. It is the subject and its socio-political biography is the predicate. In the Korean context, one may suspect that the notion of the subjecthood (主体) from North Korean Communism has sneaked into minjung theology. Once again, we should not mistake the fact that in North Korea the notion of "juche" refers to the autonomy of the national totalitarian dictatorship which uses the name of the proletariat. It is a sort of "realized" subjecthood in the form of a dictatorial state. But in minjung theology, the subjecthood of the minjung is in between the times of the "not yet" and the "already."

The minjung are not yet fully the subjects of history. However, their subjectivity is being realized through their struggles against oppressive powers and repressive social structures. In so doing, the minjung have risen up to be subjects of their own destiny, refusing to be condemned to the fate of being objects of manipulation and suppression. The minjung have their own stories to tell over against the stories or the dominant ideologies of the rulers. When we say that the minjung are the subjects of history, we are not exalting them in political terms but are affirming as authentic their identification of themselves as the masters of their own history which is told in their socio-political biography. We should neither glorify nor absolutize the minjung, for they suffer under their historical predicament. In traditional theological terms we may say that they are under and in a state of sin.

Up to now, historical writings have usually centered on the ruling power. A typical example of this is Confucian historiography. It is the chronicle of the king as the ruler. Here the people do not appear as actors in history.[1] Our proposal is that we read history from below, from the point of view of the minjung, rather than from the point of the view of the ruling power. History is the process in which the minjung realize their own destiny to be the free subjects of history and to participate in the Messianic Kingdom. This theological notion of Messianic Kingdom has been chosen to develop a minjung perspective on history.

The messianic aspirations of the people arise out of the historical confrontation between the people and the powers. The Messianic Kingdom is not an illusory or utopian dream, but is the core of the history for which the suffering people, the poor and oppressed, struggle. It is therefore concrete. Herein lies the origin and the basis of messianic language. It does not come from a dreamlike world. When we talk about messianism, we are implying a messiah who is of the people and whom the people feel to be theirs. Both terms, "messianism" and "messiah," are often used to indicate a certain "fanaticism" or to describe a hero or elitist cult. Although these negative qualities exist in the history of messiahs and messianisms, they are external to the essence of true messianism. Here, the Messiah emerges from the suffering people and identifies with the suffering people.

Theologically, the messianic expectation of the people is based upon theodicy, which is the victory of the justice of God over evil in history. The Messiah and the people actualize the justice of God in history. This historical process is a radical transformation, in which the new one arrives as the old one departs. Messianism is an eschatological phenomenon closely linked to an apocalyptic perception of history.

From our point of view, the focal point of messianism is the general resurrection of all the people (the minjung), for historical judgment against Evil and its followers. The general resurrection of all the people is a concrete vision of history in which the people realize their corporate subjectivity in participating in the Messianic Kingdom. The content of the Messianic Kingdom may be viewed as *justice, koinonia,* and *shalom* (peace or becoming whole). *Justice* is a faithful relation or a faithful interweaving of the stories of the people and power so that there is no contradiction between them; *koinonia* is the content of the creative interaction that will take place among the people; and *shalom* is the wholesome development of humanity and its well-being. These messianic categories which we have described briefly can be developed into a social philosophy which takes into account the story of the minjung and operates with a messianic view of history.

In a brief paper, it is not possible to enter into a discussion of all aspects of the large and complex issue of messianism. In this paper, we will concentrate on the conceptual difference between power-messianism and Jesus-messianism, or ruler-messianism and minjung-messianism, or political messianism and messianic servanthood. Jesus-messianism or messianic servanthood is a radical challenge to all forms of political, royal, and power messianisms. It is concerned with saving and transforming the minjung so that its subjecthood may be realized. Hence, all powers must be under the rule of Jesus the Messiah, who came to be the Servant of the minjung, who died for them, and who rose from the dead so that the minjung may rise from the power of death historically and not just at the end of time.

With this conceptual background we will turn very briefly to an examination of Korean messianic movements. The oldest significant instance of messianism in Korea came with the introduction of Buddhism, particularly the Maitreya Buddhist tradition. The Maitreya Buddha is known as the Messianic Buddha who comes from the West Paradise to rescue the people from suffering. As yet there has been no substantial study of the Maitreya Messianic Buddha movement although there are several indications of its influence in Korean history. The first such indication is the commentary of Won Hyo, a Silla scholar-monk, on the scriptures concerning the Maitreya Buddha. Won Hyo's famous doctrine that "the ordinary person is Buddha" (凡夫聖人) indicates a strong influence of the popular egalitarian ethics of messianism. Recent archaeological discoveries suggest that the Maitreya formed a decisive ideological backbone for the Unified Silla dynasty of the Three Kingdoms Period. Toward the end of that dynasty, Maitreya Messianic Buddhism influenced the popular resistance movements against dynastic regimes. One may conclude that the people in Korea have been under the strong influence of the messianic movement and ideology of Maitreya Buddhism throughout history.[2] Even during the Yi dynasty, which was dominated by neo-Confucian orthodox ideology, the idea of the Maitreya Buddha was *alive* among the people.

Recently the question has come up about the role Buddhism, especially Maitreya Buddhism, played in undergirding the ideology of the state. It is a question in the area of political messianism which attributes to the state a

188Kim Yong-bock

redemptive messianic role. The historical facts which will answer this question have yet to be determined; but Maitreya Buddhism seems to have played two rather contradictory roles during the time of the Silla dynasty.

The second messianic tradition in Korea is the tale of Hon Kil-dong.[3] Ho Kyun, a Chungin (member of the social class between the ruling yangban class and the commoners), wrote this popular novel in the vernacular language of Korea so that the common people could read it easily. The story was told and retold and was most popular during the Yi dynasty, when the ruling power was making the people suffer most.

The scenario is as follows: The alienated social hero Hong Kil-dong, like the author a Chungin, leaves home and joins a group of bandits, because he cannot fulfill his life's ambitions and goals in the existing society. Collecting a gang around him he calls it "hwalbindang" (party to rescue the poor). The hero of the story attacks the rich and distributes wealth to the poor. This creates great social disturbances. Finally, the hero is persuaded by his father to leave the country, and he goes off to an island called Yuldo—his paradise, which is characterized by the absence of social division and contradiction between the yangban class and the common people. With its picture of a messianic kingdom, the novel prompted much social imagination among the people. This novel seems to have been heavily influenced by Maitreya Messianic Buddhist ideas.

The third is the famous Donghak messianic movement. This movement emerged in the middle of the nineteenth century, when the Yi dynasty was progressively becoming decadent and the suffering of the people reached extreme proportions. During this time the ruling yangban population increased but agricultural production decreased at an alarming rate. The Japanese invasion under Hideyoshi caused many disruptions and not much land was put under cultivation. There was also a decrease in the number of common people, the productive base of society. Therefore the exploitation of the poor peasants by the yangban was extremely severe.

In this historical context, the Donghak religious movement manifested itself as a messianic religion among the common people. This may be called a truly indigenous minjung messianic religion. It played a powerful role in the Donghak Peasant Rebellion of 1895, and in the March First Independence movement of 1919.

In 1860, Choe Je-u (Choe Messiah or Choe Jesus) founded the Donghak religious movement. Although he was disillusioned and alienated from society, he was a religiously sensitive person. His basic teaching or doctrine was that humanity is heaven (人乃天). On this basis he advocated egalitarian ethical practice. He believed that there will be a second apocalypse when the whole world will be destroyed and a new era will emerge. This hope led his believers to revolutionary actions. This movement may owe something to Catholic literature which was appearing in the early nineteenth century when Catholics were being severely persecuted. However, there is no doubt that the messianism in Donghak is unmistakably indigenous. It played a powerful role in people's movements in the late nineteenth and early twentieth centuries.

The fourth is the Christian movement in Korea. Although to start with it was a Western missionary movement, it soon became a Korean Christian movement among the suffering people of Korea.

The messianic impact of Christianity upon the Korean people took place during the Great Revival of 1907. Here the messianic dynamic of this Korean Christianity unfolded itself in the successive actions of the National Liberation movement against Japanese colonial rule. Korean Christians were agents of messianism in the people's movement. Christians struggled against the Japanese Imperial Education Rescript; and they participated in the March First Independence movement of 1919. The next historical expression of the Korean Christian messianic movement was when it confronted the Japanese Imperial Authority and Japan's ultranationalism over the issue of Jinja (神社) worship. The story of martyrdom of Pastor Chu Ki-chol, a devout Christian nationalist, reveals the nature of this struggle.

The most dramatic manifestation of minjung messianism in Korea was the March First Independence movement of 1919. Korean historians have carefully documented this movement and show the minjung to be its motive power.[4] They also show that the messianic traditions of Buddhism, Donghak religion, and Christianity joined together to form a minjung messianic religious foundation which became the backbone and the dynamic of the March First movement. This movement produced an axial transformation in the history of modern Korean people; and it has become the paradigmatic or root experience of the Korean people. It supplies the motivation, scope, and direction for the minjung to create their own new future.[5]

The Christian messianic movement of the people can be understood more clearly when we see it against the background of *political messianism* in Korea during the last fifty years or so.

Basically, there are five types of political messianism in Korea. Two are traditional, namely, Buddhist political messianism, an example being the Unified Silla dynasty, and Confucian orthodox political ideology, which found expression in the Yi dynasty. One may dispute the messianic character of Confucianism; but the ideology itself contains definite messianic characteristics.

The next three experiences of political messianism by the Korean people were: Japanese ultranationalism in its colonial form; the North Korean Communist movement; and the emerging modern technocracy in Korea.[6] One might argue that modern technocracy may not be classified as messianic, but as we will show, it has strong messianic tendencies.

For the sake of brevity, we will deal with these three cases of political messianism in a schematic manner.

These three political regimes are totalitarian in different ways and to different degrees on the political level; and at the same time on the religious level each claims absolute authority in different ways by assuming divine and messianic roles *for* the people.

According to the polity of Japanese ultranationalism all values and institutions come under the Imperial Authority of the Emperor. Hence, the government, the military, business, all truth, beauty, and morality belong to the institution of Emperor. The infamous Education Rescript was an open declaration of the fact that the Japanese state, being a religious, spiritual, and moral entity, claimed the right to determine all values. This was the spirit of Japanese national polity which was combined with the doctrine of the divinity of the Emperor. This messianic motive, championed by the Japanese military as the holy army of the Emperor, launched the mission to bring the "Light of the Emperor" to the eight corners of the world.

With regard to the Communist political messianism in North Korea, we do not have all the information we need to deal with it fully. However, it seems clear that the personal messianic or cultic role of Kim Il-sung is very much emphasized. Communism is a secularized form of messianism. Its messianic role, understood in terms of the dictatorship of the proletariat, is in fact assumed by the political leader, and finds expression in a totalitarian political structure.

Finally, modern technocracy, in its Korean form, is being experienced as another form of national messianism. There seems to be a conviction that technology and science, organized into the capitalist system, can solve all the human problems of the Korean people; and the political regime integrates and controls all the economic, military, and cultural institutions. While doing this, the regime places itself and its authority above the law and criticism and claims the loyalty of the people by emphasizing filial piety, which was formerly a cardinal virtue of Japanese ultranationalism. It is not yet totalitarian and absolutist in the classical sense, but such tendencies are unmistakably present.

These three manifestations of political messianism have common characteristics, not only in their totalitarian and absolutist character, but also in sharing a common theory of contradiction. Their view of history is that there are two powers which are struggling against each other, and that one must destroy the other. One is absolutely good and the other is absolutely evil. The justice of God (theodicy) is alleged to be immanent in the established political regime, be it that of the Emperor, a Communist leader, or the military technocracy.

The theodicy immanent in Japanese ultranationalism was seldom obvious or well-defined and thus had an air of mystery about it. It showed itself, however, in opposing its internal enemies, which included liberal, political, and intellectual movements. It also waged a holy war on the so-called Western barbarians and attempted to expand the realm of the Emperor. Communism believes that its manifest destiny is to bring about the victory of the international proletariat, with imperialism (the United States) as its chief enemy. The military technocracy sees irrationality, traditionality, and chaos (instability) as characteristics of its internal enemies, who oppose its messianic claims, and suppresses them. It has Communist North Korea as its external enemy.

In claiming absolute authority, these three kinds of political messianism advocate radical reforms in society. However, these are to be carried out from the top working toward the bottom. For instance, the North Korean regime was not established by the process of a popular revolution, but rather was imposed from the outside by the Soviet Union, against the popular will of the Korean people.

These so-called radical reforms—all in the name of an earthly millennium—are undertaken with a great deal of social and political cost which has to be borne by the minjung. Indeed, the sufferings of the Korean people under these three political messianisms were and are extreme. The free subjectivity of the people is reduced to nothing in history. Socio-economic and cultural analyses of the Korean people's sufferings under these conditions bear witness to the fact that political messianism is antagonistic to the people (the minjung). They experience it as a contradiction.

Therefore, besides making and maintaining false claims to messianism, political messianism sets itself up against the minjung, who face it as a contradiction.

As we have already shown, messianism is a political process or a history in which the minjung join with the Messiah in realizing his messianic role. While political messianism attempts to make the minjung a historical nothing or an object of its messianic claims, the messianic politics of Jesus are the politics that will realize for the minjung their historical subjectivity, thus making them masters of their own historical destiny. Fundamentally, messianic politics must be understood as that of the minjung, not that of the leader, especially not that of the ruling power. The relationship between the minjung and the Messiah should be understood as a relation between the minjung as the subject and the Messiah as their function. However, the messianic function of the people should not be understood in terms of an elite who are at the top of a political hierarchy but in terms of the Suffering Servant.

To be sure, there are many images or models in the Bible which will help to illuminate this notion of messianic politics. For instance, there is the model of King David; there is the figure of the Son of Man in apocalyptic literature; and other kingly ("the anointed") images of the Messiah. However, these have a corrupting influence, for we see the Messiah as a power personality (political messianism) who embodies self-righteousness and triumphalism. However, the most appropriate and convincing of all messianic images is that of Jesus as the Suffering Servant, in the light of which we must examine and reshape other images like that of David, Son of Man, etc. What is noteworthy about the figure of the Suffering Servant is that it provides the two messianic qualities of identification with the suffering people and functioning as servant to the aspiration of the people for liberation.

Such an understanding of messianic politics will provide the means for purging Christian confessions and theologies of elements of political messianism which have come from the ideology of Christendom. The claims of Christendom did not serve the messianic politics of the people to be subjects of history; and this was deliberate. It may be one of the critical tasks especially of Third World theologians to purge elements of political messianism from our Christian confessions, proclamations, and theologies.

Furthermore, to expose the reality of political messianism in the modern state, no matter however secular they claim to be, is one of the fundamental political hermeneutics of the Christian community today.

This task needs to be performed when the Christian community seeks to serve the suffering people as Jesus the Messiah did, and when we seek to realize the hope expressed through his resurrection and his promise of the general resurrection of all the minjung. This task needs to be done in this context because the struggle to realize the messianic aspirations of the minjung is not just a religious or spiritual matter isolated from the political arena. In fact, the political field is the center stage on which the messianic struggle is carried out. Therefore, the confession that Jesus is the Messiah of the people entails political service to the people.

On the basis of the analyses given above, several tasks emerge in the Korean situation.

The first is to expose the long history of political messianism which has enslaved us and to struggle against it. This involves critical evaluations of political values, political structures, and political leadership.

The second is to rediscover the popular messianic traditions inherent in Maitreya Messianic Buddhism and Donghak religion, both through a research of extant literature and through dialogue with Buddhist and Donghak leaders who have concerns similar to ours. In undertaking this task we must remember that messianic traditions are not immune to influences from political messianism once they are linked to the ruling power. We know of this process in the history of Christianity which has justified absolute power like that of the Divine Right of the King.

The third is to evolve in a concrete way a Christian political perspective based on the following ideas: (1) The general resurrection of the people (bodily as well as spiritual) understood in terms of the messianic subjectivity of the people. (2) *Shalom* in relation to the unification of Korea. (3) *Koinonia* (participation) and justice in relation to the social and political development of the Korean people. In order to do all this we need a general understanding of Korean history and we should dialogue with secular intellectuals who seek to serve the people.

The fourth is to tackle the issue of the use of power in a political struggle. It is not simply a question of the use of violence. The issue concerns the nature and use of power in politics. Although there can be no general rule on the use of power, including force and violence, in the process of realizing the messianic hope of the people, a few general things can be said.

1. Ultimately, power, as we know it, has no ontological status in the framework of the Messianic Kingdom. Jesus not only did not use power as we know it, but he could not use power, since he himself was the embodiment and reality of the Messianic Kingdom which is the powerless status of Jesus the Messiah and the people.

2. However, as we have indicated, history shows the continuous contradiction between political messianism and messianic politics, the power and the people. Therefore, some tamed measure of political realism should be allowed, although an absolute political cynicism or "realpolitik" should never be permitted.

In considering a realistic posture on the part of Christians, the notion of people's power should be taken into account. It is infinitely creative; and various forms of it are evident especially at the grassroots level, where identification and participation with people are easiest.

The people will be the subjects of their own historical destiny. Jesus the Messiah died to expose Roman political messianism and its historical antecedents and descendants; and Jesus the Messiah was resurrected as a foretaste and affirmation of the raising of all the dead minjung to inaugurate the messianic rule of *justice*, *koinonia* (participation), and *shalom*.

NOTES

1. The traditional Korean historical books, *Samguksagi* (Historical Records of Three Kingdoms) and Royal Chronicles of Yi Korea Dynasty, are typical examples of this.
2. The Korean Buddhist scholar Ko Eun recently developed this theme under Minjung Buddhism. Maitreya Buddhism had two moments, one being the royal messianic leader and the other being the leader of the suffering people (minjung).
3. "The Tale of Hong Kil-dong" is a paradigm of the social biography of the minjung. It contains popular Buddhist and Taoist elements and is full of social imagination, humor, and satire.
4. Prof. Ahn Pyong-Jik of Seoul National University has, through socio-economic analysis, determined the constituency of the March First Independence movement to be a minjung movement.
5. For a detailed analysis, see Kim Yong-bock, "Historical Transformation, People's Movement and Messianic Koinonia," (Ph.D. diss., Princeton Theological Seminary, 1976), especially chapter 5.
6. The first draft of this paper was written in 1979. The reference is to the so-called Yushin system.

Index

Abesamis, Carlos H., xix
Abraham, K.C., xviii
adaptation, 2
agapē, 37. *See also* koinonia
Ahn Byung-jik, 180, 181
Ahn Byung-mu, xvii, 33-35, 41, 43, 138-52, 167
Ahn Chang-ho, 109
Ahn Pyong-jik, 193
Alexandra, 152
Allen, Horace N., 73-74, 81
All People's Assembly, 171, 182
Amalorpavadass, D.S., xviii
American Bible Society, 74
'am ha'aretz, 34, 42, 124, 147, 159, 180; and ochlos, 149-50
Amos, 133-37
Anderson, G.H., 10
'apiru, 33-36, 125
Appenzeller, H.G., 75, 81
April 1960 Revolution. *See* Revolution of April 1960
Aquinas, Thomas, 157
Arai, Sasagu, 180
Aristotle, 157
Asian Theological Consultation, 41
Association of the Jesus Presbyterian Youth, 79
Augustine, 157, 163-64
baeksong, 58, 68
Baikbaikkyo, 176, 182
Baikje, 175, 182
Balasuriya, Tissa, xviii
Barth, Karl, ix, xii
Basil of Caesarea, 164
Bensing, M., 181
Benz, Ernst, 180, 181
Berger, Peter, 60
blacks. *See* liberation, black; theology, black
Blair, W.M., 37, 90
Bodhisattva Jijang, 166
Boff, Leonardo, xix
Bonhoeffer, Dietrich, 17, 157
Bonsang (King), 169, 181
Boyd, Robin, 3, 10
Brooks, James H., 119
Brown, Arthur, 19, 37, 87, 92, 94, 108, 118
Brunner, J., xii

Buddha, 175; *See also* Maitreya messianic Buddhism
Buddhism, 54, 174, 187; Amita, 175, 176; Christianity and, 3, 18, 33, 42, 189; cosmology of, 175; minjung, 193. *See also* Maitreya messianic Buddhism
Bultmann, Rudolf, xii, 140, 148, 152
butchers: class of, 76, 144; liberation of, 86; symbol of, 67
Butchers' Liberation movement, 76
Byolgok, 172, 182
Byonja, 170
capitalist system, 30, 65, 171, 190
Carino, Feliciano V., 11
Catholic Farmers Association, 40, 55, 57; Andung Diocese Federation of, 55-56
Catholic Young Workers Organization (JOC), 40
Central Intelligence Agency of Kora (KCIA). *See* Korean Central Intelligence Agency
Ch'amjong Taesun, 88
Chang Chi-you, 118
Chang Il-dam, 65-68, 177, 178, 179-80
Changjori, 169, 181
Chang Kil-san, 68, 69, 176
Chang Tok-su, 115
Chang Young-ho, 55
Chassidim, 152
Che In-wham, 182
Chenchiah, Justice P., 2, 3
China: Buddhism in, 176; colonizing of Korea by, 19, 170; Japan and, 88, 110
Cho Dong-il, 182
Choe Je-u, 188
Ch'oi Ik-hyon, 89
Chon Bong-jun, 68, 69, 167, 171
Chondokyo, 77
Chong Doryong, 182
Chong Mong-ju, 98, 118
Chongum Kim Sang-hon, 88
Chon Seung-se, 61, 62
Choo Chai-yong, 19, 73-79
Choo Jae-yong, 180
Cho Se-hee, 174, 182
Chosen of Dangun Wangkom, 167, 169, 181. *See also* Yi dynasty
Chosun (Korea) Communist party, 77. *See also* communism

Christ, Carol, xvii
Christian Conference of Asia (CCA), xiv, 123; Commission on Theological Concerns (CTC) of, 1, 10, 42; dialogue of URM and CTC of, 11
Christian Ecumenical Youth Council, 40
Christian Faculty Fellowship, 40
Christian Thought, The, 40
Chu Ki-chol, 189
Chun Bong-joon, 181
Chung Chang Won, 169, 181
Chung Ho-kyong, 57
Chungin, 188
Chungin (King), 168, 181
Chungsanpyulgok, 58
Chungupsa, 58
Chungyunhoi, 103
Chunhyang, 173
Church Women United, 40
Citron, B., 151
Clark, C.A., 103, 118
clergy, dialogue of, with laity, xiii
Coalition of Human Rights movements, 41
Cobb, J., 180
Coenen, L., 152
colonization: in Asia, 5, 7; by capitalism, 65; Chinese, of Korea, 19, 170; European, x; Japanese, of Korea, xii, 19-23, 30, 33, 53, 68, 88, 89, 94-118, 169, 182, 183, 189
Commission on Theological Concerns (CTC). See Christian Conference of Asia
communism: church and, 157; during Korean War, 68; and minjung, 16, 32, 177, 180, 185-86; of North Korea, 23, 30, 183, 185-86, 189, 190, 191
Communist Youth Association, 77
community. See koinonia
Cone, James H., ix-xix, 10
Confucianism, 54, 83, 101, 114, 116, 176, 187, 189; dialogue of Christianity and, 18; discrimination of, against women, 25, 58; historiography of, 186; loyalty of followers of, 89, 90, 171; politics of, 87, 90, 171; power of scholars of, 168
Conspiracy Case, 97, 100, 117
Constantine (Emperor), 162, 163
Cosmic Christ, 2-3, 5, 6
Council of Missions, 83
Cox, Harvey, 174
Croatto, Severino, xix
dan, 64-65
Dangun Wangkom, 170, 181; See also Chosen; Yi dynasty
David (King), 191
Davis, Charles, 54
democracy, 155, 169
de Silva, Lynn, 3, 10
Devanandan, Paul, 3, 10
dignity, 127-28, 165

Donghak movement, 181, 188-89; dialogue with, 33, 42, 101, 178; language of, 116; power of, 103, 168; religion of, 189, 192; struggle for human rights and, 23, 67. *See also* Donghak Peasant Rebellion of 1895
Donghak Peasant Rebellion of 1895, 69, 75, 181, 188; deaths in, 68; *han* and, 59; inspired by Chang Kil-san, 176; political messianism and, 29-30, 52, 170-71; shift in Korean politics following, 88; suppression of, 83, 99
Doraisingh, Christopher, 1
Drury, John, xix
Duraisingh, J.C., xviii
Eagleson, John, xvii, xviii, xix
East Asia Christian Conference (EACC/ CCA), 6-8, 11; Church and Society Committee of, 6
Ecumenical Association of Third World Theologies (EATWOT), xiv, xv, xvii, xix
Elwood, Douglas J., xvii, 10, 11
Enlightenment, ix
Epworth League, 103
Essenes, 142
ethnicity, 35, 185
ethnoi, 149
Eujin, Miruk, 176
Eulsa Protectorate Treaty, 77, 171, 182
existentialism, 157
Exodus, as liberation event, 22, 34-35, 57-58, 96, 106-9, 124-30, 158-59. *See also* liberation
Fabella, Virginia, xvii, xviii, xix
Farquhar, J.N., 3
Federal Council of Foreign Mission Boards, 19, 87, 118
Gale, J.S., 84-85, 104, 118
Gasa, 172, 182
Gibellini, Rosino, xix
Gnilka, J., 152
Goff, James, xviii
Goff, Margaret, xviii
Gottwald, Norman, 180
Great Revival of 1907, 20, 90-93, 105, 189
Gritsch, Eric, 181
Gutiérrez, Gustavo, ix, xvii, xviii, xix, 57
Hague Peace Conference, 89
Haldcraft, J.G., 119
Hall, Basil, 74
Ham Sok-hon, 43, 109
han: definition of, 24-28, 51; theology of, 25-28, 55-69, 178-80
Han Jong-man, 182
Hannas, 152
Hanson, R.P.C., 164, 180
Han Wan-sang, xvii, xix
Hanyang Youth Association, 78
Han Yong-un, 171
Harrison, Norman B., 119

Hatata Takasi, 176, 182
Hegel, 35
Hellenism, 162
Herodotus, 148
Herod the Great, 152
Heum Chong, 172, 182
Hideyoshi, 99, 188
Hinduism, 3, 4
Ho Kyun, 171, 179, 181, 188
Homer, 148
Hong Kil-dong, 171, 179, 181, 188
Hong Kyung-rae, 59, 68, 69, 170
Hong Kyung-rae Insurrection, 170, 181
Hubaikje kingdom, 181
Hughes, Patrick, xix
human rights. *See* rights, civil and human
Hwalbindang, 59, 69, 171, 182
Hwang-choga, 58
Hwang Tok-yong, 118
Hyangga, 172
Hyksos, 125
Hyonjang church, 57, 68
Hyon Sang-yun, 115
Hyun Young-hak, xiii, xvi, xvii, xix, 9, 26-28, 43, 47-54
Ilchinwhoi, 103
Ileto, Reynaldo C., 11
Il Yon, 169, 181
Imjin, 170
Imo Military revolt, 75
Imsul, 170
Imsul Uprising, 181
Inda, Caridad, xvii
Independence Association, 23, 74, 75, 76, 168, 171, 181
Independence Club, 75, 87, 100, 102, 103
Independence Declaration of 1919, 109
Independence Movement of March First 1919, 69, 168-69, 181; *han* and, 26, 59; Korean Christianity and, 21, 79, 80, 118, 158, 189; leadership of, 109, 115, 171; political messianism and, 30, 118, 188-89; as struggle for human rights, 23, 77, 78, 109, 167, 193
Independence Newspaper, 74, 76, 102
Industrial Mission groups, 38
industrialization. *See* technocracy
inmin, 30, 185
Institute for Mission-Education, 57
Ito Hirobumi, 88
Jaisohn, Philip. *See* So Jai-pil
Jangga, 172, 182
Jannai, 152
Japan, Buddhism in, 176; colonizing of Korea by, 19-23, 30, 33, 53, 68, 88, 89, 94-118, 169, 182, 183, 189; filial piety in, 190; invasion of Korea by, 77, 88, 176, 188; Korean missionaries and, 80, 94; treaty of, with Paik's government, 39;

ultranationalism of, 189-90; victory of, over China and Russia, 88; victory of, over Righteous Army, 89-90
Japanese Imperial Education Rescript, 189, 190
Jeremias, Joachim, 143, 152
Jerusalem, fall of, 152
Jesamil, 40
Jewish War, 140
Jingol, 168, 181
Joachim of Floris, 163, 164
John the Baptist, 142
Jojo Yongwang, 173
Junryun, 182
Justice and Peace Commission, 40
Kabo Reformation, 75
Kaehwagasa, 182
Kal Chu-sa, 68, 69
Kang Man-gil, 181
Kantian philosophy, 157
Kapsin Coup, 75
Kasiri, 58
Katoppo, Marianne, xvii
Ken, Arai, 152
Khin Maung Din, 3, 11
Kija, 88
Kil Chin-kyong, 118
Killen, Kim, 180
Killen, Shelly, 180
Kil Son-ju, 109, 110, 111, 119
Kim, Stephen, 57
Kim Bu-sik, 169, 170, 181
Kim Chai-choon, 78, 79
Kim Chi Ha, 26, 60, 63-68, 124, 155, 166, 174, 177-79, 182
Kim Chi-kyun, 182
Kim Chong-hyon, 119
Kim Chung-choon, 43
Kim Heung-kyu, 182
Kim Hong-do, 172, 182
Kim Il Sung, 30, 190
Kim Kwan-suk, 40
Kim Kyong-suk, 56, 58
Kim Sung-jae, 43
Kim Yang-son, 91, 118
Kim Yong-bock, xiv, xv, 9, 28-29, 30-33, 34, 43, 80-119, 183-93
King, Martin Luther, Jr., xiii
Kisaeng, 182
Kittel, 148
Ko Eun, 174, 182, 193
Kofi Appiah-Kubi, xvii
Koguryo kingdom, 181
koinonia: agapē as expression of, 37; Christian, and the Japanese government, 99-104; Christian student, 40-41; as content of Messianic Kingdom, 187, 192-93; of early Korean Christianity, 24, 82, 86; emergent language of Christian,

104-18; Great Revival and, 92; of Hyon-jang church, 68; mask dance and, 27-29; political, 21, 100, 192-93; suffering of oppressed people and, 95-99; of workers, 39-41

Kongmudohaga, 58

Korea Christian Academy, 57

Korean and American Treaty of Amity, 75, 81

Korean Central Intelligence Agency (KCIA), xiii, 15, 56

Korean Christian Action Organization. *See* Urban Industrial Mission groups

Korean Christian Declaration of 1973, 79

Korean Independence movement. *See* Independence Movement of March First 1919

Korean National Council of Churches. *See* National Council of Churches in Korea

Korean Religious Tract Society, 84

Korean Student Christian Federation, 39, 40

Korean War, 68

Koryo dynasty, 68-69, 168, 169, 170, 175, 181, 182

Koryo Kayo, 172, 182

Koyama, Kosuke, xiv, xviii

Kraemer, H., 2, 5, 10

Kummel, 148

Kungye, 58, 169, 175, 181

Kurazaku, 181

Kuristo, Simmun, 119

Kwaneum, 176

Kwanghaegun (King), 168, 181

Kwangmu (Emperor), 99

Kyemyunjo, 182

Kyonggichega, 172, 182

Kyonhwon (King), 58, 69, 169, 175, 181

labor unions. *See* unions

laity, dialogue of, with clergy, xiii

laos, 34-35, 124, 139, 148, 160

Lee Chun, 89

Lee Gi-baik, 165, 167, 180

Lee Sang-jai, 95, 104

Lee Su-jong. *See* Rijutei

Lee Sung-hun, 97

Lee Wu-song, 181

Levi, 142, 144

liberal Protestantism. *See* Protestantism, liberal

liberation: in Asia, 4; black, in America, xi, xiii, xix; butchers for, 86; farmers for, 77-78; of Korea in 1945, 23, 39, 158; from oppression in Korea, 24, 33-36, 155, 157, 160, 162, 166, 169, 179, 183; theme of, in Scripture, 133-37, 146-47, 191. *See also* Exodus

Loewith, Karl, 180

Lohmeyer, Ernst, 152

Luther, Martin, 165-66

Maccabean War, 152

MacIntyre, 74

Maitreya messianic Buddhism, 32-33, 69, 169, 174-76, 182, 187-88, 192, 193

Malcolm X, xiii

Malraux, André, 164, 172, 180

Maltugi, 173-74, 182

Manchuk, 59, 68, 69

Mangsoyi, 59, 69

Mangyi, 59, 69

Manhae, 68, 69

Manjuk, 170, 180

Maoism, 30, 185

March First Independence Movement of 1919. *See* Independence Movement of March First 1919

Marty, Martin, 180

Marx, Karl: class analysis of, x, xv, xviii; definitions of, of proletariat and history, xiv; view of religion of, xv

Marxism: Asian Christianity and, 3; difference between proletariat of, and minjung, 184; and Korean Christianity, 32, 35, 42, 178; and Latin American liberation theology, 17

mask dance, 26-29, 47-54, 58, 63, 64, 69, 173, 174

mathetai, 141

McCune, George S., 98, 118

McKenzie, F.A., 118

Mendenhall, G.E., 125

messianic politics. *See* theology, political

messianism. *See* political messianism

Methodist Youth Conference, 79

Micah, 130-37

Míguez Bonino, José, xvii, xviii

mikroi, 148

Millennium, 162-63, 179

Miller, 104

Million movement. *See* One Million movement

Min (Queen), 19, 75, 99

Minamoto, 182

minjung, definition of, xvii, 16

Min Kyung-bae, 37

Min Yong-ik, 75

Min Young-jin, 43

Min Young-whan, 98, 118

Miranda, José, xviii, xix

Mission Conference (Tambaram, India, 1938), 2

Moffett, Samuel D., 118

Moltmann, Jürgen, 57

Moon Hee-suk Cyris, xvii, 33-34, 123-37

Moore, Basil, xvii

Moore, J. Robert, 105, 118

Moses, 22, 137, 141, 146, 158-59. *See also* Exodus

Muentzer, Thomas, 165-66

Munsin, 168

Musin, 168

Muzorewa, Henry, xvii

Myo Chong, 68, 69, 170, 181
Myo Chung, 170, 181
Myo Chung Insurrection, 181
Nacpil, Emerito, 1, 11
National Council of Churches in Korea, 36, 40; Declaration of Human Rights in Korea of, 79; Human Rights Commission of, 40, 57; military and, 78; Theological Commission of, 15
National Independence movement. *See* Independence Movement of March First 1919
nationalism: in Asia, 7; of Jews, 151; in Korea, 53, 93, 167, 188-89; Korean church and, 18-23; minjung, 167. *See also* colonization; unification of Korea
Nationalist movement, 169, 189
National Textile Trade Union, 56
Nestle-Aland, 151
New People's Association. *See* Sinminhoe
Niles, D. Preman, xiv, xviii, 1-11
Niles, D.T., 7, 10, 11
Nobee, 170
Nojang, 174
Northern Presbyterian Report, 96
North Korean communism. *See* communism
No Toh-sa, 81
ochlos, 33-36, 42, 124, 139-52, 159-60; *'am ha'aretz* and, 149-50; *ethnou*, 149; *laou*, 149
Oduyoye, Amba, xvii
Oh Won-chun, 55, 56-57, 58
One Million movement, 92, 96
PROK Youth Conference, 79
Paik, L. George, 21, 37, 83, 90, 91, 96, 118
Paik Nak-chun, 118
Paik Nam-suk, 119
Panikkar, Raymond, 3
Pansori, 58, 63, 69, 172, 173, 174, 180, 182
Park chang-kak, 68, 69
Park Che-sun, 88
Park Chung-hee: assassination of, 10, 15, 36; regime of, xiii, 39-41
Park Hyung-kyu, 79
Park Joon-suh, 43
Park Song-chun, 76
Park Song-ui, 172, 182
Peddlers Guild, 103
Peerman, Dean, 180
People's Rebellion, 59
Pharisees, 152
Pieris, Aloysius, xviii, 3, 11
Pieters, A.A., 103, 118
Pindar, 148
Plaskow, Judith, xvii
Plato, 157
plethos, 139
political messianism, 28ff., 112-18, 183-93; of Japanese, 31; of Rome, 193
polloi, 139

Portsmouth Agreement, 89
Presbyterian Academy in Sinchon, 97
Presbyterian Church in U.S.A., 81
Presbyterian Church of the Republic of Korea, 40
Presbyterian Mission Board, 76
Priests Corps for the Realization of Justice, 40
Protestantism, liberal, ix
Q source, 146, 159, 180
Quirinius, 152
Rabbinic Judaism, 150
racism xii, 35-36
Ramses II, 125
redaction criticism, 138-39
Reike, Bo, 152
reunification of Korea. *See* unification
Revival movement, 77
Revolution of April 1960, 23, 26, 59, 69, 78, 169, 171, 181
Rhodes, Harry A., 118
Righteous Army, 89-90, 95, 103, 170, 171, 182
rights, civil and human: Christian koinonias and, 40, 41, 65, 67, 73, 76, 80, 165; denial of, in Park Chung-hee's government, 41; desire for, generating Korean independence movements, 23, 67, 77, 78, 109, 171, 182; involvement of theologians with, 36; in Scripture, 126, 129, 130, 156-57, 165; Urban Industrial Mission groups and, 39
Rijutei, 74, 84
Ross, John, 74
Ruether, Rosemary, 180
Russia: communism of, 23; Japan and, 88, 91, 110
Russo-Japanese War, 88
Ryu Tong-shik, 37, 182
Sadaibu, 168, 181
Saint King Jun-ryun, 175
Sambyolcho, 170, 181
Samyongdang, 68, 69
Sandong Dong Methodist Church, 103
Scannone, Juan Carlos, xix
Schniewind, J., 152
Second Vatican Council. *See* Vatican Council II
Seoul Metropolitan Mission, 41
Seti I, 125
Seungdong Presbyterian Church, 76
shalom, 33, 187, 192, 193
shamanism, Korean, 18, 62, 105, 176
Shin Chae-ho, 171, 182
Shin Dol-sok, 63
Shin Dol-suk, 171, 182
Shinto worship, 30, 78
Shin Yun-bok, 172, 182
Sijo, 172, 182
Silla. *See* Unified Silla dynasty

Simon (house of Hasmon), 152
Sinminhoe, 95, 97, 103
Sino-Japanese War, 75, 83, 88
Sinsaengmyong, 115
Sobrino, Jon, xix
socialism, 32, 110
So Jai-pil, 87, 95
Sokyo, 172, 182
Solzhenitsyn, A., 178
Song Choan-seng, 4, 11
Songjong (King), 168
Sonu Hun, 97, 118
Soohjong (King), 182
Soonjo (King), 181
Sori, 168, 181
Soviet Union. *See* Russia
Speer, Robert, 87, 118
Strathmann, 152
Student Development Service Corps (SDSC), 39
Su chae-pil, 74, 75
Suh In-suk, 180
Suh Kwang-sun David, xiii, 1, 9, 38-43
Suh Nam-dong, xvi, 9, 23, 24-26, 30, 41, 43, 124, 131, 155-82
Sukjong (King), 176, 181
Sunjo (King), 168
Suwun, 68, 69
Swallen, W.L., 37, 118
Sye In-suk, 43
syncretism, 2
Syngman Rhee, 69, 104, 181
Taebong kingdom, 181
Taeguk Bookstore, 95
Tagawa, 159-60, 180
Talchum. *See* mask dance
Tamez, Elsa, xix
Tangun, 88
Taoism, 193
tax collectors: in mask dance, 49; in Scripture, 143, 144-45, 160, 161
technocracy: Korean, 30, 31, 36, 189, 190; military, 191
Terauchi, 95, 96, 97
Theissen, Gerd, 152, 180
theology: African, x, xiv; of Aquinas, 157; Asian, x, xiv, 1, 7; of Augustine, 157; black, x, xii, xiii, xiv, xvii; definition of, x; dogmatic, 6, 157-58; European, ix, xvi; feminist, x, xvii; of *han*, 25-28, 55-69; of indigenization, 18, 41; Korean, of liberation, 24, 156, 158, 166; liberal, 94; liberation, of Latin America, x, xiv, xv, xvi, xix, 16-17; liberation, of Third World, ix, xix, 192; political, 20-23, 41, 124, 157-58, 183-93; of secularization, 41, 165
Thomas, M.M., 2, 5-6, 9, 10, 11
Thomas, R.J., 74
Tillich, Paul, 28, 32, 54, 157, 180
Tji, Daniel, 79
Todd, 103

Tongkye Chong-on, 88
Torres, Sergio, xvii, xviii, xix
Treaty of Protectorate, 88, 89, 99, 102
Uibyong. *See* Righteous Army
U Kyaw Than, 11
Underwood, H.G., 75, 81
unification of Korea, 32, 33
Unified Silla dynasty, 168, 169, 175, 181, 182, 187-88, 189
unions, 38, 66
United States, imperialism of, 190
Urban Industrial Mission groups (UIM), 36, 39, 40, 41, 57, 66, 79; Inchon, 40; involvement of, with Y.H. Company, 55; Korean Christian Action Organization of, 40, 56; Seoul Metropolitan, 40; Yongdongpo, 40
Utopia, 163, 179
Van Leeuven, Arend, 5
Vatican Council II, 166
Von Rad, Gerhard, 4
Wangkon, 175
West, Cornel, xviii
Whang Song-kyu, 43
Wickremesinghe, Lakshman, 3, 11
Wilmore, Gayraud S., xvii, xviii
women: attitude of Jesus toward, 145; conversion of, 83; discrimination against, 25, 35, 62, 131, 132, 134, 185; in Scripture, 85-86, 131, 132, 134
Won dynasty, 170, 181
Won Hyo, 187
World Council of Churches, Church and Society Conference of, 166
Yang Song-wu, 62, 63
yangban, 168, 181, 188; Confucian, and Japanese rule, 95, 99; in mask dance, 48-49, 64, 173-74
Yap Kim-heo, 11
Y.H. Trade Union, 56
Y.H. Trading Company, 55-56
Yi dynasty, 181, 182, 193; arts of, 58, 69, 188; Buddhism and, 54, 187; Confucianist society of, 176, 187, 189; end of, 88, 95; oppression of, 188; policy of, toward the West, 81
Yi Kwang-su, 78
Yim Kok-chong, 68, 69
Yi Sang-jae, 74
Yi Ung-chan, 74
YMCA, 103, 104
Yongwhakyo, 176, 182
Young Men's Christian Association. *See* YMCA
Youth and Student Association Taesong School, 95
Yukdupum, 168, 181
Yun Chi-ho, 74, 95, 97, 104
Yun Hyong-kil, 59
Yushin System, 41, 193
Zealots, 145, 151
Zen, 62

DATE DUE

NOV 21 '90	
DEC 15 90	

BRODART, INC.   Cat. No. 23-221